**Maureen Cooper** is the founding director of Awareness in Action, an organisation dedicated to helping people accomplish sustainable wellbeing in their lives, with their relationships and in the work environment. Our approach views wellbeing as an inside job based on understanding how our minds work. We recognise the importance of bringing this learning into how we respond to everyday situations, so we focus on training in clarity, connection and openness.

Drawing on more than thirty-five years' experience as a professional educator, senior manager in a non-profit organisation, an entrepreneur and as an experienced practitioner of Buddhist meditation, Maureen leads workshops and training programmes in the UK and Europe.

Maureen was born in London, UK but love took her to the Netherlands, where she lives with her partner in Amsterdam.

If you want to find out more about Awareness in Action visit www.awarenessinaction.org or contact Maureen at info@awarenessinaction.org.

Also by Maureen Cooper

*The Compassionate Mind Approach to Reducing Stress*

# THE STRESS WORKBOOK

MAUREEN COOPER

ROBINSON

ROBINSON

First published in Great Britain in 2020 by Robinson

1 3 5 7 9 10 8 6 4 2



Important note
This book is not intended as a substitute for medical advice or treatment.
Any person with a condition requiring medical attention should consult a
qualified medical practitioner or suitable therapist.



A CIP catalogue record for this book
is available from the British Library.

ISBN: 978-1-47214-415-7

Typeset in Palatino by Initial Typesetting Services, Edinburgh
Printed and bound in Great Britain by Bell and Bain Ltd, Glasgow

Papers used by Robinson are from well-managed forests and other responsible sources.

Robinson
An imprint of
Little, Brown Book Group
Carmelite House
50 Victoria Embankment
London EC4Y 0DZ

An Hachette UK Company
www.hachette.co.uk

www.littlebrown.co.uk

*This workbook is dedicated to everyone who has felt stressed at times in his or her life and who has the wish to do something about it.*

*May this workbook be of use to you!*

# Contents


Acknowledgements ix

Introduction 1

**PART 1:**
**Our Starting Point**

1 How Stress Works 11

2 How Compassion Works 37

3 How our Longing for Happiness and Fear of Suffering Adds to Our Stress 68

Conclusion to Part 1 108

**PART 2:**
**Seeing Where We Want to Change**

4 Taking a Fresh Look at Our Habits 111

5 Developing a Peaceful Mind: The Basis of Compassionate Action 128

6 Identifying Our Unhelpful Habits 163

7 Adopting Beneficial Habits 190

Conclusion to Part 2 210

**PART 3:**
**Making Change Happen**

8 Compassion for Oneself – Peeling Away the Layers of the Heart 213

9 Compassion for Others – Removing Our Armour 250

10 Compassion with a Big Perspective – Removing our Blindfold 283

Conclusion: Making this Approach to Reducing Stress Part of Our Lives 301

Useful Resources 309

Endnotes 315

Index 323

# Acknowledgements

Boundless appreciation and gratitude to my Buddhist teachers who have guided me on the path all these years. It is your wisdom and compassion that enables me to write this book.

My partner, Bert van Baar, is my most trusted support and critic. As a writer himself he appreciates the ups and downs of making a book happen. As always, he has supported me through each step of this project and provided substantial and vital feedback along the way.

My sincere thanks to Andrew McAleer at Little Brown, who has been a steady and encouraging guide through the process of making this workbook happen.

Special thanks to Carole Francis-Smith for her advice on the sections regarding stress and the internet. She has been generous in sharing her Netiquette guidelines.

Many thanks to Ed Eisler who made sure that each member of his staff at JING Tea had a copy of my first book. Also, to Derek Corr, who steered me through the complex paths of internet marketing.

To my dear friends Susan Burrows and Erric Solomon, and my sister Tracey Ellis – thanks for your belief in me and constant support.

Finally, my deepest appreciation and thanks go to all the people I have encountered through Awareness in Action – those who attend workshops, take online courses, comment on blogs – you have provided so much of the material for this workbook. I continue to learn from you all.

# Introduction

We are living in highly charged, often polarised times. Social media enables world events to impact our lives with increasing intensity. As individuals, we struggle to process upheaval and change, which can seem overwhelming. Many people cite the climate catastrophe as a major source of stress, while the repercussions of voting and political decisions continue to rumble throughout the world. It is easy to feel overwhelmed and helpless.

This quote from the Dalai Lama seems very appropriate:

> *I believe that at every level of society – familial, national and international – the key to a happier and more successful world is the growth of compassion. We do not need to become religious, nor do we need to believe in a particular ideology. All that is necessary is for each of us to develop our good human qualities.*
>
> *Dalai Lama*[1]

This workbook is a manual for how to deepen our natural compassion and then to use it to help us work with stress. We will explore how we are hardwired for compassion, but our conditioning can block our expression of it. Step by step we will examine these blockages and the habits that compound them. Then we can move on to look at adopting new, nourishing habits using compassion, which will help us to work more creatively with stress.

## An Everyday Observation

Quite often we may find ourselves having to drop into our local supermarket on the way home from work. If we take the time to look around us as we push our trolleys through the laden shelves, it is not hard to find opportunities to observe many of the ways we human beings experience stress. Consider the middle-aged man in a smart suit buying an easy-to-prepare meal for one – perhaps he is recently divorced, living alone for the first time in years, and dealing with the stress of change and upheaval. Spare a thought for the young mother with a baby in a buggy and a toddler clinging round her legs. She looks as if she has not had a proper night's sleep for two or three years. The lounging teenage boy sulking around the soft drinks has an air of aimlessness and boredom about him – maybe because he left school with such high hopes and now does not seem to be able to find any kind of job that lives up to his dreams. Take care as you pass the older woman, walking carefully, who underwent major surgery two months ago and is feeling low and vulnerable as she tries to get her strength back. As we select the ingredients for our evening meal, perhaps we are rubbing shoulders with people suffering from exam nerves, having relationship problems, shouldering the care of elderly relatives – the list is endless.

Divorce, bereavement, moving to a new house and even going on holiday all rate high on the stress scale. Troubles at work, economic instability and unemployment are also possible sources. Increasingly, we find that our interactions on the internet are not as straightforward as we thought – are we projecting an image of ourselves that other people will want to engage with? People can even feel stress if caught in traffic or standing in a slow-moving queue at the airport. When we worry about our families, our health, our job, our weight, we are creating scenarios in the mind that can create stress. A short-term physical crisis such as falling over or scalding an arm can be termed stressful, as can longer-term physical challenges like facing chronic illness or disability.

Animals too face the physical eventualities of illness or death, but usually, for animals in the wild, a short-term physical emergency will either be resolved quickly or end in death. What is unique to humans is the capacity to imagine and to worry, and it is this capacity that also makes us uniquely vulnerable to stress. For example, we worry over memories of events that have already taken place and anticipate problems that may never occur. Our imagination can lead us to create scenarios that cause us real concern, until we remember that we're daydreaming and bring ourselves back down to earth. Have you ever imagined winning a large sum of money on the lottery? Inevitably you start to think about what you would do with the money and with whom you would share it. Before you know it, you're worrying about who might be offended and who might feel left out! In fact, our mind can provide a never-ending stream of potential worries and stressors all by itself.

## Terminology

The term 'stress' is one that is used so widely and frequently to describe a large variety of situations that it can be hard to arrive at a definition that satisfies everyone. One thing is clear though: when we hear someone describe themselves as 'stressed', we pretty much know what they mean and can identify with what they say. This is not always the case with the idea of 'compassion', which is perhaps not so accessible. Even harder to get a handle on is the idea that we can use compassion as a way of helping ourselves and even reducing our stress.

Compassion can be defined as the wish for everyone to be free from suffering along with having the urge to do something to bring that about. It can be misunderstood as pity, or as some otherworldly notion more in keeping with religious observance than the hustle and bustle of everyday life. It is not uncommon to hear people question how desirable, or even feasible, it is to try and be a compassionate person – isn't there a risk of being taken advantage of, or of seeming gullible? Perhaps many of us feel the struggle of trying to balance caring for our own lives and having a sense of responsibility for the lives of others. Public figures such as Desmond Tutu or the Dalai Lama can be accepted as being compassionate because they are religious figures, seemingly not subject to the demands and pressures of ordinary people. It can be hard to know how we can make a difference. Every day the news bombards us with stories of suffering, cruelty and violence that can seem overwhelming. In such a dog-eat-dog world we may wonder if taking care of number one is not the most advisable course of action.

In spite of all this, every day we also come across countless acts of kindness and concern for others that happen quietly in an ordinary and natural way as part of how we live together. Clearly, compassion is fundamental if we are to survive on this planet – we may even discover that it is the most sustainable and effective way of taking care both of number one and everyone else too – but we need to be able to understand it clearly and know how to work with it in our lives in spite of the challenges.

## Inspiration for *The Stress Workbook*

I have been a practising Buddhist in the Tibetan tradition for more than thirty-five years. This workbook draws on the approach to compassion found in those teachings. Although Buddhism is considered to be one of the major world religions, people who practise it, particularly in the West, will more often refer to it as a science of the mind, because it presents a thorough investigation of how the mind works. In Sanskrit, the term 'Buddha' means the 'one who is awake'. In waking up to how his mind worked, the Buddha saw all the ways in which we can limit the potential of our mind with concepts, habits and opinions. His subsequent teachings were practical and experiential descriptions of how these tendencies seem to become part of us, along with clear instructions on how we can uproot these patterns. By cultivating actions that enhance our confidence and peace of mind and avoiding those which cause us anxiety and fear, it is possible to live happier, more complete lives. In short, the Buddha showed a way to overcome suffering through a process of recognition that is a result of training the mind.

This approach is exemplified by the Dalai Lama in his development of a system of 'secular ethics'. He has written about this in two of his books, *Ethics for the New Millennium*[2] and *Beyond Religion*[3]. This quote from *Beyond Religion* explains the principle clearly:

> *Today . . . any religion-based answer to the problem of our neglect of inner values can never be universal, and so will be inadequate. What we need today is an approach to ethics which makes no recourse to religion and can be equally acceptable to those with faith and those without: a secular ethics.*

Both books suggest that developing peace of mind and a good heart will enable each of us to contribute to the world in a meaningful way. He often says that the Buddhist teachings on these topics are not directed exclusively at Buddhists but are relevant for everyone. This is the spirit in which this book offers an approach to working with stress through the development of compassion.

For more than thirty years, the Dalai Lama[4] has held regular meetings with scientists, psychologists, economists and philosophers under the auspices of the Mind & Life Institute,[5] founded by the Chilean-born neuroscientist Francisco Varela and Adam Engle, an American businessman and entrepreneur. During one of these meetings in 2000, the Dalai Lama made a formal request to the scientists in the room to test techniques such as meditation and compassion practices to determine whether they were beneficial for people and, if they were found to be so, to develop methods of teaching them in a secular way.

Richard Davidson, a pioneer in developing techniques for measuring brain activity, was present at this meeting. He accepted the Dalai Lama's challenge and began to invite experienced meditators to his laboratory to undergo testing there. He is now well known for his work in this area at the Waisman Laboratory for Brain Imaging and Behavior in Madison, Wisconsin. In 2012, he produced his first book for the general public, *The Emotional Life of Your Brain*,[6] based on this research. We will be looking into some of his findings as part of our exploration of using meditation and compassion to help us to reduce our stress.

As part of the work of Awareness in Action, I design and run workshops, training programmes and online courses. I also blog regularly. My speciality is finding ways to apply big principles in the busyness of everyday life. The fruit of all this is presented in this workbook in a practical and accessible form.

## Using this Workbook

This workbook sets out to explore how we can work with one of life's major challenges – stress – by recognising that it is our attitude towards it that plays a crucial role in how we deal with it. We will explore how we can change our attitude to stress: rather than trying to avoid it and hoping it will go away, we will learn to understand it, work with it and use it to develop compassion. We will see that by accepting that stress is part of life and by practising compassion we can actually reduce our experience of stress.

The word 'stress' is employed as an umbrella term to include all the aspects of life that frustrate our wish to be happy. This is not a book about avoiding stress or eradicating it from our lives. On the contrary, it acknowledges that stress is an inevitable part of being alive – and one that can provide insight into how we are in ourselves and how we interact with other people.

*The formula of the workbook is as follows:*

- Define the problem – in our case, stress – and view it from all angles.
- Identify a helpful way of approaching it – applying compassion – and explore it fully.
- Realise that in order to apply compassion we will need to make some changes in our habits.
- Examine how our mind works in order to better understand our habits.
- Engage with meditation as a means to make a space for change and develop discernment, so we can identify which of our habits are helpful and which are unhelpful.
- Learn compassion techniques and how they can help us with our stress – thereby replacing unhelpful habits with helpful ones.

*This formula is expressed through five steps:*

STEP 1 Understanding our stress instead of trying to avoid it

STEP 2 Taking a step back in order to see what is really going on

STEP 3 Trying out a fresh perspective

STEP 4 Examining our habits to see which ones help us and which ones don't

STEP 5 Taking compassionate action

## *The workbook is divided into three parts:*

### *Part 1: Our Starting Point*

The three chapters of Part 1 of the workbook are about identifying the problem we want to deal with. So, in Chapter 1 we look closely at how stress works. This will help us to understand more about stress and why it is a good idea to try and do something to tackle it.

Chapter 2 moves on to compassion and presents a broad perspective on its use as a remedy for stress. A tendency to compassion is one of our natural resources, and here we get some hints on how to develop it. As we have already seen, compassion can be defined as the wish for everyone to be free from suffering, along with having the urge to do something to bring that about.

Chapter 3 examines how our expectations of happiness and fear of suffering increase our stress. As you read, it helps to try and apply what you are reading to yourself as you go along – to make it as personal as you can – so that you can build up a clear picture of how you look for happiness and how you deal with the suffering of stress.

Two important messages stand out from these chapters:

- In terms of happiness, we need to look to developing long-term happiness, based on peace of mind and self-awareness, rather than focusing on short-term pleasure.
- In terms of suffering and stress, we need to look at our suffering to see how we can learn from it, rather than trying to avoid it.

In terms of the five steps, Part 1 focuses on step 1.

**STEP 1 Understanding our stress instead of trying to avoid it**

## *Part 2: Seeing Where We Want to Change*

Part 1 has given us a lot of information on how we experience stress. Now, in Part 2, we take a careful look at how we want to make changes, what gets in the way and what we can do about it.

Chapter 4 looks at how our mind reacts to the things that happen to us in life and how this relates to the habits we adopt. It is here that the wish to change is stressed as being important. Having decided we want to change, we need to take a step back so that we can look at ourselves clearly. We need to develop self-awareness and take a fresh look at our habits so that we can identify which ones help us and which ones cause us problems. Then we are ready to choose the ones we wish to begin to work with.

Chapter 5 examines the vital role played by meditation in this whole process. It is through meditation that we are able to begin the process of quietening and calming the mind. Then we can use our discernment to explore our habits and see how we can replace our unhelpful habits with helpful ones.

Chapter 6 delves into our habits that cause us stress – both the personality traits we have that can lead to stress, as well as how we cope with it when it happens. It may be worth going back over this chapter several times in order to get a clear understanding of your own habits related to stress.

Chapter 7 looks at developing habits based in compassion. These are likely to be less familiar to you than your reactions to stress, so again it is a good idea to read this chapter through a few times in order to familiarise yourself with these habits.

This is an important part of this book, and spending time reflecting on these four chapters will help give you a structure for how you want to work with compassion and how to apply it in your own life. You may need to revisit these areas from time to time to check your progress as you start working with the techniques.

In terms of the five steps, in Part 2 we will be focusing on steps 2, 3, and 4.

**STEP 2 Taking a step back in order to see what is really going on**

**STEP 3 Trying out a fresh perspective**

**STEP 4 Examining our habits to see which ones help us and which ones don't**

### *Part 3: Making Change Happen*

Having accomplished all this groundwork, we are now ready to directly apply some compassion techniques. Part 3 is all about making this happen in our lives. The three chapters in this section are full of different methods that you can use to train your mind in compassion. Although we have carried out many exercises as we have progressed through the workbook, the ones in this section are particularly special, as each one helps to uncover a further aspect of our compassionate nature.

Chapter 8 begins with an exploration of self-compassion and the important role it plays.

The focus of Chapter 9 is compassion for other people. It contains a range of techniques that can be used to help develop your compassion and make it stable.

Chapter 10 looks at compassion from a big perspective, when we are faced with putting other people's interests before our own. We also explore the wider implications of compassion for our society.

In terms of the five steps, we will be focusing on step 5

**STEP 5 Taking compassionate action**

## Practicalities

- Each chapter begins with the goals it will accomplish and ends with a review of the main points, and some practical tips to work with going forward.
- I recommend that you get a notebook dedicated to your responses to the exercises and tips recommended in this workbook. If you follow through, it will become a supportive companion on your journey.

# Part I

# OUR STARTING POINT

If we want to work with ourselves in any way, then we need to start from where we are. It's no good fudging this and wishing we were in a different place. We just need to begin with what we have right now – both the difficult stuff and the useful stuff.

This opening section of this workbook is all about where we are now in terms of experiencing and dealing with stress – the difficult stuff. Don't you find that it's all too easy to react to stress by trying to distract yourself from it? We just want to feel better and to avoid the uncomfortable feelings stress can bring up. This often means we go for a quick fix, such as shopping, eating foods that are delicious but not so good for us, or spending a lot of time on the internet.

This book takes the opposite approach and recommends looking closely at what causes us stress as a first step to learning to cope with it, and using compassion – the good stuff – as a way to work with it.

We will go step by step. When we discover something about ourselves that we want to change, it's tempting to want to immediately start with the solution – in our case, using compassion to work with stress. This is understandable, but if we don't put in some groundwork, we might find it hard to actualise the changes we want to make. Part 1 will establish this groundwork and provide a solid foundation for us to build on.

**In terms of the five steps, we will be focusing on the first step:**

**STEP 1 Understanding our stress instead of trying to avoid it**

# 1 How Stress Works

*A large body of evidence suggests that stress-related disease emerges, predominantly, out of the fact that we so often activate a physiological system that has evolved for responding to acute physical emergencies, but we turn it on for months on end, worrying about mortgages, relationships, and promotions.*

*Robert Sapolsky*[1]

What we are going to do in this chapter:

1. Enable you to make a connection with how stress works in you
2. Look at how the term stress came about
3. Take a brief look at the human brain
4. Consider how stress affects our thought processes
5. Explore our emotional systems
6. Consider the TYPE A personality

## Getting a Feel of How You Experience Stress

We are going to start straight away with a worksheet that is designed to help you gather some information about how you experience stress. Take your time filling it in – don't rush. You will want to refer back to this as we go forward.

## WORKSHEET

Try to pay attention to the times you refer to 'feeling stressed'.

Ask yourself what exactly you mean by 'feeling stressed' – how does it feel in your body?

I feel anxious, rushed and overwhelmed and cant think properly.

Is it because of something happening to you from an outside source?

No this is in my head, and usually due to having too much to do

Is it caused by how you are feeling in yourself? Yes because I feel overloaded

Is it something to do with your reactions to what is going on around you?

Yes, I feel overwhelmed by having too many jobs to do

What can you understand from this? I need to give myself longer to do the jobs or speed up or maybe get some help

## How the Term 'Stress' Came About

The Hungarian-born Hans Selye[2] (1907–82), is sometimes referred to as the 'grandfather of stress research'. He is credited with popularising the term 'stress', but later on, in 1976, he wrote that he thought he had confused the terms 'stress' and 'strain' because of weaknesses in his use of the English language. If this is the case, it is ironic, because since Selye's use of the term there has been intense debate over the difficulties in defining stress, which in turn has led to problems in measuring it.

Of course, even before it was named as 'stress', there was always interest in how we adapt to the struggles of life – sociologists, anthropologists, physiologists, psychologists and social workers had used a range of different terms. Once the term 'stress' was in the public domain, however, concepts such as conflict, frustration, trauma, alienation, anxiety and emotional distress were brought together under the same label, and it became a sort of umbrella term for a wide range of ideas.

The early 'mechanical' approaches to stress focused on how an animal or human responds to pressure from the outside, whereas Selye's approach was concerned with our body's response to stress and the internal pressures that can result. The 'psychological' view that came later favoured the study of the dynamic relationship between the outside causes of stress and the responses we have to it – thus combining the three elements of the body's response to stress; the internal pressures that can result from that stress, and the psychological view.

The trouble is that in everyday practice the term stress can be used to describe all these different meanings. Someone may describe an unpleasant situation they are exposed to as 'stress', but use the same term to label their reaction to it, such as chest pain, or indeed the end result, which could be an ulcer. We can talk of 'feeling stressed', which indicates our own reaction to an outside pressure, and of 'having a lot of stress', which makes it sound like a simple external factor. In fact, we are talking about the same thing.

However intense the debate about terminology, there is little doubt that the concept of stress has taken a firm hold in our society. There is a wealth of statistics that paint a disturbing picture of how common stress is, particularly in the workplace.

**Here are some statistics from the Mental Health Foundation's 2018 study:**[3]

- In the past year, 74 per cent of people have felt so stressed that they have been overwhelmed or unable to cope.
- 49 per cent of 18 to 24-year-olds who have experienced high levels of stress felt that comparing themselves to others was a source of stress, which was higher than in any of the older age groups.
- 36 per cent of women who felt high levels of stress related this to their comfort with their appearance and body image, compared to 23 per cent of men.

**According to the Health and Safety Executive 2019**[4]

- Stress, depression or anxiety accounted for the loss of 12.8 million working days in 2019
- In 2018/19 stress, depression or anxiety accounted for 44 per cent of all work-related ill health cases and 54 per cent of all working days lost due to ill health.

## How stress works in our bodies

### TIPS

As you read this part of the chapter, try to imagine the physical effects that are being described happening in your own mind and body over and over again.

The chances are that if you are using this workbook you are already thinking about how to reduce the stress you have.

Becoming familiar with the biology of stress can be another building block in our effort to understand stress more thoroughly.

Humans respond to stress just like other mammals do. The purpose of the stress response is to protect us in times of danger and keep us alive. The stress response has evolved as a way of returning the body to a state of balance after it has suffered an attack.

When we lived as members of tribes of hunter-gatherers on vast savannahs, our lives were infinitely less complicated than they are today, and at the same time dramatically more dangerous. Animal predators, unfriendly tribes, the perils of hunting and the demands of a life lived at the mercy of the elements all presented immediate life-or-death situations needing instant action. A gazelle attacked by a cheetah will experience the same set of physiological responses that humans do when feeling threatened, but in the case of the gazelle, the stress response is short-term – lasting either till she outruns the cheetah, or the cheetah gets its meal.

The trouble is that in humans this response has not been updated to suit our current lifestyles. In today's complex world, few of us find ourselves chased by a sabre-toothed tiger, and yet our body's stress response is still geared to deal with exactly this kind of emergency. Our body goes into the same response mode when we are faced with bad traffic, late-running trains and slow service in restaurants, but instead of the experience being short-term and relatively infrequent, we go through these and similar episodes several times each day.

It is this repeated low-grade arousal of the stress response, the sense of a continual simmering of activity, that is the greatest threat to our wellbeing. What makes the picture even more complex is that humans have the capacity to think and stimulate ideas, fantasies and images in the mind, which they then can ruminate on, going over and over them in their minds. This is a very common source of stress that we need to look at in more detail.

Before we go any further though, let's take a moment for you to identify your own main sources of stress and reflect on how you feel this stress in your body.

| What are your main sources of stress? | How do you experience them in your body? |
| --- | --- |
| Jobs I need to do every day | Feeling I have to rush, and having very little time for breaks. |

## A Practical Example of How Stress Works in Our Bodies

Here is an everyday example of how we can experience a stress response to a perceived threat. It's designed to bring home the impact stress has on our bodies.

Imagine that you have enjoyed a pleasant evening out with friends – so good in fact that you lost track of time and missed the last bus home. There are no taxis about and so you find yourself making the journey on foot – it's dark, there are not many people about, and you need to pass through some unfriendly looking streets.

Suddenly you hear a noise behind you. Your threat and self-protection system is activated – your heart begins to beat a little faster, you become aware that your breathing is more rapid and the meal you so enjoyed a few hours ago now feels heavy in your stomach. At the same time, you feel a surge of energy and a sharpening of your senses.

The first thing you want to know is whether or not the noise represents danger, and the process of working this out requires activities of the brain such as sensation and memory.

These are located in the cerebral cortex, part of the 'new' brain.

You can check the areas of the brain as they are mentioned in the simple diagram opposite.

If the noise is indeed considered to be a threat, emotional responses such as fear and anxiety are generated in the limbic system in the brain in order to process the information. The limbic system is part of the evolutionary 'old' brain and is responsible for directing behaviours required for survival such as fear, aggression and sexual reproduction.

It includes such areas as the hippocampus, which is located within the temporal lobes and is concerned with memory and detecting threats, and the amygdala (1), which is located near to the hippocampus (2) and is concerned with emotionally charged or negative stimuli.

The amygdala functions like an alarm bell: if the noise behind you sounds a lot like the noise you heard in that scary movie you watched recently, it will pulse a general warning throughout the brain and fast-track signals to your fight-or-flight neural and hormonal systems. In this way the limbic system can activate the hypothalamus (3), which is located just above the brain stem in the middle of the brain and controls the stress response.

The structure of the brain

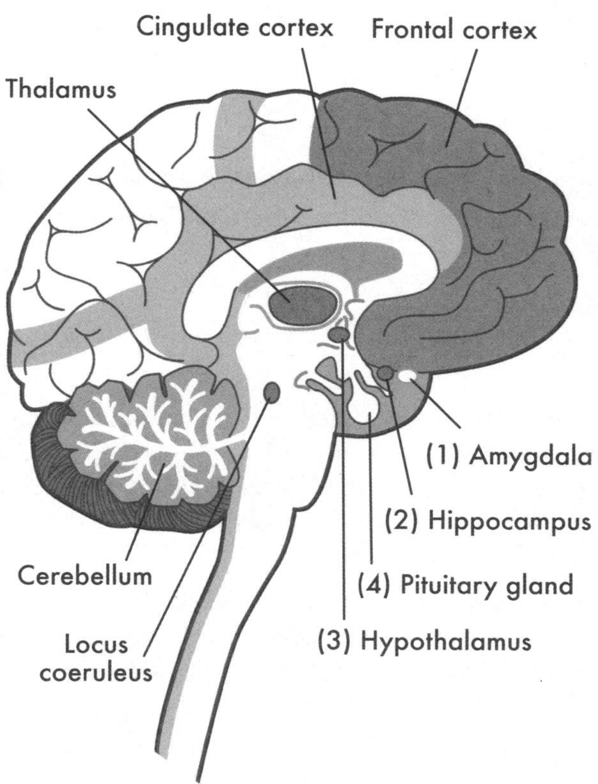

We are accustomed to the beating of our heart, the digestion of our evening meal, our breathing and blood circulation, the regulation of our temperature all going on without our conscious control.

**This is the work of the automatic nervous system**, which can be thought of as our survival nervous system because without it we would be at best very ill and at worst, dead. It is this system that is activated by the hypothalamus once a threat is identified.

**The automatic nervous system consists of two systems: the sympathetic nervous system (SNS) and the parasympathetic nervous system (PNS). Different emotional states cause different activation of each – feelings of anxiety and stress are associated with the SNS, whereas relaxation is associated with the PNS.**

So, when that noise behind you gives you a fright on your late-night walk home, it is the SNS that kicks into action, releasing the neurotransmitter noradrenaline to activate the internal organs. It is responsible for increasing your heart rate, releasing glucose into the blood and slowing digestion in order to prepare your body for action. The PNS will do the opposite – it slows the heart rate, stores the glucose in the liver, and returns the digestion to normal once you feel the danger has passed.

If the noise gets closer and louder, and the situation seems acute, the hypothalamus activates the adrenal glands to release adrenaline[5] into the bloodstream in order to prepare for fight or flight.

**This is part of what is known as the 'sympathetic adrenal medullary response system' (SAM).** This response system has been likened to striking a match – it takes little effort, but its effect does not last long. Whichever way we decide to respond to this frightening noise – whether we fight or run – we will need a plentiful supply of energy and oxygen to our brain and muscles in order to meet the challenge, and this is exactly what the SAM system is designed to accomplish.

However, if the hypothalamus judges the stress to be chronic and needing sustained attention over time, it stimulates the pituitary gland (4), which puts into process a series of reactions culminating in the production of another hormone, corticosteroid. This enables the body to maintain steady supplies of blood sugar to help cope with prolonged stress.

**This is known as the 'hypothalamic-pituitary-adrenal axis' (HPA).** The image used to describe this stress response system is of lighting a fire – it takes effort to get it going but once it's alight, it can remain effective for a long time. The HPA axis is only activated in extreme circumstances. So, if we start to quicken our pace in order to get away from the noise behind us but it seems to draw closer however fast we go, our HPA system might kick in.

An important thing to realise is that this reaction will depend on our own personal threshold for stress – how we react to challenging events. If we are habitually nervous, the noise we are trying to escape will conjure up all kinds of frightening images that could lead to the activation of the HPA axis, but if we are used to long solitary walks in nature, we may be more accustomed to unexplained noises and the HPA axis would not kick in. The bottom line is that the more readily the HPA axis is activated, the more impact the stress will have on our mental and physical wellbeing.

| **What have we learned from this example?** | **Your insights** |
|---|---|
| The response to threat comes largely from the old brain | |
| Analysing what is happening takes place in the neocortex – the newer part of the brain | |
| When you experience threat, the SNS takes over to prepare your body for action | |
| Your body is prepared for flight or fight – some systems are stimulated (heart-rate increased, glucose pouring into the blood), others are closed down because they are not needed (digestion, reproduction, immune system) | |
| Our body's reaction can be short-term SAM, but there is also another reaction which lasts much longer (HPA) | |

## How Stress Works with Our Thinking Brain

### *1. We go over and over things in our minds*

| | Does this happen for you? |
|---|---|
| About two million years ago, pre-humans started to get smart. We evolved the ability to think, ruminate, anticipate, imagine and predict. Whereas the gazelle will calm down quite quickly after it has escaped from the cheetah, we humans are likely to think, 'What would've happened if I'd got caught?' Frightening fantasies and images may come up in our mind as a result. Perhaps we wake up in the night and think, 'What would have happened if I hadn't seen the cheetah? What if I get caught tomorrow? What about letting the children go out – maybe it's too dangerous?' So for us the threat has not passed away. We play it over and over in our minds and in this way constantly maintain and stimulate our stress response. | |

### *2. Our minds are pulled back into the past and ahead into the future.*

| | Does this happen for you? |
|---|---|
| In addition, humans have evolved the ability to understand and think about themselves as individual selves. We can worry about so many things to do with our individual self – such as whether or not people like us, whether our job is secure, whether we will be able to pass our exams and so on. The sense of self gives rise to a constant monitoring of potential threats to our 'self' both now and in the future. We have a capacity to worry about all kinds of things linked to our 'self' identity. So, this thinking brain constantly pulls us away from the present moment into the past and the future. | |

To put it simply, humans create loops in the mind where an emotion or a frightening event can trigger a series of thoughts and attention-focusing, and these in turn maintain and strengthen the emotion. These loops are the basis of many forms of stress and also of mental-health difficulties. The reason for this is that people find it very difficult to get out of them – and the greater the threat, the tighter the loop. So, people find the mind going back and back and back to the thing that is stressing them, over and over again.

Generally, it is not helpful for us to berate ourselves for falling into the trap of dwelling on things because that will only make us feel worse. Moreover, trying to tell ourselves to stop it doesn't usually work. This is why in this book we are going to set out some exercises that will help you to break up these loops. The very good news in all this is that we do have more choice in how we respond to them than we think. We will see that by using mindfulness, meditation and compassion exercises we can begin to change the way our mind responds to threat and difficulty.

You already identified your main areas of stress but let's go a little deeper. Try to identify two or three of your main thinking loops that recur again and again and cause you stress.

______________________________

______________________________

______________________________

______________________________

______________________________

______________________________

## How Stress Works with Our Emotional Systems

If our thoughts, imaginations and ruminations playing on our emotions can create loops, then it's quite important to think about what kinds of emotions they can play on. It is helpful to think of at least three basic types of emotion linked to different functions.

Professor Paul Gilbert has developed a therapeutic approach called the Compassionate Mind Approach.[6] An element of this approach is to understand our Three Emotional Systems.

These are:

- The threat and self-protection system (sometimes called the threat-focused regulation system).
- The incentive and resource-seeking system (sometimes called the incentive/resource-focused regulation system).
- The soothing and contentment system (sometimes called the non-wanting/affiliative-focused regulation system).

We will look briefly at each one in turn.

### *The threat and self-protection system*

The first types of emotion are linked to threat, and evolved to help us detect threats quickly, pay attention to them and take defensive action. Typical 'threat' emotions are fear, anxiety, anger and disgust.

It is useful to think about how the threat system interacts with our other emotions – especially positive emotions. In fact, the threat system is designed to knock out our positive emotions when it is triggered.

For example, if you're walking in the forest looking for a nice spot to have lunch and you think you see a tiger, you are going to have to forget lunch, pay very close attention to the tiger and prepare yourself to run quickly. Keeping your attention on how wonderful your lunch is going to be, or where you're going to sit to enjoy the sunshine, is absolutely not the thing to do! The moment the potential threat of the tiger appears, all that goes out the window. So, threat naturally turns off positive emotions. However, it does more than this.

There are two very important processes that happen in the threat system:

1. The system itself tends to make mistakes because it uses what is called 'a better safe than sorry' process.

How does this work? Imagine you are a rabbit in a field nibbling at a nice lettuce when you hear a sound or see a movement in the bushes. What's the best thing to do? The answer is to run, because although nine times out of ten the sound will be perfectly innocent, occasionally it will be a predator. If you watch birds on the lawn eating your breadcrumbs, you will see just how sensitive to threat they are. They will often leave a very good meal of breadcrumbs because they fly away at any hint of danger.

The interesting thing is that as we get stressed, this tendency increases, so when under pressure we are even more likely to focus on threats. So here we can see that the threat system can jump to the wrong conclusions, causing us all kinds of trouble.

2. The second thing the threat system can do is even worse, because it can lead us to think of things that upset and stressed us in the past.

Imagine you go Christmas shopping. In nine out of ten shops the assistants are very kind, smile at you and show real interest in helping you buy a good present, so you leave the shop really happy. However, in one shop the assistant is talking to her friend and seems very uninterested in serving you, behaving quite rudely, as if you're a bit of a nuisance. Then she tries to sell you a present you don't really want and ends up short-changing you. On your way home, who is it that sticks in the mind – whom do you tell your partner about when you reach home? It's the rude shop assistant, of course. We've all done it at one time or other – the threat system will make you dwell on the one rude person rather than the other 90 per cent of people who were kind and helpful.

Just think about what's going on in your brain and the loop you are getting into. It does not even need to be a recent event because we can ruminate about things that happened months or even years ago and, in this way, constantly stimulate our brains into stress.

### Exercise: Answer these three questions

Think about what would happen if you noticed this thinking loop occurring and made the decision that you didn't want to keep replaying this stressful situation?

______________________________________________

______________________________________________

What do you think would happen in your brain if you deliberately noticed your unhelpful thinking and chose to refocus on the smiling and helpful people?

______________________________________________

______________________________________________

Supposing you replayed again in your mind the real sense of interest the majority of shop assistants had and your own pleasure in the whole experience?

______________________________________________

______________________________________________

The threat system is like a magnet and it can so easily pull our attention away from a more positive focus if we're not careful. When it does that our mind and our body become more stressed. Learning to become aware of when we are doing this is a first step in choosing to react in a different, more positive way.

## *The incentive and resource-seeking system*

Incentive or 'drive' emotions such as enthusiasm, determination and the wish to succeed help us to go out and do things. They create feelings of pleasure and enjoyment from achieving and having; they give a sense of excitement and anticipation. When something really major happens to us we can become very excited, mentally and physically.

Imagine for a moment winning the European lottery and being worth €100 million! How would you feel? The chances are you would get a rush of chemicals such as adrenaline and dopamine in your brain and body. These have the effect of making you very stimulated. You would find it hard not to be constantly thinking about your money and what you were going to do with it. In fact, you would probably have a few sleepless nights. This reaction would be perfectly natural but can be difficult for us to manage.

Interestingly, many scientists now recognise that in our society, 'drive' emotions are often seen as the source of happiness, pushing us to go after what we want. Society encourages us to buy things because that's how our economic system works, and so we are being constantly enticed to do more, have more, try harder. However, as we will see later when we look more deeply into happiness, even the pleasure of winning the lottery doesn't last for ever. Within a few months people are often back to where they were in terms of their levels of happiness.

We also know that sometimes people become very driven and high-achieving because underneath the surface they are quite insecure. They are frightened that if they don't achieve things other people won't accept or want them. So, for some people the fear of rejection is a reason for constantly trying to prove themselves.

People who rely too much on the drive system also run the risk of getting exhausted and burnt out and collapsing. They can even get depressed when they feel they can't achieve enough. Indeed, it's not uncommon to find that depressed people have an underlying sense of inferiority which they try to make up for by endlessly trying to prove themselves. As long as they are achieving, they feel OK, but the moment they can't do so or are forced to slow down, for instance because of illness or incapacity, depression can come.

It can also happen that when people get stuck solely in 'drive' system functioning they run the risk of behaving in quite immoral and unhelpful ways. Recent revelations about the behaviour typified in the banking culture illustrate this. So 'threat' and 'drive' systems need balancing, and it turns out that there is indeed a third emotional system that can do this.

### *The soothing and contentment system*

It's clear that animals – including ourselves – cannot always be running away from threats or rushing around achieving things. Sometimes animals need to rest and to be in a state of quiescence where they are neither under threat, nor in a state of seeking or achieving – we could say they are in a state of satisfaction or contentment. It used to be thought that these states simply related to the 'threat' and 'drive' systems being turned down for a while, but more recent research is showing that contentment can accompany very profound, positive feelings. It is linked to calmness, peacefulness and wellbeing – very different types of positive emotion from typical 'drive' emotions such as achievement and excitement.

These 'soothing' types of emotion are especially linked to the production of endorphins and oxytocin. We will look at this in more detail later on in the book. For now, it is enough to know that the soothing and contentment system is linked to the parasympathetic nervous system, whereas the drive and threat systems tend to be linked to the sympathetic nervous system.

### *From contentment to compassion*

We will begin to look into compassion in detail in the next chapter, but let's take a moment to see how it fits with what we have been talking about here. Compassion is sensitivity to distress – turning towards it and trying to alleviate it, rather than trying to avoid it – but it is also linked to affiliation, or a sense of connection, and friendliness.

There is a fundamental story here that helps us to understand how these 'soothing and contentment' emotions are linked to compassion, and why they have a very powerful influence on our 'threat' system. The moment when mammals evolved to engage in live birth – where the parent, usually the mother, provided care to their offspring – was a very important one in evolutionary terms. It became very helpful for the offspring to spend periods of time in a state of quiet and sleep, out of harm's way. Significantly, the presence of the mother, along with elements such as bodily contact, has the automatic effect on the infant of calming them and stimulating their 'soothing' emotions.

As children grow older, the presence of their mother is enough to provide a sense of safeness and calm, which allows for play and explorative behaviour. Commonly, if the mother leaves or moves out of sight of the child, its 'threat' system is activated. The return of the mother stimulates the soothing system and deactivates the threat system again. The basic narrative is that in childhood, access to a loving 'other', such as a parent or carer, plays a very important role in how stressed we feel and how easily we calm down.

Although the full story is complex, we now know that kindness and love operate through specific systems in our brain and have very specific effects on the threat-stress system. When a baby is distressed, the mother will respond to the distress call and the baby will in turn calm down in response to a cuddle from its mother.

## Worksheet 3.1 – How your three systems function

| | Threat System | Drive System | Soothing System |
|---|---|---|---|
| How often is this system triggered? | | | |
| What tends to trigger it? | | | |
| How long does it stay activated for once triggered? | | | |
| How powerfully do you experience this system when triggered? (1 is weakly, and 10 powerfully) | | | |
| What type of thoughts do you have when in this system? | | | |
| What do you want to do when this system is triggered? | | | |

From *The Compassionate Mind Workbook* (page 36) with the permission of Chris Irons and Elaine Beaumont.

> Think about this in your own life:
>
> If you are distressed, how often do you turn to somebody you think cares about you and loves you?
>
> How much does their ability to listen to you and understand you give you the feeling that they value and care for you?
>
> How much does this help you to calm down?

We now know that low affection from the parent figure can even affect our genetic make-up as well as how our brain matures – it's that powerful! From the day we are born to the day that we die, the loving kindness of others will have a huge impact on the quality of our lives.

It is not just the kindness of other people but also our own kindness to ourselves that can calm us down. This is because kindness stimulates a very important emotion regulation system in our brain – one that evolved to respond to loving and kindness.

We can depict these three basic emotion systems as three circles that are constantly interacting.

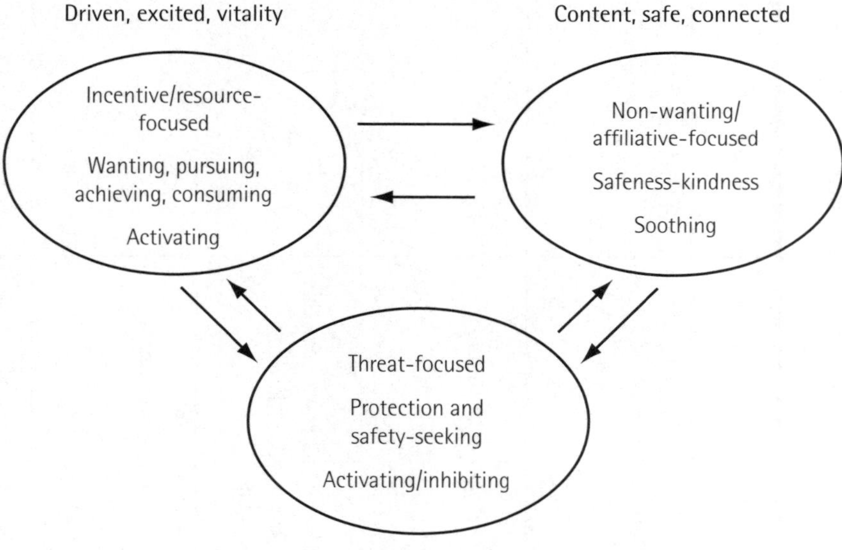


**Diagram 1:** The interaction between three major emotion regulation systems

From *The Compassionate Mind* by Paul Gilbert (2009), reprinted with permission from Little, Brown Book Group

It is not that one system should always dominate, but rather that they should be able to operate in such a way that they feed into each other and balance each other out. The ability to feel anxiety and anger at appropriate times is important, as is the ability to have drive, excitement and ambition, but so too is the ability to be able to calm down and to regulate our behaviour. To rest and to find peace and stability in our own mind is essential; to know how to feel safe in, and calmed by, our relationships with others and ourselves. Many of the exercises in this book will help you to bring these three different emotional regulation systems into balance. To do this will provide you with a greater sense of inner peace and stability.

### *The downside of the stress response*

We have seen that our whole stress response system has evolved to help us escape short-term physical emergencies, such as being chased by a sabre-toothed tiger or attacked by a hostile tribe. In order to survive an event like that our bodies would have needed to respond very fast and work very hard.

The points in the following box describe:

1. How the body gears up to cope with stress – what works harder and what shuts down.
2. The changes in life expectancy now from when we were living as hunter-gatherers and what this means for us today.
3. The effects of a constantly stimulated stress response.

As you read through, think carefully about your own life and your own habits. We will be looking deeply at our habits in Part 2 of this workbook. Getting a handle on how your habits work will help you to identify how you experience stress and what your stress habits are.

**1. The main purpose of the stress response is to get energy to our muscles in the quickest and most effective way possible.**

Our heart rate, blood pressure and breathing rate all increase in order to transport glucose and oxygen to the critical muscles. The flip side of this is that when the body is mobilising to face immediate danger it puts a halt on long-term projects – which would divert energy from the priority of the moment – in order to survive:

- Digestion is a slow process and there is no time to benefit from it during times of stress, so it is shut down.
- Growth, reproduction, tissue repair and the immune function are also put on hold.
- In addition, our experience of pain is blunted under stress, enabling us to continue to run, or fight, even if we are injured.
- Various shifts occur in our cognitive and sensory skills, improving our memory and sharpening our senses so that we can draw on memories of similar emergencies and be totally alert to what is going on around us

All these activities are extremely important for your long-term survival but will not help you if you want to run away from that noise.

**All our energy is focused on the moment and on staying alive.**

**2. In our lives as hunter-gatherers we would not have expected to live for more than thirty-five or forty years, and our encounters with hostile tribes and sabre-toothed tigers, although traumatic, would have been fairly infrequent and short-lived.**

How different from our lives now, when our life expectancy is more than doubled and the causes of stress that we encounter can come in myriad forms over and over again.

Nowadays, this response is being activated repeatedly and over longer periods of time, so as we have seen, it can be the stress response itself that begins to cause us problems.

- If we keep mobilising energy and never store it, we will tire easily and put ourselves at risk of some form of diabetes.
- A cardiovascular system that is frequently overstimulated will result in hardening of the arteries and increase the risk of heart disease.
- Repeatedly shutting down digestion leads to ulcers, colitis and irritable bowel syndrome.
- An interrupted reproductive cycle will take longer and longer to regulate itself and can result in amenorrhea (menstruation stopping) and infertility.
- A suppressed immune system means we are more likely to contract infectious diseases and be less able to fight them.

### 3. The impact of a constantly stimulated stress response

Next time we are out late and hear a noise behind us, we are more likely to treat it as a threat because we have been so recently frightened.

- The threat system is responding with its 'better safe than sorry' approach.
- The same repeated stress activity wears down the hippocampus, which is concerned with keeping clear records of our experience.
- The hippocampus is also one of the few regions of the brain that can grow new neurons (nerve cells that receive and send electrical signals over long distances within the body), but steroid hormones released as part of the long-term stress response, prevent this, impairing the ability of the hippocampus to produce new memories. This means that our memory does not work as well as it used to.
- The production of dopamine, which has a lot to do with our sense of attention, and feelings of enjoyment and pleasure, is also lowered over time by these hormones.
- Repeatedly activating the stress response can therefore have a detrimental effect over time. It is a kind of vicious circle – the more frequently the body responds to stress, the more reactive the amygdala becomes to apparent threats, which in turn increases our tendency to stress, which sensitises the amygdala still further. This is likely to result in a heightened sense of fear and anxiety

**We can see therefore that in a biological sense stress undermines our happiness and threatens our wellbeing.**

As we have seen, the body works hard whenever we experience any kind of stress. Because of this it can provide us with vital clues as to when and how we are stressed – clues that can help us become more self-aware and therefore equipped to tackle the habits that we fall into when we are stressed. We can think of our body as a kind of *stress barometer* that provides evidence to show how we are being affected by stress.

**Try this exercise:**

When you are feeling stressed, pay attention to your body and notice where the stress is making itself felt.

Perhaps it is a tightness in the chest, or a sinking feeling in the stomach?

Has it lodged in your neck, or in frequent headaches?

When you have located the physical feeling associated with stress, firstly just notice it and then try and consciously relax that area.

At the same time, ask yourself if there is another way to respond to the stressful situation and lessen the impact on your body.

## The Role of the Internet in Our Stress Response

We have looked at various kinds of threat that we can experience and how, for the most part, they tend to be very different from what our ancestors might have experienced on the savannah. Let's take a moment to reflect on something that our ancestors did not even dream about but that has become a vital part of our lives in a very short time – the internet.

Research on the effects of internet exposure are still in their early stages but already it is clear that the norms of how we communicate as human beings is changing. I have several work colleagues with whom I share quite a profound working relationship and yet I have never actually met them in person! We are becoming used to having numerous relationships at a distance, and at the touch of a few keys. Information pours into our devices in a constant stream. New research is showing that already this kind of access is changing how we store, process and even value knowledge.[7]

Interaction on the internet can also be experienced as threatening.

**Take email for example.** A harsh, or challenging email can cause our amygdala to respond as if to a threat and, if we are not paying attention, it can lead us to lash out in response. This kind of thing can become quite contagious. When that happens, we can quickly find ourselves in a spiral of negative interaction.

When we are not engaging with another person face to face, it is easier to de-personalise the exchange and cause us to lower our usual standards of care and concern.

It is important to be able to hit the PAUSE button with this kind of exchange:

- Take time to process the email.
- Write a draft reply.
- Wait for a while before you finalise it.
- Read it again slowly before hitting send.

Have you had a recent example of feeling threatened by an email exchange?

What did you learn from it?

**Then there is the increase in public shaming through social media.** There is nothing new about the ritual of public shaming, but with the internet the safety valve of witnessing the effects of your criticism is removed. The kind of outpouring of attack and criticism we see from time to time on Facebook and Twitter is reaching a higher level of hostility.[8] As a result, people can lose their jobs along with their reputations. This can have devastating repercussions for an individual. In the online world, everyone is a public figure, and everyone is a target. The conversations that used to be reserved for our friends, family members and communities are now open for scrutiny, criticism and even persecution by anyone with a Wi-Fi connection and a temper. This takes the fear of ostracism outside of the public sphere and places it squarely in our homes.

This workbook is all about helping us reduce stress in all aspects of our lives. We don't know yet the full impact of the internet on our lives, but the evidence is already there that shows it to be a possible source of threat.

We will pick up on this topic in Chapter 8 where we look at self-compassion.

## A Word About the Type A Personality

In the 1950s, two cardiologists in San Francisco, Meyer Friedman and Ray Rosenman, observed that the chairs in their waiting room were wearing out at an alarming rate. Growing tired of frequently replacing them, they sought the advice of a new upholsterer, who drew attention to the kind of damage the chairs had suffered. The front area of the seat cushions and the armrests were torn to shreds because the patients in the waiting rooms were literally on the edges of their seats, fidgeting, impatient to be seen, clawing at the armrests. It was not until several years later that the penny dropped and Friedman and Rosenman saw the connection between their waiting-room chairs and the term 'Type A personality', which they had invented to describe people who are competitive, high-powered super-achievers, time-pressured, impatient, critical and hostile. 'Type B', on the other hand, is the term they came up with to describe people who do not have these characteristics and who are laid-back, seek harmony, have inner motivation and a creative attitude towards mistakes. In one study that they carried out in the 1970s, a group of 3,000 healthy men were observed over an eight-and-a-half-year period. According to the findings, twice as many Type A subjects developed heart disease as Type B.

However, Friedman and Rosenman's findings were not confirmed by subsequent studies. By the end of the 1980s, it was agreed that although personality traits are more useful in determining whether or not someone is at risk of heart disease among those who have their first heart attack relatively early in life, as we get older a first heart attack is more to do with levels of fat in our bodies and smoking. Later studies identified a high degree of hostility as a more reliable predictor of coronary heart disease and atherosclerosis, along with higher rates of mortality with these diseases.[9] More recent studies have shown that hostility is associated with a significant overall increase in mortality across all diseases, not just heart disease.

In this chapter we have traced the stress response as it cascades through the body. We have seen that if it is activated too often, or too readily, the stress we are experiencing is going to have a deeper and more lasting impact. This is what tends to happen with people who have high levels of hostility. A Type A person is going to look on life as a series of provocations and frustrations that they will interpret as requiring immediate and often hostile responses, whereas for other people the same events may well appear as minor irritations. A Type A personality's emotion regulation systems will be repeatedly firing on full alert even in such trivial situations as finding oneself in the slowest queue in the supermarket checkout. If we are a Type A person, on our late-night walk home, we are more likely to remain irritated, even when we find out that the noise behind us is only a stray cat rummaging among the garbage bins; even though there is no danger, we keep the stress response going by cursing the cat and our own fearful imaginings. A Type B person is more likely to allow themselves to experience relief and then find some humour in the situation.

Which Personality Type do you identify most closely with
– Type A or Type B?

The good news is that no one needs to stay as a Type A. If you are a Type A personality, as soon as you take the vital step of beginning to notice your behaviour and are willing to take steps to change it, you can begin to learn how to reduce your stress levels. We will explore this further when we look into stress habits and look at how developing self-awareness is a good place to start to work with stress.

| What we have learned in this chapter | Your reflections |
|---|---|
| • Understanding how stress affects our body can help us decide to do something about our stress levels.<br>• Our stress response is the same as that of any other mammal and evolved to help us survive in the demanding conditions of life as a hunter-gatherer several thousand years ago.<br>• Humans have the capacity to produce ideas, fantasies and images in the mind, which they then can ruminate on. This is a very common source of stress.<br>• Humans create loops in the mind where a negative emotion or a frightening event can trigger a series of thoughts, which in turn maintain and strengthen the emotion.<br>• In the Compassionate Mind Approach, it's helpful to think of at least three basic types of emotion linked to different functions. These are:<br>  * The threat and self-protection emotion system<br>  * The incentive and resource-seeking emotion system<br>  * The soothing and contentment emotion system<br>• The stress response activates all the emotion systems in our body that are needed to stand and fight, or run away – for example, our heart beats faster, our blood courses through the body more quickly, energy is released into our bloodstream and muscles.<br>• At the same time, many of our other systems shut down under stress because they are not needed for short-term | |

| | |
|---|---|
| survival – for example, this can affect digestion, fertility, the immune system, and growth and repair of the body.<br>• However, in modern times we may experience stressful situations several times every day and so the stress response is activated over and over again. Added to this, we live much longer than we did as a hunter-gatherer and our bodies can get worn out by the repeated response to stress.<br>• There is a lot of research into the relationship between stress and illness. It appears that the stress response itself could become a factor in our susceptibility to disease.<br>• A connection between hostility and heart disease has been firmly established.<br>• The more we can notice our own behaviour and how we respond to stressful situations, the better we can get a handle on how to work with it. | |

## TIPS TO TAKE INTO EVERYDAY LIFE

1. We need to notice when we are stressed.
2. It does not help to try and ignore our stress, or distract ourselves from it.
3. Best is to 'lean into' our stress to understand it.

# 2 How Compassion Works

*I believe that at the most fundamental level our nature is compassionate, and that cooperation, not conflict, lies at the heart of the basic principles that govern our human existence.*

*The Dalai Lama*[1]

What we are going to do in this chapter:

1. Reflect on the definition of compassion
2. Explore the idea of fundamental wholeness
3. Learn what it means to train the mind in compassion
4. Understand the biology of compassion

*Exercise*

What does the following story tell you about compassion?

______________________________

______________________________

There is a traditional story that is told in different versions in several different world religions, including Judaism, Hinduism, Christianity and Buddhism. A seeker of the truth is curious to know the nature of heaven and hell, so he requests his guide to show him. The guide leads him to a large room filled with a table piled high with delicious food and surrounded by people. Each person is holding a spoon with a long handle, so long that it is impossible for him or her to put food in his or her mouth. Everyone is quarrelling and miserable, hungry and desperate. The seeker sighs as he is led away and declares that now he has seen hell.

Next the guide says he will show him heaven and leads him into another room just like the first one, with people sitting around a sumptuous banquet holding their long spoons. The astonished and disappointed seeker declares that this is what he has just seen in hell. His guide advises him to look more closely, and as he does so he notices that instead of each person struggling to feed themselves, they are using the long spoons to reach across and feed each other. Everyone is getting plenty to eat and is relaxed and happy. 'This is how heaven is,' the guide explains.

It is easy to see our world as being dominated by people struggling to use their long spoon solely for their own benefit and to miss the numerous instances of people helping each other. Certainly, the potential for selfishness, greed and violence exists in all of us, but it sits alongside a core of altruism and kindness that can lead us to perform compassionate acts even for strangers. We can feel overwhelmed by the speed and volume of sad and tragic news pouring into our homes through television and the internet, but amongst this avalanche of suffering come frequent accounts of kindness and bravery on behalf of other people – think of aid workers supporting people afflicted by war and famine, or the kindness and bravery of first responders. Human nature is founded in compassion and, although it can be challenging for us, we need to work out some practical understanding of it so that we can apply it in our ordinary lives.

Most religions place compassion at the heart of their doctrine, each expressing its own version of what is known as the Golden Rule,[2] or the ethic of reciprocity:

Always treat others as you would wish to be treated yourself.

Perhaps its most common expression is in the words of Jesus Christ:

Do unto others, as you would have them do unto you.[3]

These simple words carry a message of critical importance for the continuation of the human species and as such they constitute the basis of the United Nations Universal Declaration of Human Rights.[4]

**As you go about your day, try to act according to the Golden Rule.**

How did it go?

What was difficult?

What worked well?

In this book we will primarily be working with Buddhist ideas about compassion.

Central to these ideas is an understanding of compassion as *the ability to feel another person's suffering as if it is your own, to wish for them to be free from it, and to be prepared to help them in that endeavour.*

This definition is based on an understanding that all people suffer and that it is not possible for us to maintain an attitude of indifference in the face of this. We will see that developing this kind of understanding has a profound effect on how we experience the difficulties of life and the stress that can result. Training our mind in this way helps to calm the emotional systems that lead to stress and strengthens those that help to alleviate it.

## Exercise: Ask yourself: Does this definition make sense to you?

| Yes, it does | No, I have concerns |
|---|---|
| ______________________ | ______________________ |

**There are several special qualities in the Buddhist approach to compassion**

- In the first place, it is not based on a set of moral guidelines, nor does it rely on a system of belief.

  ______________________

- It is a step-by-step training of the mind based on logic that combines human feeling with reason.

  ______________________

- Because of this system of logic and emphasis on reason, it goes hand in hand with a modern, scientific approach. We will be looking into some of the findings from Western scientific research as we go along.

  ______________________

- As this approach is not belief-based, people of different religions or those who are not interested in religion at all can practise it.

**Taking as its starting point our natural inclination to love and kindness, developing compassion is about learning to consider others as well as yourself.** This enables us to engage in a way of living that will bring enormous benefit to ourselves as well as others. Although it may sound surprising, by concerning ourselves with the suffering of others it is possible to find a key to reduce our own suffering. Stress is certainly one of the great sufferings of modern life. One of the things we will learn in this book is how to apply the logic of compassion to our experience of stress, and so try and gain some clues as to how to transform it and reduce our feelings of stress and the impact it has on our lives.

## Two Aspects to the Definition of Compassion

When we look closely at the definition of compassion, we can see that it has two parts:

The first is:

**The ability to feel another person's suffering as if it is your own and to wish for them to be free from it.**

The idea is that we turn *towards* suffering rather than away from it.

- We need to be motivated to engage with suffering and the causes of suffering.

This is important because:

- If we wish people to be free from suffering, we need to know something about what it is and how it works.
- Our tendency is often to turn away or become overwhelmed by suffering.
- Even when we think about our own stress, we are not always prepared to turn towards it, to really engage with it and get to know it.

We need to learn to *pay attention to suffering,* which in this case is the stress that arises within us, and to try to form an emotional connection to it. This is important because:

- It's far easier to crack open a bottle of wine at the end of the day than to try to get to the heart of what is making us feel stressed and to make difficult changes in order to improve our situation.

When we do manage to connect emotionally with suffering and the sources of suffering, *are we able to tolerate it, and make sense of it, or do we close down?*

This is important because:

- In order not to close down, to be able to think about our own feelings and the feelings of other people, we need to develop an empathic understanding of our own minds.
- Genuine empathy needs imagination and it requires us to put in some cognitive work. Example: if we see a beggar in the street, we might spend a few moments imagining that we are that beggar – cold and in a state of despair; or caught up in a cycle of drugs or having some kind of mental illness.
- It is a process of getting familiar with the mind of another from inside. This is what empathy is – the process by which we come to know the minds of others deeply and without judgement.

The second is:

**To be prepared to help them in that endeavour.**

Here we are trying *to do something* about alleviating suffering.

Example: a doctor when confronted by a new patient. The doctor must first pay attention to the nature of the patient's difficulties, the symptoms and pains, but then his attention needs to switch to relieving the causes of the problem.

This is important because:

- If we only turn towards pain and try to engage with it empathetically, sooner or later we will get burnt out and overwhelmed.
- The key is to have some insight into what's actively helpful.
- We can learn to pay attention to what is helpful, learn to reason in ways that are helpful and also to behave in ways that are helpful.

This of course involves *courage*. Compassionate behaviour means directly confronting stress and suffering in ourselves and in others, and taking actions to relieve it and its causes.

Within the Buddhist tradition there is recognition that the more understanding you have of how your own mind works in relation to experiencing suffering, the more able you are to help others. *Training our minds* is the road to the understanding that enables us to alleviate stress – it's what this book is all about.

*Exercise*

Now you have read about the two aspects of compassion, go back to the definition of compassion:

***The ability to feel another person's suffering as if it is your own, to wish for them to be free from it, and to be prepared to help them in that endeavour.***

Has your understanding of the definition clarified, or deepened?

---

---

## Fundamental Wholeness

When we are feeling overwhelmed by the pressures of life, it is not easy to feel fundamentally well and whole, but this is another important aspect of Buddhist ideas about compassion, and one that can help us as we try to understand both stress and compassion.

*Picture a jar of water: the nature of the water is clear.*

If we add a drop of blue ink to it, then it changes into a blue liquid. If we add red ink, then it becomes red. If we drop in some mud and gravel and then shake the whole jar, the water stops being clear and becomes a swirling mass of particles and muddy liquid. If we put the jar down, then all the mud will settle at the bottom and the water will become clear again.

*This is how it is with us* – our mind in itself is calm and clear, but experiences can stir us up and obscure that calmness and clarity to the extent that we hardly remember that it is there.

Stress is a major way to 'stir ourselves up'.

It is possible, therefore, to draw a distinction between a person's fundamental nature and their actions. While this nature is basically 'whole' and well, our actions are subject to confusion, mistaken perception and self-interest. This can make them seem harmful or negative.

Making this distinction can bring a tremendous sense of relief, because it removes judgement and brings us and everyone else within the embrace of compassion. How wonderful to realise that however frustrated we can be with ourselves, underneath it all we are perfectly well and whole.

*Exercise*

Try out the glass of water example:

Take a glass of water and experiment with adding colour to it or stirring it until the water is opaque and then watch it settle.

Can you relate this to how your own mind is?

________________________________________

________________________________________

________________________________________

________________________________________

Let's look a bit more closely at what we mean by 'wholeness'. It has three aspects:

- The understanding that ourselves and everything else are interconnected
- The quality of awareness
- The natural capacity for compassion

Let's now take a closer look at each of these three aspects.

## *1. The understanding that ourselves and everything else are interconnected*

As you read this book, you will probably be sitting down on some kind of seat.

Let's examine this seat more closely.

**1. Consider**

The materials that have been gathered to make it

The people who have worked on it

The calculations and arrangements made in order for it to be sold and brought to where you need it

*Your seat cannot exist independently of all these causes and conditions that brought it into being – it depends on them all for its existence.*

**2. Consider:**

Where is its 'seatness' to be found?

Is it in the legs?

Is it in the base?

If we remove the back, is it still a seat, or does it become a stool?

These legs, cushion and back are not a seat on their own – they only become one when they are put together.

*Without the different parts there is no seat, but without the idea of a 'seat' the parts do not make sense.*

**3. If we continue to analyse this seat we can see that the notion of 'seatness' is not a continuous, independent one. Consider:**

A child may see a seat as a climbing frame, or a castle.

Woodworm see it as food.

Mice may make their homes in the upholstery.

*The seat only becomes an object to sit on to work or relax when it is used for that purpose. It does not exist as a seat in and of itself.*

We are not used to thinking in this way most of the time, and it is even harder to apply the same sort of perception to ourselves.

**Try it for a moment.**

### Reflection exercise: Reflect on each of these statements

*We were born due to the previous meetings of countless ancestors before us.*

*If we change just one ancestor, then we would have been a different person.*

*Where does your sense of 'self' manifest – is it in your body, in your head?*

*Think of how this body of ours looks to a child, a dog or a visitor from outer space.*

*Consider how your body has changed through all the years you have been referring to it as your 'self'.*

*Consider how your experiences have grown and changed since you were a child.*

Clearly, we are also not independent and unrelated to our environment and all the people in it.

This way of thinking shows our ordinary perception of the world around us to be limited. Not to take interdependence into account is a form of over-simplification. Thinking about the interdependence of things, however, is not easy: it challenges our tendency to see things as either black or white, desirable or unpleasant. We need to be prepared to question our habitual reactions and accept that we can misperceive things – things that could help us as we try to reduce our stress.

## TIPS

During your day, pause from time to time and reflect on how interconnected we all are.

You might consider all the people involved in getting the cup of coffee you are drinking to you.

You could also think of all the people who contributed to the books in the bookstore where you are browsing.

Or all the people involved in designing, making, transporting and selling the clothes you are wearing today.

If we begin to apply this new perspective of interconnectedness to our own lives, we can appreciate that compassion is not an optional extra but rather the only sane and responsible way to live. Simply for reasons of enlightened self-interest we can see that it benefits us to have compassion for all the other people we share this planet with. The story of people feeding each other with long spoons at the beginning of this chapter is a good example of this. The Dalai Lama sometimes calls this attitude being 'wisely selfish'. We might not be ready yet to put other's interests before our own, but we can start to appreciate that our interests and the interests of other people are intimately related.

In Chapter 7, when we look at how to develop new habits of compassion, we will explore this further.

## *2. The quality of awareness*

This second aspect of 'wholeness' is our capacity to see things clearly, as they are, but without opinion and judgement.

**This quality of awareness is with us all the time**

- it is what enables us to know when we are stressed, for example, but most of the time
- it is buried under layers of thoughts and feelings about what we are experiencing.

---

In spite of this, there are times – when we are by the ocean, perhaps, or enjoying an inspiring view – when we can get a clear glimpse of our own awareness, unencumbered by the limitations imposed on it by the clutter in our minds.

---

This is the awareness that we can learn to develop through meditation, as we shall see later.

---

The example of a crystal can help us to understand this. If we hold a crystal and look into it, we can see through it clearly, but if we hold it up against a coloured cloth, then the crystal takes on the colour of the cloth.

In other words, it reflects everything – beautiful things and ugly things, things we like and things we don't like.

Whatever it reflects, the crystal itself does not change – it stays pure and unaffected.

This is how our awareness is.

---

**However much stress and anxiety we experience that might appear to cloud our minds, these are external factors, and the basic clarity of our awareness remains unaffected.** This is very helpful to remember as we try to work with our stress.

### *3. The natural capacity for compassion*

The third aspect that describes our fundamental 'wholeness' is our natural capacity for compassion. Compassion is an expression of who we are as human beings, not something we need to acquire from outside.

Let's look at some ideas that help to support this.

Firstly, we human beings are social creatures and place a high value on affection:

- From the moment we are born we rely heavily on the kindness and care of our mother, without whose help we could not survive and grow to maturity.
- As we progress through life, we look for affection in family, friends and partners.
- We are more readily drawn towards people who are able to express affection towards us.
- As we grow older and face sickness and reduced energy, we come increasingly to rely on the affection of others.
- When the end of our life approaches, we will need affection and kindness to support us.

*Now think about our natural ability to connect deeply with the suffering of others.*

It does not matter which culture, religion or country we live in, if we hear a cry of pain, or see a child suffering, our immediate response is a feeling of empathy and concern.

Maybe we are not able to do anything with this feeling and it quickly goes away, but this does not undermine its intensity or the reality of the feeling of connection.

*Moreover, whoever we are, we are all trying to live happy lives – our inclination is to seek happiness rather than pain.*

There are many scientific studies that show that adopting healthy, positive habits as part of our lifestyle has a beneficial effect on our wellbeing, and when we feel emotions such as anger, hatred, jealousy and pride they can have a corresponding detrimental effect. We can experience this directly by observing how we feel when we are in the grip of a powerful negative emotion, as opposed to the peace we feel when we are engaging in acts of kindness or care.

Reflect on the idea that we are all fundamentally whole.

Training the mind in compassion combines the deep feelings we have for the welfare of others with a chain of reasoning, thereby providing a firm basis for action. In fact, it is said that the Buddhist view is interdependence, and the action this inspires is altruism.

## Exercise: Remembering fundamental wholeness

Reflect on the idea that we are all fundamentally whole.

How can you apply this to yourself and others as you go through your day?

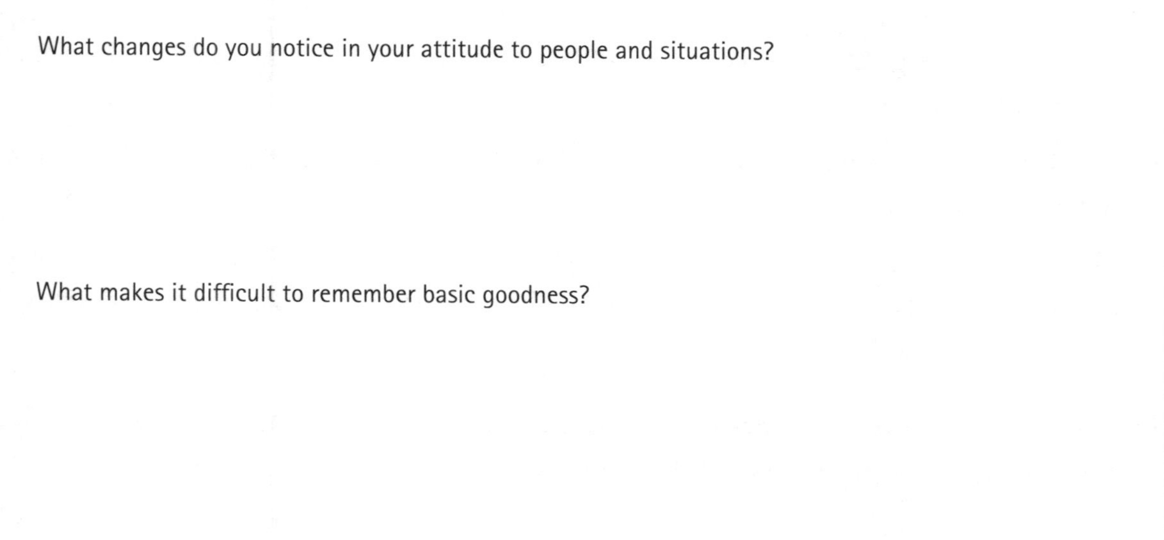

What changes do you notice in your attitude to people and situations?
What makes it difficult to remember basic goodness?


## Training the Mind in Compassion

This altruistic action is expressed as the wish that all beings, whoever they are, should be free from suffering and find reliable happiness, combined with the commitment to make every effort to bring this about.

**For us to be able to contribute the effort required for this, we need to focus on ourselves by training our minds.**

What does this mean?

- Learning more about how our minds work
- Understanding what suffering is and what it entails, as well as how we can work with it ourselves
- Developing awareness so that the full capacity of our mind is available to us[5]

**When we decide to place compassion at the heart of our lives in this way, it has an immediate effect on how we view ourselves, other people and the world that we share.** So, as we begin to use compassion to reduce our own stress, we are starting out on a journey that will lead us to develop the ability to help other people work through their own stressful situations. As we do this, we will find that our own experience of stress is relieved. We will explore this further in Part 3.

Training the mind in compassion starts from where we are now and leads us through a step-by-step process that gradually reveals our self-focused habits, and at the same time provides ways to access our innate compassion.

- In this way we develop the courage and skills to address any unhelpful habits we may have as we become more aware of them.
- The training takes into account from the beginning that changing our habits is not always an easy or speedy process, and that we are likely to get side-tracked from our goal and frustrated by our slow progress.

**The techniques in this book begin at a fairly basic level and gradually become more challenging, but you can work at a pace that suits you.**

- You can work with any of the techniques for as long as it takes, and your effort will still have tremendous benefit.
- It is never too late to begin to train yourself in compassion, and there is no one to judge your progress.
- The aim is to connect with your own fundamental wholeness, your natural capacity for kindness and affection, and then to extend that feeling in ever-increasing circles until it is universal.

> Much of our stress comes from struggling to keep things the way we would like them to be. When we change this perspective to drawing on our sense of wellness and natural kindness, a sense of ease and space opens up. This enables us to gain greater insight into our difficulties and see them not as isolated incidents in our own lives but as part of the pattern of human life, affecting everyone.

**The stages in training the mind in compassion are:**

1. **Trying not to cause harm**
2. **Melting the ice in your heart**
3. **Seeing other people as just like you**
4. **Putting yourself in the other person's shoes**
5. **Seeing others as more important than yourself**

### 1. Trying not to cause harm

If compassion is the wish to help everyone become free of suffering, it can seem like a tall order. The first step is to focus on what you *can* do rather than trying to aim for seemingly unobtainable goals. Perhaps you do not feel ready to be a force for good, but you can at least try to limit the harm you cause.

Think about all the small acts of selfishness and irritation we are all prey to in our daily lives – from pushing ahead in the queue at the supermarket to hissing at other drivers who get in our way. Compassion training works at all levels – body, speech and mind – so you need to look at all the things you do, all the words you say, and all the thoughts you think.

Every time you are able to disarm a self-centred reaction you are managing not to cause harm – to yourself, as well as to others.

---

**How would you go about trying not to cause harm?**

**2. Melting the ice in your heart**

The second step is about accessing our natural capacity for kindness and altruism more deeply, thereby beginning to melt away the self-protective instincts that block our ability to communicate with others.

There are four techniques we can use here, traditionally known as the Four Immeasurables:

- The generation of immeasurable equanimity (or lack of bias)
- Loving kindness
- Compassion
- Joy

These Four Immeasurables are important because they help us to strengthen our compassion 'muscles' by giving us the chance to practise showing compassion beyond the range of the people close to us, and the people we like. They help to make our compassion more robust and reliable.

You start by applying each technique to yourself, then continue by sharing these feelings with those close to you, and then gradually widening the circle until your feeling becomes unlimited and without bias – in other words, immeasurable.

---

**What impression do these Four Immeasurables make on you?**

We will look at these techniques in more detail in Chapter 9 and explore how working in this way can help to reduce our feelings of stress.

**3. Seeing other people as just like you**

To understand the third step, we can begin by remembering that everyone we meet just wants to be happy and not to suffer – and, the truth is, that is exactly the same for us as well. Because our heart has begun to soften with practising the Four Immeasurables, we are more capable of remembering this in a practical way so that we do not always put our own interests and wellbeing first.

We would like to take others along with us and have them share the same things that we want for ourselves. With this step, we take our own concern for our personal welfare and share it with others. We want to do this because we see each person as being just like us – not in the specific details of their lives and circumstances, but in them having the same hopes and fears.

---

**What are your feelings about seeing other people as just like you?**

This step will be explored in Chapter 10.

**4. Putting yourself in the other person's shoes**

With this step we are ready to go further and actually allow ourselves to imagine what it is like to be another person, to try and experience how they feel, to discover how things are for them.

---

**Think of someone that you know and take some time to try to put yourself in their shoes – when you are able to do this, what do you learn?**

We will look at this further in Chapter 10.

**5. Seeing others as more important than yourself**

This last step is really the culmination of compassion training from a Buddhist viewpoint. It is a profound step and not easy to do. It requires a deep understanding of interdependence – how we relate to everyone around us – and long meditation experience, and so we will just touch on it in this book.

However, in order to visualise it, think of the occasions in which people risk their lives to save others, sometimes people that they do not even know. Surely that shows at least a willingness to embrace the possibility of seeing others as more important than oneself.

---

**Are there times when you see somebody else as being more important than yourself?**

## The Biology of Compassion

We are going to close this introductory chapter on compassion with a short look at how compassion works in our bodies

Jerome Kagan, a Harvard psychology professor, writes[6]:

> *Although humans inherit a biological basis that permits them to feel anger, jealousy, selfishness and envy, and to be rude, aggressive or violent, they inherit an even stronger biological basis for kindness, compassion, cooperation, love and nurture.*

On the one hand, we only need to spend some time watching the news on television to feel depressed and hopeless about the state of the world and our fellow human beings. There are the terrible scenes of war and slaughter, imprisonment and torture, and the reckless cruelty of leaders more interested in maintaining their own power than caring for the people for whom they are responsible.

Then on the other, the Dalai Lama often cites the basic human instinct to seek happiness as a proof of the goodness of our true nature. This instinct runs very deep in all of us – we simply wish to be able to live a happy life. Love, affection and the sense of being connected to others are inextricably linked to this search for happiness. When we experience these feelings, we experience happiness and a deep sense of wellness.

**Let's take some time now to explore how our brain has developed, bearing in mind as we do that this evolution is not always a smooth process that can just throw out any previous mistakes and start again! It develops by amending and adapting what is already there. This can lead to tensions and contradictions that we have to find ways to come to terms with.**

**The 'old brain'**

Also known as the Reptilian Brain, it consists of the brain stem and cerebellum.

- It is the area that controls motor movement coordination, balance, equilibrium and muscle tone.
- It controls the body's vital functions such as our heart rate, breathing, body temperature and balance.

Reptiles were not complicated creatures:

- Their sole focus was to survive
- They were entirely motivated by self-interest

They were concerned with fighting for territory, defeating any challengers, finding enough food to eat, and securing a place of safety in order to mate and reproduce.

Although reproduction was a priority for reptiles, relationships were not, and after their mating fulfilled its purpose, the animals parted. After the female laid her eggs, neither parent had any interest in nurturing their young, not hesitating to eat them if the occasion arose.

Not surprisingly, the young that survived were tough and capable of fighting for their lives.

We have inherited these characteristics. They are located in the hypothalamus – a key area of the brain in terms of the stress response, as we saw in Chapter 1. By preparing us for fight or flight, this part of the brain helped to ensure our survival.

**Think carefully – can you recall a time recently when you were probably operating mostly from your old brain?**

________________________________________

________________________________________

This mode of life was to change with the advent of mammals that gave birth to offspring who were more vulnerable and needed parental care in order to survive.

*This departure from the lifestyle of the reptiles represents the first seeds of what would become a biological basis for compassion in humans.*

The question of survival was still the overriding priority, so these new mammalian instincts did not replace those of the reptile but existed alongside them. However, the skills required in caring for young, engaging in an increasingly social group, and longer-term mating all led to the growth and development of the cerebral cortex – the outer covering of the cerebrum, the layer of the brain often referred to as grey matter.

By the time we get to the arrival of humans, the area of the old brain was completely enveloped by and buried within it.

**The 'new brain'**

This is a part of the cerebral cortex concerned with sight and hearing in mammals, regarded as the most recently evolved part of the cortex.

It includes but by no means is restricted to our neocortex and is concerned with the higher functions of reasoning, for example thought and language.

It is altogether more complex, subtle and multi-faceted than the 'old brain'.

---

For the most part the new brain is able to stand back from and regulate the primitive instincts of the old brain, but not always. There are times when the old automatic impulses override our more recently acquired skills of reason and discernment and we find ourselves at the mercy of our aggression and self-interest. If you've ever driven home at the end of a long and tiring day and found yourself yelling abuse at another driver for cutting in front of you, then you have experienced what we are talking about here.

Worse still is when we employ our new-brain skills in the service of old-brain interests, for example when someone with a good understanding of finance uses their skills to embezzle the company they work for, thereby being overwhelmed by instincts of greed and self-interest.

---

Can you identify a recent experience of your old brain impulses overriding the skills of your new brain?

**Buddhist teachings on compassion return again and again to the image of a mother caring for her young – offering nourishment as an act of unconditional love without the expectation of anything in return.**

The mother and the baby are drawn together instinctively in affection and love – the baby's need of love in order to survive matching the instinct that the mother has to care for her offspring.

---

The Dalai Lama comments[7]:

> *What we see . . . is a relationship based on love and mutual tenderness which is totally spontaneous. It is not learned from others, no religion requires it, no law imposes it, no schools have taught it. It arises quite naturally.*

---

What we know of the story of our evolution bears this out.

---

In the case of the earlier mammals, a mother's care was a rough and ready means of keeping her young alive, but over time parental skills developed as parents learned to engage in behaviour that benefited their children, such as stroking them and teaching them to look after themselves.

---

Human parents also developed the ability not only to protect their young but also to influence their development through the care and support they provide.

---

These increasing skills led to the development of larger and larger brains, which meant that human babies had to be born prematurely in order to navigate the birth canal. Because of this, babies came to need the support and care of the whole community as well as their parents.

---

A human mother had no fur for her baby to hang on to, making it necessary for her to carry it herself. There were times when she had to put the needs of the baby, for example for food and rest, before her own.

---

In this way, the care given to a child developed from an automatic instinct to ensure its survival into something more voluntary, based on feeling.

The seeds of compassion were beginning to sprout.

## The Beginnings of Empathy

Along with the need to produce and rear healthy offspring, our ancestors living in small tribes in harsh conditions had a pressing need to cooperate in order for the tribe to survive the challenges of finding food, scaring off unfriendly tribes and protecting themselves from predators.

**The instinct to care for one's young needed to extend to include the tribe as a whole.**

This involved the development of empathy, the ability to 'tune in' to another person and to share their concerns. It is not hard to see that it was much easier to survive as part of a tightly knit supportive tribal group, rather than trying to keep oneself alive as a lone agent out on the grasslands.

Cooperation based on empathy was effective in ensuring the genes for these traits passed on to future generations, so gradually influencing how our brains further evolved. So human beings have developed as intensely social beings that thrive on friendship and close personal networks.

There is now a lot of research showing that we function at our best and are happiest, with low stress and strong immune systems, when we feel loved and valued (rather than feeling marginalised) and are kind and loving (rather than being indifferent to others or hating them).

To feel part of our social relationships and networks, it helps to know that others are concerned for you and will help you (and know how to help you) if you need them to. It also helps that they know you feel the same about them and that you are a reliable and helpful 'friend'.

*This sharing of our empathic concerns for each other is core to the development of friendship and mutual caring and has helped make us the species we are today.*

We will be going into this in more detail when we come to Part 3 and begin to look at some techniques that we can use to develop compassion.

---

Can you identify your own primary social networks? Can you see the dynamic of receiving support and being a helpful friend playing out in your own life?

**There are several recent studies that have examined the biological roots of empathy.**

One study of the brain activity of mothers looking at photos of their babies[8] showed unique activity in the region of the brain associated with positive emotions. However, it seems that this response is not confined to parents. Joshua Greene[9] and Jonathan Cohen[10] of Princeton University found that when subjects contemplated harm being done to others, a similar network in their brains lit up.

A further study[11] monitored brain activity while participants were engaged in helping someone. Activity was found to have been triggered in the areas of the brain that 'turn on' (or, as sometimes described by scientists, 'light up') when people receive awards or experience pleasure, showing that helping others provides us with the same pleasure as when we receive something we like.

This will come up again in more detail in Chapter 9 when we discuss the benefits of volunteering.

## Research on Compassion

There is an increasing interest among scientists in studying compassion. Some of the findings are very new and still emerging. To understand the biological underpinnings of compassion, it is useful to note some of these research projects.

### *Neuroscience*

Richard Davidson has carried out extensive research on the changes in the brain that are brought about by training in meditation and compassion techniques. This is a vitally important area of research, which we will return to throughout this workbook.

### *Mirror neurons*

In 1996, Giacomo Rizzolatti, a neuroscientist at the University of Parma in Italy, and his team published their findings of research carried out on monkeys.

While investigating brain activity related to planning and carrying out movement, the team accidentally discovered that the monkey's brain lit up in just the same way whether it moved itself or watched the lab technicians moving. When someone returned from lunch with an ice cream and ate it in front of a monkey, its brain fired as if it was moving the ice cream to its own mouth.

The brain of the monkey contains a special class of cells, which have come to be termed 'mirror neurons', that fire when the animal sees or hears an action and when the animal carries out the same action on its own. This discovery was exciting in itself, but even more exciting was the research that followed. It showed that humans have the same kind of cells but more sophisticated, more flexible, smarter, and more highly evolved than those found in monkeys.

Before this important discovery, scientists believed that our brain used logical thought processes to interpret and predict other people's actions.

*However, this research is giving rise to the belief among researchers that we understand other people not only by thinking, but by feeling as well.*

If I see someone touch you on your arm, my brain will light up as if I am being touched – the only things that prevent me from thinking it is me being touched are the sense and pain receptors on my skin. In fact, if my arm is anaesthetised so that these sense receptors are not working, and I can then actually 'feel' the touch on your arm as if it were my own. These findings are enabling researchers to learn more about how we develop empathy.

One of Rizzolatti's team suggests that we live in a more 'we-centric' space than we realise – one that takes into account the importance of the group – rather than the popular belief that each of us is an island unto ourselves. Understanding mirror neurons is not only changing the idea of how we see others but how we understand ourselves.

## *The wandering nerve*

This is the nickname given to the vagus nerve – *vagus* is the Latin for wandering. It actually consists of two nerves which are the longest in the body, starting in the top of the spinal cord and then meandering through the body to connect the facial muscle tissue, the thorax, and all the major organs of the body – the heart, lungs, kidneys, liver and digestive organs.

It plays an important role – influencing the muscle contractions in the stomach that are required to digest food and serving as a natural brake on the heart rate, keeping it relatively low. Recent research has shown that it also has an involvement in monitoring inflammation in the body.

The vagus nerve is sometimes referred to as the 'caretaking nerve' because of its connection with compassion. It is worth noting that the vagus nerve is unique to mammals.

Dacher Keltner, professor of psychology at the University of California, Berkeley, cites three conclusions that support this description, drawn from studies carried out in his laboratory.

1. They found that when people are listening to someone describe an experience of suffering, they give a tiny quarter-second sigh from time to time that acts as an expression of concern and understanding and which in turn comforts and soothes the speaker. This is the work of the vagus nerve, stimulating the muscles of the throat, mouth, face and tongue to make the reassuring sounds.
2. The vagus nerve reduces the heart rate from a possible 115 beats per second to an average of 72 beats per minute. This means that when we are alarmed or frightened and our heart races, preparing the body for fight or flight, the vagus nerve acts to calm it, making it more possible for us to respond in a gentle manner.
3. It is believed that the vagus nerve is related to the release of the hormone oxytocin, which is connected to the experience of trust, soothing and love.

Scientists believe it evolved in order to support the care-giving skills of mammals for their young. It is still early days in terms of understanding the full impact of research into the vagus nerve, but indications so far point to it as being an important support for compassionate activity.

### *Oxytocin*

The hormone oxytocin is known to play an important role in relaxing mothers during childbirth and assisting breastfeeding, but recent research indicates that it plays a wider role in our lives. Oxytocin is produced when we are touched, when we are warm and through vibration (such as a good massage).

It also acts to calm the stress response – when it is released blood pressure is lowered, which helps us to shift from the muscle-boosting stress arousal state to a restorative mode in which our energy can go into storing nutrients, growth and healing.

A surge of oxytocin does not last long, but we can prolong its benefits through loving, stable relationships. Each time we hug, or share an affectionate moment, it causes oxytocin to be released over and over again – which in turn soothes and calms our nervous system. It is a self-nourishing cycle.

---

As Dacher Keltner writes:[12]

> *Being compassionate causes a chemical reaction in the body that motivates us to be even more compassionate.*

---

| What we have learned in this chapter | Your reflections |
|---|---|
| • The Golden Rule: Always treat others as you would wish to be treated yourself.<br>• Compassion is the ability to feel another person's suffering as if it is your own, to wish for them to be free from it, and to be prepared to help them in that endeavour.<br>• There are two psychologies of compassion: the psychology of engagement and the psychology of alleviation.<br>• Our mind is naturally calm and clear, but experience can stir us up and obscure that calmness and clarity to the extent that we hardly remember that it is there.<br>• Our nature is fundamentally whole and can be said to have three aspects:<br>  * The understanding that ourselves and everything else are interconnected.<br>  * The quality of awareness.<br>  * The natural capacity for compassion.<br>• When we decide to place compassion at the heart of our lives, it has an immediate effect on how we view ourselves, other people and the world that we share.<br>• Training the mind in compassion starts from where we are now and leads us through a step-by-step process that gradually reveals our self-focused habits and at the same time provides methods for accessing our innate compassion.<br>• The stages are:<br>  * Trying not to cause harm<br>  * Melting the ice in your heart<br>  * Seeing other people as just like you | |

  * Putting yourself in the other person's shoes
  * Seeing others as more important than yourself

- The instinct to seek happiness runs very deep in all of us – we simply wish to be able to live a happy life. Love, affection and the sense of being connected to others are inextricably linked to this search for happiness.
- Our 'old brain' is concerned with survival – we have inherited it from our reptilian ancestors.
- With the advent of mammals and the need to nurture their young, the first seeds of a biological basis for compassion took root.
- The 'new brain', the neocortex, is concerned with the higher functions – reasoning, thought and language, for example. It is altogether more complex, subtle and multi-faceted than the 'old brain'. For the most part, the 'new brain' is able to stand back from and regulate the primitive instincts of the 'old brain'.
- Humans have a natural tendency for empathy – the inability to bear another's suffering without wanting to try to help.
- Current research is coming up with interesting data which shows that compassion is part of our physiological make-up and that, when we engage with it, our health and wellbeing improves.
- How we work with ourselves is key in determining whether our capacity for kindness and compassion can become stronger than our instinct to protect ourselves and survive at any cost.

### TIPS TO TAKE INTO EVERYDAY LIFE

1. The Golden Rule (page 38) is a useful way to remember compassion as you go about your day.
2. Take time to reflect on where things come from that you are using and remember all the people involved in making them.
3. Remember that you are hard-wired for kindness.

# 3 How our Longing for Happiness and Fear of Suffering Adds to our Stress

*I believe that the very purpose of our life is to seek happiness. That is clear. Whether one believes in religion or not, whether one believes in this religion or that religion, we are all seeking something better in life. So, I think the very motion of our life is towards happiness.*

*The Dalai Lama*[1]

What we are going to do in this chapter:

1. Consider how both our longing for happiness and our aversion to suffering can cause us stress
2. Look at some happiness research
3. Examine ways in which happiness can be trickier than we thought
4. Look at how our disappointments with happiness cause us stress
5. Explore the inevitability of suffering
6. Look at some of our assumptions that lead to suffering
7. Consider how suffering can contribute to our learning and growth

The definition of compassion that we are working with is:

**The ability to feel another person's suffering as if it is your own, to wish for them to be free from it, and to be prepared to help them in that endeavour.**

We've said that in order to understand suffering we need to lean into it and not turn away. The trouble is that as human beings we want to be happy and to avoid suffering, so this can be difficult. Strange as it may seem, our longing for happiness and fear of suffering can be a considerable source of stress for us. That is what we are going to look into in this chapter.

## Exploring Happiness

We will begin with exploring happiness. Try this exercise to give yourself a starting point. Give yourself time to dig below the surface a little and come up with meaningful answers that will provide useful information for you.

What makes you happy?

________________________________________

________________________________________

________________________________________

What gets in the way of your happiness?

________________________________________

________________________________________

________________________________________

Would you say you are a happy person?

________________________________________

________________________________________

________________________________________

### A changing perspective

Recent research is showing that our levels of happiness and wellbeing have wide-reaching effects across many areas of our lives – including on our ability to make satisfying relationships, on our health and even on how long we may live.

**Previously**, conventional wisdom held that if we worked hard, we would become successful, and happiness would be our reward in time when all our goals fell into place.

**Now** research findings from the fields of neuroscience and positive psychology indicate that it could be the other way around – that happiness fuels success and that the happier we are, the more successful we become.

So, happiness is not just about feeling good, and the question of what makes us happy becomes increasingly important.

Our levels of happiness are not merely haphazard and subject to luck.

*In fact, if happiness is lifted out of the domain of short-term good feelings and developed as something stable and longer lasting it can become a foundation from which we can learn to cope with stress.*

**Let's take a look at how happiness research has developed.**

## Positive Psychology

In 1998 Martin Seligman chose his term as president of the American Psychological Association as an opportunity to launch what is now called 'positive psychology'. Along with researchers like Ed Diener, and Mihaly Csikszentmihalyi – the architect of the notion of 'flow' (the moments when we are engaged in an activity that is completely absorbing and satisfying for us)[2] – Seligman has worked to refocus psychology on nurturing talent and improving life, rather than dealing only with treating mental illness.

In the absence of any universal measurement of happiness and wellbeing, psychologists measure happiness levels through self-reporting in which people answer questionnaires detailing how happy they are. **Seligman has created a General Happiness Scale**[3] asking people to rate themselves on a score of 1–7 on four questions.[4]

## Ability to Measure Brain Activity Patterns

A recent important development is that scientists can now measure brain activity patterns associated with happiness. We can see that particular moods or emotions are accompanied by distinctive patterns of electrical and chemical activity in various regions of our brain. Brain activity patterns associated with happiness are quite different from those associated with sadness.

When subjects are shown images designed to make them happy – such as pictures of a smiling baby – there is heightened activity in the left pre-frontal cortex, which is situated just behind the left eye. When shown upsetting images – such as pictures of a baby in pain – there is a corresponding increase in activity in the right pre-frontal cortex.

These differences in left–right brain activity also show up when people are engaged in ordinary activity. 'Left-siders' report more positive thoughts and memories and they smile more, whereas 'right-siders' report the opposite.

The impact of being able to investigate our brain's reactions in this way has elevated happiness studies to a new level. Serious research on happiness and wellbeing is now a growing and productive field. It includes a wide range of interests – brain scientists advancing our understanding of how happiness works, clinicians seeking to help patients avoid depression, social scientists interested in measuring happiness across the globe, and economists examining how people choose to spend their money.

## The Relationship Between Happiness, Resilience and Longevity

In April 2006, the BBC presented a series of six programmes on happiness called *The Happiness Formula*.[5] As part of their investigations they set up what they termed 'a happy lab' to run various experiments.

In one experiment they asked people whose happiness levels they had already tested to see how long they could keep their hands in ice-cold water. At one end of the scale was a young man whose happiness score had been quite low and who managed thirty seconds with his hand in the water. One of the women who had scored highest on the happiness questionnaire still had her hand in the water after six minutes when the tester asked her to take it out.

**This simple experiment provided convincing evidence of what research is showing – that people with a higher level of happiness and wellbeing have greater resilience and more staying power than their less happy counterparts.**

We also know that happier people have lower levels of the stress hormone cortisol, high levels of which are linked to type 2 diabetes and hypertension.

What evidence do you find in your own life that indicates that when you feel well in yourself, your resilience is stronger?

Perhaps even more remarkable is the relationship between happiness and wellbeing, and longevity.

An intake of nuns into a nunnery in Milwaukee in the USA during the 1930s was the subject of a now-famous study. The nuns were asked to write a journal of their lives up until they entered the convent. Some of the journals were joyful and optimistic, others less so. The researchers counted the number of times each nun used a positive or negative word and on the basis of their score divided the nuns into 'happy nuns' and 'not-so-happy nuns'.

After joining the order their lives were almost exactly the same – same food, same work, same routine, but not the same life expectancy. Among the less-positive nuns, two-thirds died before their eighty-fifth birthday, whereas 90 per cent of the happy nuns were still alive. On average the happy nuns lived nine years longer than the not-so-happy nuns.

In an interview on the BBC's *The Happiness Formula*, Ed Diener, a positive psychologist, points out that smoking one packet of cigarettes a day takes on average three years off your life. Discovering this has transformed how we treat cigarette smoking in society, yet with happiness levels we are talking about a difference of nine years.

The presenter of *The Happiness Formula* travelled to visit the nunnery and to attend the 102nd birthday party of sister Helena, one of the happy nuns. When she was asked for the secret of her long life her answer was this:

Be accepting of everything that comes to you.

In this simple statement she summed up an attitude of patience and contentment. She was less vulnerable to the vicissitudes of hope and fear that for many of us dominate our interactions with the world. **Here is a clue as to the kind of happiness that is worth cultivating and which will help increase our resilience in terms of managing stress.**

### Exercise: Be accepting of everything that comes to you

Choose one day in the week and take this statement as a focus for your day.

What difficulties do you experience in trying to do this?

What effect does it have on your levels of stress?

### The happiness set point

There is an ongoing discussion about what is called the 'happiness set point'. This is a sort of genetic baseline for our level of happiness and wellbeing that we slip over and under as we go through different experiences throughout our lives. We inherit this set point from our parents, and it has an influence on how we handle happiness in our lives, but not on our overall capacity for happiness.

The theory states that only 50 per cent of our happiness levels are determined by this set point, and 10 per cent by life circumstances. That leaves the remaining 40 per cent within our power to change – so there is plenty of room to manoeuvre.

**This research gives scientific endorsement to the notion that we have a considerable role to play in deciding on our own level of wellbeing, and consequently on how we manage stress.**

## What the Happiness Research Shows Us

The happiness research bears out what our life experience shows us – we might intend to be happy; we might take concrete steps to bring this happiness about, but it does not always work. The disconnect between our wish for happiness and how it plays out in our lives can be a source of considerable stress.

**Let's look at two of our main beliefs about happiness and then examine what the research shows.**

### *1. If I had more money, then I would be happier*

> One of the key findings highlighted by the British economist Richard Layard in his groundbreaking book, *Happiness*, is that over the last fifty years, the standard of living in the US and Western Europe has roughly doubled, while levels of happiness have stayed the same.

Let's look at some reasons why. . .

#### a) We get used to having things

An ongoing social survey carried out in the United States[6] on a cross-section of Americans monitored the choice of items that people considered necessary for a good life. Participants were asked to list what they considered their 'essential' items and then tick the ones they already possessed. The list of items included things like a house, a car, a TV and a holiday home.

The survey was repeated with the same group sixteen years later. During this time people went from possessing, on average, 1.7 to 3.1 of the items on their list, whereas the items deemed necessary for the good life increased from 4.4 items to 5.6 items.

So, revealingly, sixteen years later people considered that their circumstances fell as far short of the good life as they always had – even though they owned more of the items on their list.

One of the most startling results to emerge from research into happiness is that big lottery winners, after experiencing an initial period of euphoria, tend to return to their normal levels of happiness within a year. The huge rise in their financial and then material resources is not enough to lift their happiness levels long term.

**The trouble is that we adapt to what we have and so become used to it, and when the gloss of having it fades away, we want something more.**

The process of adaptation we experience with material possessions seems to work in the same way for life experiences – so career moves, lifestyle changes or new relationships, rather than transporting us to new levels of happiness, eventually settle down until they become simply part of our normal pattern of happiness.

The good news is that this also seems to hold true for many things we would wish to avoid – redundancy, accident and romantic disaster. This is something it would be helpful to remember when we are in the thick of anxiety about a job interview or the high of a new love affair.

However, if we feel that happiness is always just beyond our reach it is going to leave us feeling frustrated and disappointed and increase our stress.

I have a strong memory of setting up my first home after university and buying a washing machine. It felt so incredible to have a washing machine of my own and not have to go to the laundrette that I sat and watched the whole washing cycle as it went through its stages.

Now my washing machine is a basic part of the equipment in the house and I just rely on it to do its job. It no longer feels like a miracle.

---

Do you have a story like this from your own life?

## b) We compare what we have with what others have

Students at Harvard University were asked which of two imaginary worlds they would prefer to live in: the first was one in which they would earn $50,000 per year while everyone else earned $25,000; the second was one in which they would earn $100,000 a year and everyone else $250,000. Most people preferred the first choice and opted for a lower actual income that was still higher than most other people's.[7]

**We compare ourselves with our peers, people with roughly similar lifestyles – the lives of the super-rich are far beyond our reach, while many of us feel comfortably far away from the very poor.**

Studies of Olympic medallists show that bronze medallists tend to be happier with their medals than silver medallists because they compare themselves to people who did not get a medal at all, while silver medallists believe they just missed a gold.[8]

Changing one's point of reference from comparing one's situation to someone less well-off to someone more well-off can be quite stressful. One illustration of this is the case of East Germany. The standard of living for East Germans improved considerably after re-unification in 1990, but happiness levels fell, because instead of comparing their standard of living with other members of the former Soviet Bloc, people compared themselves with the more prosperous West Germans. Previously they had been able to see themselves as better off than their neighbours, but after unification they themselves were the poor neighbours by comparison.

Richard Layard sums this up:[9]

> *The things we get used to the most easily and take for granted are our material possessions . . . Advertisers understand this and invite us to feed our addiction with more and more spending . . . If we do not foresee that we get used to our material possessions, we shall over invest in acquiring them, at the expense of our leisure . . . As a result, our life can get distorted towards working and making money, and away from other pursuits.*

We could interpret 'leisure' here to include time for reflection on what we actually want out of life, while we work out the connections between how much we struggle to acquire more possessions and our stress levels. Perhaps working so hard to gain a certain standard of living exacts such a high price from us that it is hard to actually appreciate and enjoy the fruits of our labour.

Can you think of a time when you were contented with something in your life and it was undermined because someone else had something you thought was better?

## *2. If I could just have things the way I want them, then I could be happy*

There is evidence to show that when we look at our material circumstances, in other words the things we think we need in order to be happy, we are not skilled at seeing things objectively, or in proportion to their long-term effect on our wellbeing.

Do we fare better when we contemplate how things have been for us in the past, or when we try and gauge our needs in the future? Ideally, we should be able to accurately review how our past experience has been in order to reasonably predict which choices to make in the future, but a growing body of research is showing that this is not the case. We know, of course, that the future has not happened yet and all we have to go on is our present circumstances with our current likes and dislikes. **The trouble is that we rarely take into account how our preferences or circumstances may change – we don't consider that our future selves may see things differently from the way we do now.**

A friend of mine worked for an independent company that was taken over by a multinational. He was in middle management and was one of the people from the old company that the new bosses considered worth keeping on and promoting.

He was very anxious to get the job – both for his family's security and for his own career path – and was sure that it would bring him happiness. After a period of anxious waiting he was offered a two-year contract at a higher level of management than before. He had been so worried about the outcome that the relief of getting the job was almost an anti-climax.

Now, several months later, he is working longer and longer hours in an increasingly competitive and unfriendly environment and struggles to find a level of satisfaction in his work. He is plagued by the fear of not being able to maintain the pace and style of the 'new' company, even though he does not feel in sympathy with much of their approach.

In his old role, he was one of a group of middle managers who supported each other, whereas now he is more senior and alone, with only the top bosses to compare himself to – so he is constantly trying to keep up. His belief that the new job would bring him happiness is an example of how poorly my friend was able to predict how it would turn out for him.

We've said several times that happiness can be unpredictable and tricky – and indeed my friend did not accurately predict what would bring him happiness; instead, he adapted very quickly to the desired outcome when it arrived and now suffers from comparing his situation with people in seemingly better ones.

In remembering the past, the way we experience how things end seems to be particularly tricky.

To demonstrate this, the psychologist Daniel Kahneman conducted an experiment similar to the one described above but with a notable difference: Participants were asked to place their hands in cold water, but for one group the temperature was raised right at the end of the experiment.

For the first group the water was at 14°C and the experience lasted 60 seconds. For the second group the water was at 14°C for 60 seconds and then the experience continued for an additional 30 seconds with the temperature of the water raised to 15°C.

When asked which trial people wanted to repeat, the majority chose the second one – the one with a longer period of discomfort.[10] People chose more pain over less because their experience was defined by its ending – in this case, the water becoming marginally warmer.

A different kind of ending could be having a pleasant evening out with a friend – a delicious meal, good conversation, a great movie, but then, when we go to collect our car, we discover we have been given a parking ticket. The unpleasantness of the parking ticket will override the positive experience and colour our whole recollection of the evening. In our memory it will become, 'that evening I got a parking ticket'. In addition, as we saw in Chapter 2, we are programmed to remember negative experiences longer than positive ones because from an evolutionary perspective this helps us to survive. However, if we get caught up in this pattern it can be a painful source of stress.

### Anticipating what will make us happy

Think of a time when you were planning an event that was designed to make you happy, for example a holiday, an outing, a party, decorating your bedroom. Try to remember:

What worked and what did not?

---

What went according to plan and what did not?

---

What was better than you hoped?

---

What was worse than you hoped?

---

Were there any surprises?

What can you learn from this in terms of planning for happiness?

## Our Wandering Mind and Unhappiness

Our tendency to remember events inaccurately and to wrongly anticipate the future has a lot to do with our habit of not paying full attention to what we are doing, but rather going through the motions on a kind of automatic pilot. If we are not fully paying attention in the present then it is going to be hard to gather all the clues we need to make decisions for the future, or to remember clearly enough to assess the past accurately.

A recent research programme contributed startling evidence of the link between this habit of allowing the mind to wander and dissatisfaction.

Towards the end of 2010 Daniel Gilbert carried out a research study with his doctoral student, Matthew Killingsworth, at Harvard University. Killingsworth designed an iPhone app that contacted 2,250 volunteers in an age range of 18–88 from a variety of socio-economic backgrounds. At random intervals during the day people were asked the following four questions:

- How happy they were at that moment.
- What activity they were engaged in.

- If they were thinking about their current activity.
- If they were thinking about something else that was pleasant, neutral or unpleasant.

The results showed that for almost half their time, the volunteers were thinking about something different from the activity they were engaged with.

**The study concluded that people spend 46.9 per cent of their waking hours thinking about something other than what they are doing, and this mind-wandering typically makes them unhappy.**

If we think about this in terms of our own lives it means we are missing almost half of our experience on a regular basis – quite an extraordinary statistic.

Killingsworth and Gilbert write:[11]

> *A human mind is a wandering mind, and a wandering mind is an unhappy mind. The ability to think about what is not happening is a cognitive achievement that comes at an emotional cost.*

Although the human mind has this capacity to wander, it is capable of much more. The habit of wandering can be addressed by using mindfulness and meditation, which have the effect of enabling the mind to calm down and settle. When this happens the mind's capacity to see clearly is enhanced, increasing discernment and leading to a greater degree of self-awareness. With increased self-awareness we are able to see our habits more clearly and make better choices as to how we wish to behave. This is one of the first steps towards self-compassion.

### The wandering-mind experiment

Try out the wandering mind experiment for yourself.

1. Set your watch, mobile phone or computer to set off a buzzer at random times during a twelve-hour period and have a notebook ready to record your responses.

When the buzzer goes, ask yourself these questions from the study:

- Am I happy at the moment? (You could set a scale of 1–10)
- What am I doing?
- Am I thinking about what I am doing?

Keep a note of your responses

---

2. At the end of the day count up:

- How many times you asked yourself these questions.
- How many of the times you were happy.
- How many of the times you were thinking about something else apart from what you were doing.

Calculate:

- How much of the time you were focused on what you were doing.
- How much of the time you were happy.
- Notice the relationship between the two.
- Notice which activities you were paying full attention to.
- Notice when you were happy and when you were not.

## The Complexity of Modern Life

Both as a society and as individuals, we are always looking forward and trying to improve – we would like things to get better and better. It's undeniable that in terms of improved healthcare and housing, of advances in medical science, and better education, most of us who live in the developed world have much to be thankful for.

Technology is a good example. The technological developments of the last sixty years have changed our lives in ways we could never have imagined, and continue to bring almost weekly innovations – innovations that carry the promise that they will save time and energy so we can accomplish more, with less effort.

Fill out this worksheet to see where you stand with technology contributing to your happiness.

| Question | Is your happiness increased? | Do you feel indifferent? | Do you become more frustrated? |
|---|---|---|---|
| How much time do you spend on your phone each day? | | | |
| How much time you spend on your computer? | | | |
| How do you feel when there is a problem with your internet? | | | |
| Do you enjoy social media? | | | |
| Do you upgrade your phone every time there is an update? | | | |
| How often do you use Siri, Alexa or Google Assistant? | | | |
| What are your conclusions? | | | |

Then there is the question of choice.

American psychology professor Barry Schwartz, author of *The Paradox of Choice*,[12] claims that the huge amount of choice available to us is in itself a source of worry and stress for two main reasons:

- First, that we can never gather and absorb all the information available in order to make a good decision about which energy plan, digital camera, or holiday option to choose.
- Second, that the moment we make our choice and buy it we have regret that there may be a similar option out there for a much better deal.

Schwartz once calculated, on a trip to his local electronics store, that the range of available hi-fi separates – speakers, tuner, amplifier, CD player, tape player – meant that he could construct a possible 6.5 million different stereo systems.[13]

A recent article in *Mail Online* entitled, 'The tyranny of choice: Do we really need 38 types of milk?'[14] includes the following figures:

In Tesco it is now possible to buy no fewer than 38 types of milk. Some of it is flavoured with strawberry, banana or Belgian chocolate; some has active bacterial flora; some has extra omega-3 . . . And that's before you get to the aisle with 154 flavours of jam, or the one with 107 varieties of pasta.

There is a quandary here: by trying to improve our living standards and make everything happen faster and with less effort, we run the risk of creating so many options, possibilities and choices that we expend a lot of energy and worry just trying to manage it all. For example, my Facebook page is a source of delight, but it can also be a source of pressure as I struggle to keep up with all the articles and movies that people send me. All this support exists to enable us to feel in touch, and yet it creates this nagging fear of falling behind because there are simply not enough hours in the day to absorb all that there is on offer.

## Pleasure, Happiness and How it Gets Complicated

In evolutionary terms, pleasure acts as an incentive for keeping us alive. Most people would list sex and food among their main sources of pleasure – both activities cause the brain to release the chemical dopamine that makes us feel happy. While eating keeps us alive, sex ensures our species will continue. This search for good feeling has helped to keep the human race going, but these feelings were designed to be temporary. If we only mated once and never needed to again, we would see a startling fall in the birth rate. So, pleasure is something that is so enjoyable that we want to experience it again and again, but it starts out as a temporary state with a specific purpose, not something that will last for ever.

Sadly, we often seem to find this hard to accept, and our search for wellbeing and happiness can become narrowed down to the pursuit of pleasure and the attempt to hold on to it once we get it – or at least to repeat it as often as we can. There is nothing wrong with enjoying pleasure – we can see how good it can be for us – but grasping on to it is another thing entirely.

Unfortunately, when advertising and peer pressure hook into our delight in pleasure things can turn sour. Instead of increasing our wellbeing, the search for pleasure can become a source of worry and even stress as we strive for the perfection dangled in front of us but always just out of reach, or attempt to hold too tightly to what we already have.

A simple experiment illustrates this point.

Participants were given a choice between a mug and a sum of money. They were asked to say how much money they would need in order to prefer the cash to the mug.

They agreed on a sum of $3.50.

Then the participants were given the mug to keep and asked how much money they would need to give it up – the average went up to $7.12.

Once we feel something belongs to us, is 'ours', then we place a much greater value on it and want to hold on to it.

The trouble is that we so often mistake transient pleasurable experience for lasting happiness that we can neglect our human capacity for something deeper and more fulfilling. We are no longer functioning at the level where our happiness is based on survival alone, and yet we so often settle for the quick fix, pleasure-based route to happiness, without taking into account the full range of potential effects.

If we feel a bit low, we have a choice about how we cope with it.

| CHOICE 1 | CHOICE 2 |
|---|---|
| Find something to distract us – surf the internet, have a coffee, watch the news | Acknowledge we feel low<br>Be gentle with ourselves<br>Look for the cause |
| What is your own habit in these moments? | |

Much of the happiness research that has been described in this chapter bears out the temporary nature of pleasure and how this differs from our expectations.

Let's review the conclusions:

- Do we really need all that we think we do in order to be happy?
- As our lifestyle improves, we set the bar higher in terms of what we want to achieve, often adding to our stress and rarely feeling deeply satisfied.
- The pleasure of attaining a goal does not last and is undermined by how we view the achievements of other people.
- What we think will bring happiness often only brings short-term pleasure and too infrequently adds to a deeper feeling of contentment.
- Our habit of distraction means we are not sufficiently skilled in learning from our experience or foreseeing how to be happy in the future.

**However, the research also shows that happiness is important for our wellbeing – our resilience to difficulties such as stress – and even impacts on our longevity. We need to make a shift away from short-term, quick-fix solutions to achieving happiness and instead take a look at a more enduring state of mind.**

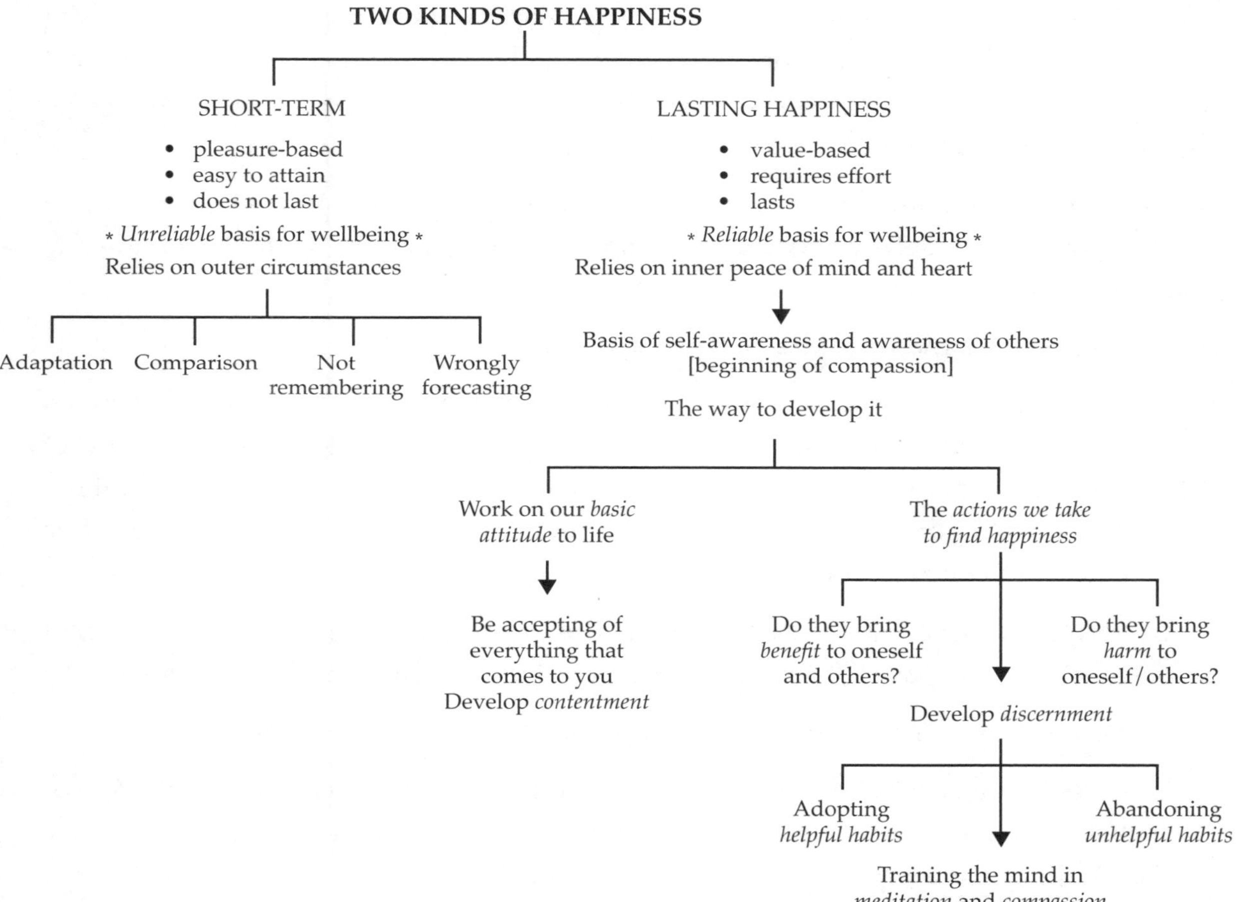
TWO KINDS OF HAPPINESS
SHORT-TERM
• pleasure-based
• easy to attain
• does not last
* Unreliable basis for wellbeing *
Relies on outer circumstances
Adaptation
Comparison
Not remembering
Wrongly forecasting
LASTING HAPPINESS
• value-based
• requires effort
• lasts
* Reliable basis for wellbeing *
Relies on inner peace of mind and heart
Basis of self-awareness and awareness of others [beginning of compassion]
The way to develop it
Work on our basic attitude to life
Be accepting of everything that comes to you
Develop contentment
The actions we take to find happiness
Do they bring benefit to oneself and others?
Do they bring harm to oneself / others?
Develop discernment
Adopting helpful habits
Abandoning unhelpful habits
Training the mind in meditation and compassion

## Lasting Happiness

We could say that there are two kinds of happiness: the short-term, pleasure-based experience and a more lasting happiness.

The first kind is much easier to attain than the deeper happiness, which requires effort but once established serves as a reliable basis for wellbeing. Although in seeking short-term pleasure we are trying to improve our lives, ironically the fruits of this search often have adverse effects because repeatedly we are let down by the results. The harder we try, the tighter the spiral of effort–disappointment–stress–renewed-effort becomes. The trouble is that initially our strategy works – as the research shows, short-term happiness does give us a rush of pleasure. This is the trap that we fall into again and again.

Developing lasting happiness is much harder – there is rarely an initial flood of pleasure, although there can often be a sense of relief that, at last, we have found something we can count on. However, we need to work at it regularly and over the longer term. On occasion it can seem beyond our ability to sustain this feeling, and then it is so much easier to simply go and buy the latest gadget in order to feel better about life.

**Giving ourselves the time and space to explore and develop this lasting happiness is one of the deepest acts of self-compassion we can engage in and marks the first step in using compassion to reduce stress.**

How do we access this deeper kind of happiness?

1. We need to recognise that it is not about looking outwards but depends on having an inner peace of mind and heart. This is the basis for self-awareness and the awareness of others – the foundation of compassion – that enables us to view our actions and those of other people with greater clarity. It can be developed by working with both our basic attitude and with the actions we take while trying to be happy.

   To start with, take our basic attitude to life. This is going to be influenced by our happiness set point (see page 73), but remember there is 40 per cent room for manoeuvre.

   Recall what Sister Helena advised: 'Be accepting of everything that comes to you.'

   She is describing a kind of contentment that could be seen as a basic attitude to life that enables us to deal with patience and a favourable outlook with everything that comes. This is not about being a doormat, but about developing a willingness to engage with life as it comes, rather than trying to insist that it somehow be different. We could say it is the foundation of peace of mind and heart, and the more we can cultivate it, the more reliable it becomes. It has the potential to be a safeguard against stress.

2. Then we can begin to look closely at the actions we take in order to be happy.

   **There is a simple question we can use here as a measure of whether or not our actions will be a source of lasting happiness:** ***Do they bring real benefit to oneself and others, or not?***

   Actions that bring benefit automatically result in happiness and, as we will see later, are important elements in training our compassion. We need to develop a clear sense of discernment to enable us to analyse our actions clearly in the light of this question, and to identify the habits that lead us away from lasting happiness even if they initially seem to bring pleasure.

**Try this out for yourself.**

Think through your day so far and make a list of 10 things you did.

Divide the list into things that brought benefit and things that did not:

BENEFIT NO BENEFIT

Then mark the ones that made you happy.

This is the way to start the process of training our own mind to become more useful to us. It is the first step in learning to become compassionate towards ourselves, and the first step towards coping with stress.

In fact, as we increase our ability to discern in this way, we begin to cut through our normal responses to stress. This is because we learn to recognise that such responses are not useful for us, or for others. We may not be able to achieve this all in one go, but we can learn to notice our responses more and more often and to remember them more quickly. This is what training the mind is – abandoning unhelpful habits and adopting new, more helpful ones. This brings us back to self-awareness, which we will come to in Chapter 8.

As we learn how to work with our mind to understand our own happiness, the next natural step is to increase our understanding of other people and their wish for happiness.

## Exploring Suffering

In our look at happiness we have seen that there is always a tension between our longing for happiness and our fear of losing it. It is this tension that can lead to stress. Let's look more closely at what we mean by suffering.

---

> *It may seem strange that some people's first move into compassion is through their rage at and sense of injustice about the suffering of life.*
>
> *Professor Paul Gilbert*[15]

---

### *Knowing that we suffer*

We are all hoping for happiness, but at the same time fearing that we may not be able to achieve it or hold on to it, and there lies the cause of a great deal of our suffering. An important first step in working with stress is to be able to see what causes us pain and suffering. Instead of trying to turn away, we need to lean into the pain, to understand it and to see how to learn from it.

**The big sources of pain and distress in our lives are not hard to spot because they stare us in the face.**

- From the moment we are born, our bodies are on a conveyor belt of change, growth and eventual disintegration. No sooner are we 'grown up' and able to enjoy the independence of adulthood, than our bodies start to age and develop unwanted wrinkles, extra bulk and various aches and pains.
- Unfortunately, most of us will face serious illness at some time in our lives and, as we all know, at some point our time will run out and we will die.
- Depending on where we live, natural disasters can strike at any time – floods, earthquakes and drought affect large areas of the planet.
- In some parts of the world, people live under the burden of famine, war and social unrest.
- Throughout our lives, we will be subject to a number of sources of unhappiness rooted in the society we live in – economic collapse, political upheaval, crime and violence.
- Then there are mishaps and accidents – things we try to avoid do happen; things we don't want to be taken from us are lost. For example, we may fail an important exam even though we worked hard for it; our car may come off the road on a foggy night; the promotion we've planned for may be given to someone else; and the friend we love dearly may go to live in another country.

All of this is the backdrop to our lives. We hope it will never happen to us, but we know it could – or if not to us, then to someone we care about.

This lends a sense of insecurity to everything we do.

Perhaps we have a feeling that life is just not that easy to get a handle on, and people and situations can change in ways one never imagined. This feeling can increase with experience when we have been hurt, failed to take up certain opportunities, or carry regrets and memories tinged with sadness.

It is no wonder that we can feel stressed from time to time, and that in modern times stress has become one of the most widespread manifestations of suffering.

**Added to this, we also experience all kinds of everyday small travails that in themselves do not seem to amount to much but which, when we add up all the wear and tear they impose on us, can also be sources of stress.**

- Whether you live in the sun in Australia, or in the chillier climate of Northern Europe, you still need to wake up, shower, dress and get to work most days.

- Food does not arrive prepared and nicely served on the plate – we need to shop and cook and, even worse, wash up!
- Only a small minority of people get their houses cleaned for them, or their clothes ironed.

> We may look at someone else and think that their lifestyle has to be easier, or happier or less stressful than our own. Often that is just not the case.

**THE PROBLEM**

- We fear suffering, and because we are afraid of it, we try and pretend it is not there.
- We focus on pursuing happiness. That way we never get to the bottom of what might be causing us pain, never mind trying to do something about it.

**THE SOLUTION**

- Self-awareness – see our helpful and unhelpful habits
- Gain insight into actions that will be beneficial.
- The realisation that everyone is in the same situation – everyone has their own kinds of suffering and stress, whoever they are, however they live – is one of the foundation stones of compassion.

**RESULT**

- If we can try to look at our lives realistically and see our suffering clearly – with tenderness and a gentle humour – then we have the possibility to learn some important things about how we live.
- Our pain can become an inspiration to make changes in order to reduce our stress.
- When we are able to see suffering and stress as an inevitable part of life and so learn to take it less personally, then we are able to relax to some extent.
- In that relaxation comes an easing of our focus on ourselves and so there is room to see how things are for other people and how we are all in the same boat.
- Realising this can touch a deep tenderness in us, as we see how pervasive suffering is.
- Just as we wish not to suffer ourselves, we are moved to want to help relieve other people from their suffering – this is the basis of compassion.

**Reflection exercise – take a while to reflect on these three statements.**

**Ask yourself if they resonate with your own experience.**

- It is hard to truly care about how other people suffer if we are not able to look at our own difficulties in the first place.
- If we are tightly focused on avoiding recognising and understanding pain and simply want to feel good about life, then we are creating an unrealistic worldview that closes off our capacity for compassion.
- Instead of protecting us, as we imagine it will, avoiding suffering prevents us both from healing our own pain and at the same time distances us from others.

**Make a note of your findings.**

## How Things Are and How We See Them

### *Interdependence*

*Everything is closely connected but we act as if we were separate.*

In Chapter 2 we looked at how interdependence underpins the whole logic of compassion, but we tend to live our lives as if we were an independent unit. We want to feel that we have our life under our own control. This can be seen powerfully in the current dialogue about climate change. On one level we understand that human behaviour is endangering the planet, and yet it is hard to make sense of it on an individual level. We know we are called on to change some of our habits, but we are not comfortable with admitting they are necessary.

Albert Einstein describes this feeling and relates it to developing compassion:

> *A human being is a part of the whole called by us universe, a part limited in time and space. He experiences himself, his thoughts and feeling as something separated from the rest, a kind of optical delusion of his consciousness. This delusion is a kind of prison for us, restricting us to our personal desires and to affection for a few persons nearest to us. Our task must be to free ourselves from this prison by widening our circle of compassion to embrace all living creatures and the whole of nature in its beauty.*

*Reflection exercise: Take some time to think deeply about this quote*

What do you understand from it?

**As you get ready for bed tonight think about the following:**

- All the people involved in making the appliances that you switch off before sleeping.

- Where your clothes were made.

- Where all the ingredients for your toiletries come from.

- Think of all the farming, harvesting, transport, haulage, advertising, selling and so on that has gone into these items being within your reach, and all the thousands of people involved.

- What do you take from this?

## *Change*

Everything is impermanent and changing but we behave as if things will last for ever.

Something we can definitely rely on is that change is part of life. We can take the example of our own self as an illustration of this.

The person we were when we were ten years old is not the same person that we are now. Not only do we look very different, with altered life circumstances and interests, but the physical make-up of our body has almost completely altered as well. In fact, the person that we were yesterday does not have all the experience of the person we are today – even the last twenty-four hours will have brought a wealth of thoughts, feelings, impressions and activities that have moved us on from where we were this time yesterday. How we are at home is rarely exactly the same as the person we are at work. When we are in a parent role, we are not the same as when we are with our own parents, or with our lover, or friends.

This self that we see as 'me' or 'myself', that in my case carries the label 'Maureen', is in fact not one single independent entity but a mass of interconnected elements that are themselves interconnected to other sets of elements, and so on. It is so easy to assume that this self, this 'Maureen', is a constant entity moving along through life rather than a combination of ever-changing facets that shift every moment in relation to a variety of other shifting and changing people and circumstances.

**Question: What can you think of that does not change?**

______________________________________________

______________________________________________

______________________________________________

______________________________________________

______________________________________________

______________________________________________

______________________________________________

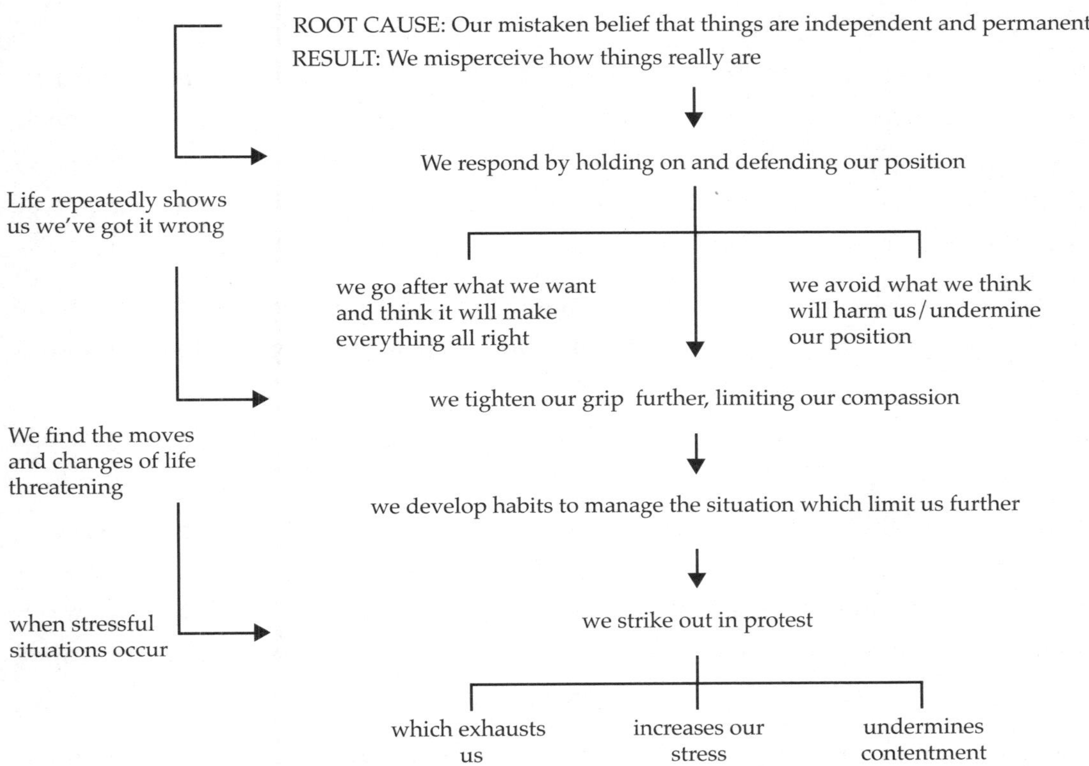
UNDERSTANDING WHAT CAUSES SUFFERING
ROOT CAUSE: Our mistaken belief that things are independent and permanent
RESULT: We misperceive how things really are
We respond by holding on and defending our position
Life repeatedly shows us we've got it wrong
we go after what we want and think it will make everything all right
we avoid what we think will harm us/undermine our position
we tighten our grip further, limiting our compassion
We find the moves and changes of life threatening
we develop habits to manage the situation which limit us further
when stressful situations occur
we strike out in protest
which exhausts us
increases our stress
undermines contentment
THE SOLUTION * We need to become aware of these habits in order to understand why we suffer and learn to replace them with useful habits *

Our inability to view life in this way is the basis of suffering. We all do it. The point is not to feel bad about it but to realise what we're doing and try something different.

Lacking awareness of the way that we are connected to circumstances and to other people, and avoiding the reality of impermanence and change, means that we assume things are one way when they are in fact quite different. Because we don't acknowledge the constant flow of change throughout life, we try to hold on to our position by going after the things we think will strengthen us and by avoiding the things we think will harm us or cause us stress.

Even though life constantly moves and changes, we are not able to see this as the natural course of events but tend to see it as threatening, and so we tighten our grip even further, which limits our compassion. Instead of taking things as we find them without judgement, which we find painful, we develop increasingly sophisticated habits in order to avoid facing reality. These habits then cause us further suffering as they limit us more and more.

When we are faced with stressful circumstances, it becomes all too easy to strike out in protest rather than see such events as an inevitable part of life that affects us all. It is extremely hard work to maintain this limited attitude (that refuses to acknowledge interdependence and impermanence) in the face of all the evidence of real life. It exhausts us and leads to all kinds of stressful reactions, which undermine our ability to feel contented.

Becoming aware of the habits we learn in a misguided attempt to keep ourselves safe, and understanding that they cause us pain, are the first steps in learning how to change them.

## Transforming Our Suffering

If our limited view of the nature of things is one of the causes of suffering, then it follows that changing this view will help reduce stress. This ties back into one of our central themes – the importance of awareness. We saw in Chapter 2 how awareness is an element in our fundamental 'wholeness' and a crucial element in our wellbeing. But we need to develop it, to bring it out; we can develop our awareness through meditation.

By practising meditation, we can uncover the ways our mind overlooks change and impermanence, interconnectedness and interdependence, and all the patterns we fall into because of this.

We have learned that research carried out on distraction and the wandering mind has revealed that for almost half of our waking hours we are not paying full attention to what we are doing. When we are distracted in this way, we miss what is going on around us because our mind is not settled enough to see clearly and understand events. However, our mind has a need to keep the narrative of our lives constant, and to fill in any gaps, so that these lapses in concentration are filled in with assumption rather than fact. These assumptions build up as further layers of misperception, clouding our awareness and leading to more unhelpful habits of thought.

## A SCENARIO

Imagine having an argument with someone at work who frequently annoys you.

Perhaps your colleague is late for a deadline and this is going to put you in a tight spot. This is not the first time this has happened. In fact, you think the person is a pretty lazy worker and is given too much leeway from your joint boss.

As your colleague tries to explain to you that they are late with their piece of work because they were up all night as their daughter was being sick, your mind is whirring with feelings of resentment and irritation. Because of all these thoughts and emotions, you do not really listen to what they are saying and miss the chance to express sympathy and work out a solution to the problem together.

Our tendency is not to realise we are doing this. We do not recognise that we have failed to pay attention to the full situation, and instead are indulging in a stream of judgement.

## RESULT

The relationship between you and your colleague deteriorates further, having missed an opportunity to come closer. It means that the next time there is a misunderstanding between you, you will remember how resentful you felt, and your colleague will remember how unsympathetic you were.

You have both been pushed further apart and your negative opinions of each other have taken a firmer hold.

---

Can you think of a similar situation from your own life?

In meditation, our mind calms down and begins to settle, so it becomes possible to see what is going on with us, and around us, more clearly. In this state, we are more likely to recognise that some of the habits that we have developed as a means of self-protection are not only useless to us but sometimes even harmful. Our self-imposed limitations are unnecessary, and obstructive. Meditation allows our mind to settle into its natural state of awareness. It has been found to be one of the most effective and sustainable ways of reducing stress – in other words, once we learn to meditate, we have a technique to hand which can help us to address stress as it happens. As a means of helping us develop peace of mind, meditation is also a way to develop lasting happiness. Because of this, learning to meditate is one of the most profound acts of self-compassion possible.

We will look at how to meditate in more detail in Chapter 5.

## Tools to Help Us

In meditation practice and compassion training, we can find a series of methods that can help us reduce the suffering of stress and transform our attitude towards it. Too often, we are not in the habit of using our mind to achieve contentment, but it is possible to learn how to do this and the tools exist to enable us to do so.

- As we have discussed in this chapter, firstly we need to be able to see our problems clearly from the basis of a peaceful mind and compassionate heart.
- Furthermore, we need to see that the causes of these problems are in part connected to our own emotions and that how we react to the situations we get into is connected to our inner state of mind.
- In the example of the work colleague we just looked at, we can see that there was an emotional reaction that triggered an exaggerated reaction, which made the situation worse.
- How we react to particular situations will help determine how they turn out.
- If we wish to work with difficult circumstances, then we need to work on what is going on inside us – our emotional reactions and opinions about what is happening to us.
- The good news is that we are not hardwired into our habits. We can reduce stress because we have the ability to transform our thought processes.
- As we shall see when we look into neuroplasticity in later chapters, our brain is malleable and can change in relation to our experience.
- It is possible to change how we respond to what life throws at us and therefore to change how we feel.

Here is a story of how we can use meditation and training the mind in compassion to make this happen.

---

**Paul was a CEO of an organisation supporting the homeless in the UK.** He had been hired to turn it around after a period of poor management and loss of volunteer support.

He was passionate about his work and cared deeply about the people his organisation was set up to help. However, instead of this being inspirational for his staff, he often came over as judgemental, hard to please and a poor listener.

Paul was not able to communicate his own inspiration because his enthusiasm made him feel vulnerable to accusations of naivety, and yet he badly wanted to succeed. Instead of engaging his staff in his vision for the organisation, he adopted a top-down management style based on his word as law.

After his first six months in the job, several of his staff were sufficiently frustrated to think about looking for new jobs and the volunteer numbers were not improving. Unable to see the connection between his style of leadership and the behaviour of his staff, Paul was ready to let them go and hire replacements, but at this point his deputy Martin intervened.

**Martin had attended a training course on communication skills for managers that included meditation and compassion training.** Plucking up his courage, he went to see Paul and during a long and difficult meeting managed to broach the topic of Paul's negative style of communication.

Martin tried to get Paul to see that by not opening up to his staff about his vision for the organisation, he appeared not to trust them, and that by being so bossy and judgemental he was undermining their self-confidence.

Paul was shocked. He had been so caught up in his passion to help the homeless, his feelings of vulnerability and his fear of failure that he had not realised the effect his behaviour had on others. He had not seen the extent of his own stress in striving to succeed and he certainly had not seen that *his* stress was *causing* stress to his staff.

Martin helped Paul to see that there was a problem in the first place, and then he gave him an insight into how his own state of mind and emotional habits were a factor in the disappointing results he was getting from the staff and volunteers.

Slowly Paul was able to see that what he thought was a straightforward lack of enthusiasm on the part of his staff was in fact the result of a combination of his own hopes and fears and those of his staff. The staff just wanted a boss who would guide them creatively and enable them to do a good job but in his very wish to do a good job himself, Paul was stifling enthusiasm and causing himself stress.

**After his initial conversation with Martin had broken the ice, Paul took him into his confidence and asked him to share with him some of the techniques of communication he had learned on his course.**

Then Paul spent quiet time at home over a weekend trying to identify the habits he had fallen into which had proven to be so unhelpful.

He recognised that it would help him and others if he was able to talk to his staff about his vision in an inspiring way without fear of feeling exposed. He thought about delegating more work and adopting a more consensual form of decision-making. He even tried a bit of the meditation technique that Martin had shared with him and was surprised to find that it helped him to relax more and to sleep better at night.

Furthermore, he came to see that he and his staff were engaged in a joint venture to help the homeless and that if he could not express some empathy for the people he worked with, he was not going to be of much use to their clients.

Like many of us, Paul needed help to recognise that there was a problem, but once he saw it, he was able to accept his part in it. Having done that, he took time to work out the causes of the problem and the part his habits had played in it. He decided on steps to try and improve things and was open to new methods such as meditation to help him to do this effectively.

What do you think about Paul's story?

Can you equate it with anything going on in your own life at the moment?

## Perceiving suffering

Last year a friend of mine was diagnosed with cancer. Fortunately, it was in its early stages and treatable but, still, the experience of having cancer is intense, frightening and sometimes lonely. She had surgery, which went well, and was then prescribed radiotherapy. She described to me what it was like to be a patient in a radiology outpatients' department of a large, busy hospital. Having been through several weeks of convalescence, suddenly she found herself part of a community of people all undergoing the same kind of treatment. Her own treatment consisted of twenty-eight daily visits excluding weekends. Over the course of this time she often ran into the same people having their daily session and saw that there was a sense of everyone going through something together. She told me that being with people who were recovering from cancer, just as she was, was a profoundly moving experience. There were people there she felt she could have made friends with and there were others with whom she felt little in common except the experience of this illness.

The patients were from all kinds of cultural backgrounds and social classes. There were people older than her and some younger. Some people came with their sons or daughters, others with their husbands or wives. All these differences faded into insignificance, she said, as each was joined by the experience of going through cancer. Each person was facing their own fears and anxieties about their illness and the changes in their lives. No one wanted to be in the hospital and yet, faced with the necessity of treatment, each person was facing it with their own courage and fortitude.

Suffering is an inevitable part of life, and our circumstances and who we are change all the time. It is natural to long for happiness and wish to avoid pain, but in the process we can find ourselves mistakenly grasping at happiness and trying to push away any suffering we encounter, increasing its power to hurt us as well as depriving ourselves of the opportunity to learn something about ourselves.

Every circumstance has a cause and effect – some actions will lead to happiness, others to unhappiness. It is by working with these causes that we will learn to transform the suffering of stress. At the same time, the way in which we perceive the difficulties that come our way determines how we deal with them and the effect they have on us. If we take them personally and feel that our troubles are worse than anyone else's, then we are shutting ourselves off from being able to change our reactions.

Stress is one way to respond to suffering, but it is only one of a range of responses that we can draw on. The trouble is that we can get into the habit of getting stressed. It is helpful to be able to see how this happens so that we can try a different approach.

<table>
<tr><th>What we have learned in this chapter</th><th>Your reflections</th></tr>
<tr><td>

<ul>
<li>Everyone wants to be happy and to avoid pain and suffering, but how we go about trying to be happy does not always bring the results we hope for and can even result in stress.</li>
<li>Happiness is trickier than we thought and much less reliable – hoping for it can even be a source of stress – whereas suffering can present us with challenges that can in the end be beneficial.</li>
<li>Recently scientists have discovered how to 'measure' happiness by monitoring blood flow to the emotional centres of the brain.</li>
<li>Current research into happiness shows us that:
<ul>
<li>Technology has not resulted in giving us more free time</li>
<li>The amount of choice we have can be overwhelming</li>
<li>Improvements in our standard of living do not necessarily lead to an increase in happiness</li>
<li>We adapt to what we have and then want more</li>
<li>We compare what we have to what others have</li>
<li>We remember causes of happiness inaccurately and are not good at forecasting what will make us happy in the future</li>
</ul>
</li>
</ul>

</td><td></td></tr>
</table>

* 40 per cent of our potential for happiness is in our own hands
* Happiness can improve our resilience and even our chances of living longer
* 46.9 per cent of the time we are not focused on what we are doing, and this makes us dissatisfied

- There are two kinds of happiness:
    * Short-term, easily attained, pleasure-based
    * Lasting happiness, requires effort, value-based
- Lasting happiness can be developed through peace of mind and heart, and self-awareness.
    * It is a powerful source of self-compassion and a starting point for compassion for other people
    * Contentment is a good starting point
- Recognising and understanding the causes of our suffering will help us to change it.
- Stress is a manifestation of suffering.
- Recognising that suffering is an inevitable part of life touches a deep tenderness in us, which is the basis of compassion.
- Suffering is caused by our misperception of how things are – we think things are independent – in other words, capable of standing alone and never going to change – when the opposite is true.
- We can address this misperception by developing our quality of awareness through the practice of meditation.
- Meditation is one of the most effective ways to work with stress and is an act of self-compassion.

## TIPS TO TAKE INTO EVERYDAY LIFE

1. Try to be aware when your wish to be happy gets tricky.
2. Remember that everyone wishes to be happy and not to suffer.
3. Ask yourself whether you are emphasising long-term or short-term happiness.
4. Observe how you respond to difficult situations – do you push them away, distract yourself from them or try to find out what is going on?

# Conclusion to Part 1

The step we have covered in Part 1 of this workbook is:

**STEP 1 Understanding our stress instead of trying to avoid it**

We have looked carefully at what we understand by both 'stress' and 'compassion' and learned how our physical make-up is related to both. We have seen that as we go through life, we tend to hope for happiness and fear suffering. Happiness turns out to be both more important and more elusive than we think it is, whereas suffering is an inevitable part of life. We experience stress when our pursuit of happiness is interrupted and the suffering that we do not want comes to us anyway. If we can learn to develop resilience in the face of suffering, there are the possibilities for learning and wisdom. So, there are other options open to us apart from a stress response, and in Parts 2 and 3 we will look at what those are.

# Part 2

# SEEING WHERE WE WANT TO CHANGE

This is the part of the book where we begin to look at how we want to change. We've seen the reality of stress and how it can affect us, and we have seen how working more closely with compassion can help us on many levels. However, the ways in which we experience both stress and compassion will depend on how our mind reacts to situations that we face, and so it is useful to spend some time looking at how our mind works.

If we are going to make changes in how we deal with stress, we are going to have to drop the habits that increase our stress and look at replacing them with those that help us reduce those feelings – such as using compassion techniques.

At the same time, to be able to work with compassion in an effective way, we need to look into how we are. Compassion is not easy; it requires courage to open our hearts. While we work with ourselves in order to do that it is possible to misunderstand compassion as a way of keeping it at arm's length. I find this quotation from Pema Chödrön's book, *The Places That Scare You*, very helpful to reflect on:[1]

> *Compassion is not a relationship between the healer and the wounded. It's a relationship between equals. Only when we know our own darkness well can we be present with the darkness of others. Compassion becomes real when we recognise our shared humanity.*

So, we do not look down on people that need our compassion. Instead, we search our hearts to see where our own weaknesses and fragility are. The more we reflect, the more we understand how deeply connected we all are.

In Buddhism, the idea of training the mind is well understood. With research being undertaken into meditation and compassion, science is beginning to move in the same direction – with the idea that spiritual skills can be learned through practice, in the same way a person would learn to play an instrument.

Tania Singer was the director of the Max Planck Institute for Human Cognitive and Brain Sciences in Leipzig, Germany. She conducted a large-scale longitudinal contemplative mental training study, The ReSource Project, which is based on years of dialogue between Western clinical psychology and Eastern contemplative traditions.

This is how she describes the findings:[2]

> *The data shows that already after three months of mental training where people focused on cultivating either present-moment attention or socio-emotional qualities like compassion and cognitive perspective taking of others, you can induce structural changes in brain networks associated with these specific skills. This is compelling because people in the study are on average about 40 years old and face significant stress at work and are often balancing the demands of raising children. In addition to brain changes, we also found that such training can reduce social stress and increase prosocial behavior and altruism. What our findings suggest is that instead of being born as an egoist and being stuck as an egoist, these mental exercises can change your outlook on the world – and you can change from an egoist to someone more compassionate and in touch with the realities and possibilities of his or her life very quickly.*

So, the scientific evidence for the effectiveness of training the mind is available to endorse what contemplative traditions have known for over two thousand years. It can help to give us confidence as we work through this investigation of our habits.

In Chapter 4, we will examine how our mind works and look at what we understand by 'habits' and how to go about changing them.

Chapter 5 introduces mindfulness and meditation techniques and explains how these techniques can help us use our mind in ways that are more useful for us and help us to change our unhelpful habits.

In Chapter 6, we will look more closely at the unhelpful habits we need to let go of, and in Chapter 7 examine at the new habits we need to adopt in their place – the habits of compassion.

**In terms of the five steps, we will be working with steps 2–4:**

**STEP 2 Taking a step back in order to see what is really going on**

**STEP 3 Trying out a fresh perspective**

**STEP 4 Examining our habits to see which ones help us and which ones don't**

# 4 Taking a Fresh Look at Our Habits

*Mind is its own place and in itself*
*can make a heaven of hell and a hell of heaven.*

*John Milton*[1]

What we are going to do in this chapter:

1. Consider how our minds work
2. Look at how we react
3. Make a formula for change
4. Explore our habits

## The Mind that Experiences Stress and Compassion

How our mind reacts is an important factor in determining how we are affected by the suffering that life can throw our way, as well as the stressful situations that we all have to face. We have already glimpsed the importance of the mind in working to reduce stress and develop compassion.

This is a fundamental theme in using compassion as a means of working with stress: **In order to really get to grips with our stress and develop compassion, we need to be aware of and ready to change how our mind responds to our experience.**

It is more than likely that we have all had experiences that bear out the quotation above from the poet John Milton. Perhaps we may call it our 'mood', but we know that if we are in a positive frame of mind we feel that we can handle more or less anything that comes along, whereas if we are feeling down, even going out for a birthday treat can seem like nothing more than an obligation. How our mind reacts will determine how we will engage in whatever we are doing, but for the most part we rarely realise this and look to factors *outside* ourselves as the causes of whatever mood we may find ourselves in.

In this chapter we will start to look at ways of working with our mind more systematically before moving on to meditation techniques in the next chapter.

Accepting that our mind needs training is a process in itself. After all, we use our mind all the time and it seems to more or less keep up with everything we require of it – why bother to ask it to do more? In order to answer this question, let's begin with a simple exercise.

### *Exercise: 'Watching' our mind*

Take a moment now to look up from the page and 'watch' your mind – just observe its movement and activity for a few moments.

Now, break it down into three steps:

1. Connect with your *body* and allow yourself to 'check in' with it, to become aware of how it is feeling.
    - Do you have any discomfort, any tightness? Perhaps you feel hungry, or a little tired, or just simply relaxed.
    - Just notice these feelings without judgement if you can.
2. Next, check in on your *mood.*
    - Is it relaxed, or a little tense?
    - Just notice the emotions that move through your awareness.
3. Finally, notice the *thoughts* that come and go in your mind.
    - Can you let them come and go, or do you follow after them and create stories, or loops in your mind?

Perhaps your response to this exercise goes something like this?

- You start out by thinking about my asking you to do this and form an intention to try and go along with it, but maybe random thoughts also come into your mind.
- You might start thinking about what you are going to do this evening – for example, if you need to go shopping for supper – then you remember that you cooked last night as well but because your partner is working late tonight you offered to cook again.
- You feel a bit put out about this and then immediately feel guilty because you did offer.
- At the same time, you remember that you are going away for the weekend in the countryside and you spend a few moments reflecting on how much you are looking forward to it – except, oh gosh, you meant to buy a new pair of decent walking shoes, now when can you manage to find the time to go shopping?
- Just as you are trying to work that out, you notice that your back is aching and that actually you are feeling a bit tired and your mind jumps back to having to cook the supper.
- You wonder if getting a takeaway would be a good idea and then you remember that your favourite place has closed down and you'd need to try somewhere new – mmm, risky . . .

Do you get the picture?

This exercise shows us that part of the trouble with our mind is that we keep it so occupied there is rarely an opportunity to just let it be. Most of the time our experience of our own mind is covered over with layers of thoughts and feelings and subsequent thoughts about those thoughts and feelings. Then there is sensory information pouring in all the time, such as the noises and smells around us, and this gets caught up in the tumble of activity going on, which means that the way we process this information can get quite skewed!

We are so used to our mind being hyperactive that we take this state for granted and believe that that is how the mind naturally is, but this is not the case – in fact, it would be more helpful to take a step back and observe our mind. This way we might get some kind of a handle on how our mind behaves and learn to access its innate power and intelligence. When we don't do that, our mind will run wild.

How often do you settle down to a task requiring concentration, only to find yourself daydreaming, checking your email or making another cup of coffee? We have developed a habit of letting our mind roam around, and we have been perfecting this habit for such a long time that it seems to be normal. It's as if long ago, in a moment of boredom, we hired an entertainer to keep us always occupied and busy, but then he moved in, became one of the family and refused to leave – and now we are stuck with him!

The movement of thoughts and emotions is natural to the mind – there is nothing wrong with it. Remember in Chapter 2, when we compared how a human behaves after getting away from a sabre-toothed tiger to how a gazelle would behave – once the gazelle is safe, it settles down and continues to graze. A human would worry if the danger had really passed, whether they should move to another part of the savannah and so on. We noted that humans are specially evolved to think, imagine, plan, anticipate and ruminate. Often these mental activities stimulate our threat system, which makes it even harder to settle down. Indeed, this is why we need *training* to focus and take control of our attention.

## Two Habits We Have with Our Thoughts

- We treat our thoughts and emotions as solid and real, giving them tremendous power over us.
- We have thoughts we like and become attached to, but we also have thoughts we feel bad about or are even frightened by. These are the mental loops we discussed earlier – we all know what it is like to have a worry nagging away in our mind and what it feels like to churn it over and over looking for a solution. Actually, we are making it worse by focusing on it more than ever.

This leads to two aspects of mind:[2]

| **The experiencing aspect of mind** | **The evaluating (judging) aspect of mind.** |
| --- | --- |
| The aspect of our self that is living in the present – fresh, awake and experiencing each moment as it happens.<br><br>*Remember in Chapter 2 the example of the glass of muddy water to illustrate the essence of our minds? (see page 43)* | Based on memory and concerned with making our life into a continuous story – keeping score and maintaining records.<br><br>*We are more familiar with this aspect of our mind.* |

It is in the evaluating aspect of mind that we go over and over events that have happened in the past, and plan and anticipate events still to come, trying to turn our stream of experiences into a continuous whole in order to make sense of them. In so doing, we cover up the individual moments of our experience, numbing our perception and dulling our reactions. We'll find out more about this when we look at mindfulness in the next chapter.

This research is strikingly consistent with Buddhist ideas about the mind, which in simple terms makes a distinction between the busy, distracted aspect of mind and the clear, unobstructed quality of awareness that is the mind's true nature. In spite of all the activity of our thoughts and emotions, the clear awareness or our essential nature is always available to us and, as we learn to access it, we can learn to tame the activity of our minds.

## The Metaphor of the Sky and the Clouds

Here is another way to understand this relationship of our natural mind with our thoughts and emotion.

Imagine a clear blue sky with the sun shining brightly. Very simply, the mind in its natural state is like this – calm, spacious and limitless like the sky, with a clear, sparkling awareness that could be compared to the sun. We can take the analogy further and say that the rays of the sun are like our capacity for compassion arising from our natural state of awareness.

Now imagine a sky that is overcast and pretty cloudy – this is more like how the mind is on a daily basis. The clouds represent our thoughts and emotions, with all our inclination to dwell on our thoughts, our hopes and fears, our habit of wanting one thing and not wanting another, and of clinging to the past while also anticipating the future. Just as on a cloudy day, we can almost forget there is a clear blue sky above the clouds, so when our mind is occupied with all kinds of thoughts and emotions, we can forget what our natural state really is.

Some days, perhaps we can see quite a bit of sky and there are attractive fluffy clouds moving across it. These are 'good' days for us, when we are not feeling too stressed or busy and can keep a sense of proportion. However, we all know what a stormy sky looks like, with dark, boiling clouds that seem to loom right down on top of us. These are the times of real mental turmoil and distress when our stress levels can seem unmanageable and it feels like there is no way through.

The thing to do here is to change our perspective. Generally speaking, we view the sky from the perspective of the ground, whereas when we travel in a plane and look down on the clouds everything looks quite different. A panorama of clouds viewed from above appears quite beautiful and enticing. The cloud cover may be thick, but it is lit by the sun and moving in all kinds of fascinating patterns and shapes. It does not look threatening or frightening in any way.

### Exercise: Changing perspective from the clouds to the sky

Sit quietly and take a few moments to look at the sky.

Reflect that your natural mind is limitless, spacious and vast like the sky.

Now look at the clouds and think of them as being like your thoughts and emotions that come and go but never change the sky.

Try to view the clouds from the perspective of the sky – fleeting, always changing, insubstantial.

Now try to observe your thoughts in the same way, from the perspective of your natural mind.

Learning to look at the clouds from the perspective of the sky involves changing our habits and does not happen overnight but, the thing is, once we are able to do it, even for a few moments, it brings tremendous benefit and quickly becomes much easier to do.

Changing perspective in this way can be compared to observing our mind from the viewpoint of its natural qualities of spaciousness (as represented by the sky) and awareness (as represented by the sun). Instead of restricting the mind with endless activity, this shift in perspective opens up a space that provides the opportunity to change how we react to things.

Remembering that there is more to our mind than all this busyness completely changes the possibilities open to us. It starts to seem possible to be able to take that step back in order to look at how our mind is, and when we do, to be able to regard our thoughts and emotions as transient, so there is no need to try and hold on to them. Working with our mind immediately seems like a worthwhile, even essential, endeavour. We will look at this in a more practical way when we look at techniques to help us apply compassion to stress in Part 3.

## Choosing How to React

There is an old Cherokee folk story that you might have come across. It's a wonderful tale and offers a helpful insight into how we can choose how to react.

An old chief is walking with his grandson, pointing out different features in the landscape and sharing stories.

At one point the old man says to the boy, 'You know, most of the time I feel as if I have two wolves living in my heart. One is fierce and wild, a mighty hunter and fearsome fighter, filled with the power to hate. The other one is gentle and tender, filled with the power of love. Sometimes it feels as if these two wolves are doing battle inside me.'

The child asks, 'Grandfather, which wolf will win?'

His grandfather replies, 'Whichever one I feed.'

| Think of a recent time when you fed the angry wolf instead of the gentle wolf. Can you identify why the wolf was angry – what did it need? | And when you fed the gentle wolf instead of the angry wolf? |
| --- | --- |
| ______________________ | ______________________ |
| ______________________ | ______________________ |
| ______________________ | ______________________ |
| ______________________ | ______________________ |

The Cherokee story is backed up by this quote from Viktor Frankl, who was an Austrian neurologist and psychiatrist as well as a Holocaust survivor and author:[3]

> *Everything can be taken from a man but one thing: the last of the human freedoms – to choose one's attitude in any given set of circumstances, to choose one's own way.*

So often in life we can feel that we have very little choice in the situations that we face, and this can make us feel a loss of control, or even a sense of helplessness. Frankl's observation, based on the terrible events he witnessed in the concentration camps of the Second World War, is that whatever we face and however hemmed in we are by our circumstances, we can still choose how we react. The choices we make will depend on our mental state at any given moment – if our mind is suffused with anger and pain, we are more likely to respond with aggression, but if our mind is calm and clear, we have the possibility of reacting with compassion. This is not easy, but learning to change our habits gives us the choice as to how we want to react. While we are bound by our habitual ways of reacting to things, we will keep repeating the same old patterns – and the more often we re-tread the same patterns, the more entrenched they become.

When we feel stressed, our response is often to turn away from the feeling by trying to suppress it, by denying it, or by trying to distract ourselves from it and comfort ourselves. How often have you gone shopping or switched on the TV to distract yourself from feeling stressed? These are classic responses and there is nothing wrong with them in the short term. Sometimes taking a short break from our stress can help to give us perspective. However, if distraction is our main strategy for dealing with stress, then it is a different story. Continuously trying to avoid the issue and provide ourselves with short-term comfort can reduce our ability to choose how we truly want to react because we are preventing ourselves from seeing clearly what the situation requires. This means we aren't able to be discerning about how we wish to react – we are simply avoiding the problem.

So, the first step in reducing our stress is to learn to *turn towards our stress*, to face it, to work out what is causing it and to try to see what lessons it is showing us. Just doing this brings about an important change. Although it is likely to be hard to do at first, and may show us things about ourselves that we are not very comfortable with, it is a vital first step in learning to use compassion to deal with our stress. After all, we need to diagnose the complaint in order to be able to heal it.

As Christopher Germer, a clinical psychologist who teaches and practices mindfulness-based psychotherapy and self-compassion, writes in his book on self-compassion:[4]

> *Leaning into our problems with open eyes and an open heart – with awareness and compassion – is the process by which we get emotional relief.*

Two key words here are 'awareness' and 'compassion'. We are not leaning into the problem in order to fixate on it or worry it over and over in our mind. Our goal is to acknowledge our stress and to try to see how it arises and what we do when it does. If we really get a handle on how to do this and understand its benefit, it will help inspire us when the task of facing our stress feels difficult. This is important for the long term.

| Think of a recent time when you felt stressed and you tried to distract yourself from it. | Think of a recent time when you felt stressed and you tried to lean into it. |
|---|---|
| | |

What was different about the two experiences?

Which helped you more?

## A Formula for Change

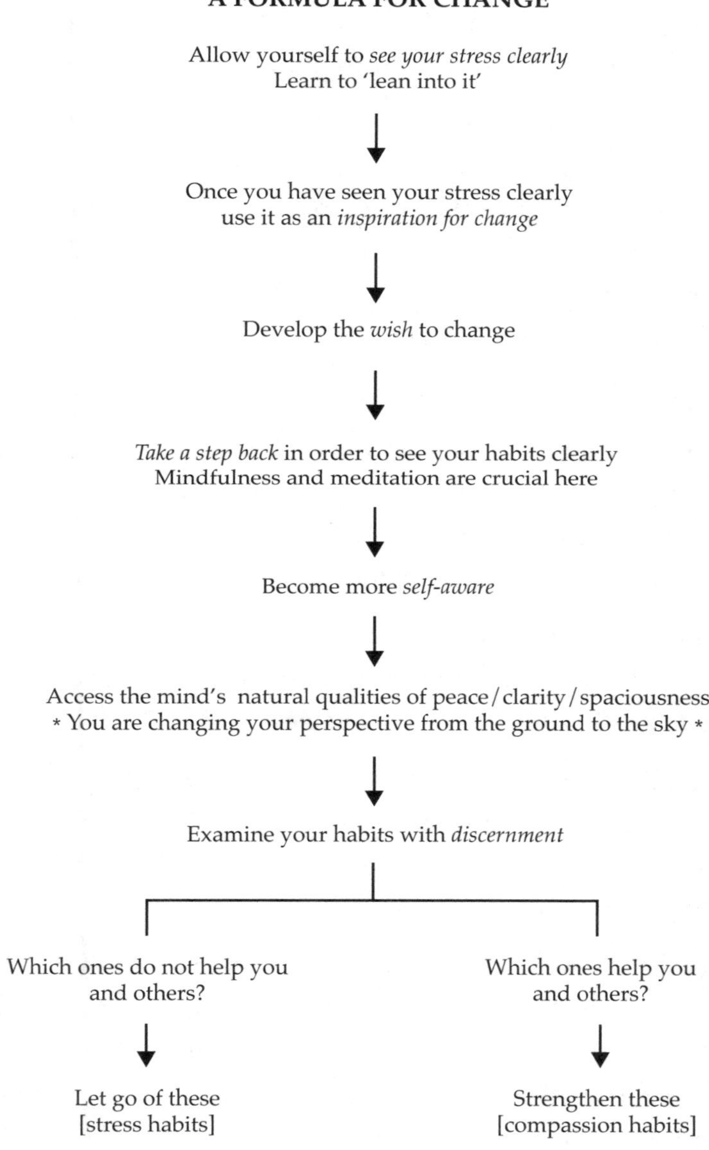
A FORMULA FOR CHANGE
Allow yourself to *see your stress clearly*
Learn to 'lean into it'
Once you have seen your stress clearly
use it as an *inspiration for change*
Develop the *wish* to change
*Take a step back* in order to see your habits clearly
Mindfulness and meditation are crucial here
Become more *self-aware*
Access the mind's natural qualities of peace/clarity/spaciousness
* You are changing your perspective from the ground to the sky *
Examine your habits with *discernment*
Which ones do not help you and others?
Which ones help you and others?
Let go of these [stress habits]
Strengthen these [compassion habits]

The process of using compassion to change how we experience and react to stress is based on learning to understand our habits and letting go of the ones that make things difficult for us. Many of us have numerous habits when faced with stress that are deep-seated – we have been perfecting them for quite some time, after all! Although compassion is natural to us, how we practise and express it is often diluted by our lack of awareness of ourselves and other people, along with a misunderstanding as to how it can help us. It can seem an overwhelming task to learn how to change our attitude – where do we begin?

After we have learned to *lean into* stress and therefore to see it and understand its causes more clearly, we aim to develop the *wish to change*. We have seen that one of the most potent qualities of compassion is that it gives us the courage to try something different – something that will enable us to understand how and why we suffer and even develop the capacity to transform it. This is the attitude we need to adopt with relation to our habitual reactions to stress – to take them as *an inspiration for change*.

Let's look at a step-by-step process of reflection that will enable us to do that.

First, we need to *take a step back*. It is hard to see clearly when our mind is caught up in all its habits. Taking a step back allows us some space to see more clearly, which is the basis of self-awareness. One of the most effective ways of creating some space in our minds is through meditation practice. In the next chapter we will look at how to do this in more detail.

As we begin to develop self-awareness through meditation it becomes more possible to *access the qualities of our natural mind*, the mind that is not constantly overwhelmed by activity. These qualities include peace, clarity and spaciousness.

Once we have re-engaged with these qualities of mind, we are ready to *look at our reactions to stress from the perspective of the sky*, rather than the ground. This means taking a fresh look at what causes us stress and how we experience it. The key here is to be discerning – to be able *to see clearly which habits help us and which don't*.

After you have reflected on your own habits in this way, you probably have a reasonable idea of which ones may be causing you problems. Now it is a matter of deciding which one to choose to start working with. You can work with all of them over time, but to give yourself the chance to make a good start it helps to identify just one to begin with. As you do this, you'll be asking a lot of yourself and it is important to be able to feel a sense of accomplishment, to feel that change is happening. So, it is a good idea not to begin with your most stubborn habit, as that is likely to need more attention. Instead, choose something that definitely gets in your way but that you feel you can get a handle on reasonably quickly.

### An example of how to work with looking at habits in this way

When we go through this process in workshops people often ask for an example of what a habit is in this context. Perhaps it might be useful if I share one of my own that is occupying my attention at the moment.

As someone who works for herself, I have a lot of freedom to make my own schedule. I enjoy this very much but sometimes find it difficult to balance the routine tasks such as email and travel planning with more demanding projects like designing workshops and writing. My tendency is to want to clear the decks of all the mundane stuff and then devote a large chunk of quality time to the projects. Of course, this is hard to do, and I constantly find days that were supposed to have been cleared in this way being taken over by unexpected demands. When this happens, I experience a build-up of tension. If I don't catch this early on it can make me feel overwhelmed. As if that is not bad enough, I then find myself piling on the misery by listing *all* the tasks I need to do in a given period, including doing the ironing and cleaning the windows, until my feeling of being overwhelmed feels really justified! It's a pattern that can end taking a lot of time and energy, as you can imagine.

What I am trying to do instead is to change the basic dynamic that I set up between my routine and my more creative tasks. If I have a clear idea of what I hope to achieve within a certain time then I find there is actually plenty of time to plan the tasks around my energy levels – if I am slow to get started in the mornings, I can knock off a batch of emails until things start flowing, and then I can switch to something more substantial. If I get stuck with a workshop design, I take a break and do something less demanding such as arranging flights and travel schedules. Working this way allows me to relax and work in a more organic, less forced way, following my own natural rhythm – which is, of course, much kinder to myself.

On the occasions this breaks down, I try to notice if I am piling on the pressure with all my lists. Because I have studied this habit of mine – rather than distracting myself from it – and identified my habits that help, and the ones that don't, it becomes possible to apply remedies along the way. It is always good to have a range of remedies in case one doesn't work straight off.

Of course, each person's habits, their responses, and how they are affected by them will be different – your habits may be overworking, putting yourself down, or perhaps letting yourself become more irritable than you want to be. Whatever it is, you will find it easier to work with if you take the time to identify and understand your habit clearly and work out how you are going to try and address it.

## Support for Working with Habits

Once we have identified the habits we want to address, then we need a strategy for changing them. We will be looking at how to build up new, compassionate habits to replace the unhelpful habits around stress in the next chapters, but here are a few introductory remarks.

Wanting to apply compassion to our stress might sound like a tall order, but it is good to remember that learning to work with our habits in this way is just like any other kind of training that we might undertake. If we join a gym and start an exercise programme, we know that we will need to work hard over a sustained period of time in order to get results, and even then, if we cut back on our routine the benefits will not stay. It is the same if we decide to learn a new language, or take up a musical instrument – these things require effort and practice and there is a big difference between doing the minimum to get by and really trying to achieve a sufficiently high standard until playing the instrument or speaking the language feels like second nature.

---

Daniel Goleman, who has written extensively on emotional intelligence, writes:[5]

> *[A] new way of thinking, feeling, or acting feels unnatural at first, something like putting on someone else's clothes. At the neural level, a person is forcing the brain to go along a path less-travelled.*

---

In the second sentence, Goleman is referring to a relatively new development in neuroscience – the idea of neuroplasticity, the discovery that the brain changes in response to experience. Up until about twenty-five years ago it was thought that once the brain matured it could not change and, except for some deterioration, remained the same until the end of our lives. The discovery of neuroplasticity turns this assumption on its head because it demonstrates that the brain continues to change in response to experience throughout our whole lives. How does this change happen? The actions we take can expand or contract the neural activity in different regions of the brain – we can stimulate activity in quiet areas and calm down overly busy ones. The parts of the brain we use more frequently tend to develop more than the parts we do not use often, so it can be said to provide a map of the kind of life we are living.

As Goleman points out, what we now know about neuroplasticity underlines what we also know about our ability to change our habits. Realising that we can 'rewire' our brain makes clear that our endeavour to change is not simply a lofty ambition but is rooted firmly in the realm of science. The new habit will feel like an effort at first but as we persevere, we will be able to rewire our brain to support what we are doing.

Imagine that you live on one side of a forest and your best friend lives on the other side. You visit each other regularly and have worn down a path through the undergrowth between your homes that is easy to find and easy to follow – in fact, you could do the journey with your eyes shut. Now imagine that one day your friend moves to another house on a different side of the forest. Your old path is of no use to you any more and you need to make a new one by treading down undergrowth and repeating the same journey many times. The journey takes more effort and concentration and does not have the sense of ease of your former route, which continues to look inviting. However, after a few months, not only is the new path beginning to look well established, the old path is showing signs of neglect and beginning to grow over. This is the same process that happens with our neural pathways. Gradually over time the new helpful habit will make new neural connections and the connections associated with the old, unhelpful habit will weaken, making it easier to drop.

So, when we have identified our habits through the *formula for change* and are ready to begin to work with them, there are several practical steps we can take to help us.

First of all, as we have seen, it helps if we can be aware of the habits we wish to change so we need to bring them fully into our awareness. We can therefore try to *lean into* our problems with stress, rather than trying to avoid them.

Then we can understand that external events are connected to what is going on in our minds and that if we wish to work with difficult outer circumstances, we need to work on what is going on inside us – our own minds.

Having decided what we want to change, we need to decide on a new way of responding and then practise it at every opportunity. If we feel confident enough, we can ask friends and family to give us feedback on how we are doing. For example, we may be trying to listen more carefully to what people are saying to us and to interrupt less often. We can ask people to tell us how they think we are getting on.

As we work in this way, we can feel confident that gradually new neural pathways are being developed in our brain that will help us to sustain our new, more helpful habits. This is because our brain is plastic, changing according to our experience, and our mind transformable. We are not hardwired into our habits and change is possible.[6]

We will come back to neuroplasticity several times in this book as it is an important scientific discovery that supports the whole idea of being able to change oneself. We started out in this chapter looking at how our mind works and the importance of being able to train it to be more useful for us. Our habits are a result of how we use our mind and how our mind reacts to the events and situations we face. Training the mind requires us to work at several different levels at once, from the level of understanding what our mind is doing, through to identifying our habits and applying the techniques set out in this book. It takes time and effort, but the good news is that as soon as we begin, we can start to experience the difference.

| What we have learned in this chapter | Your reflections |
|---|---|
| • How our mind is determines how we engage in whatever we are doing, but for the most part we rarely realise this and look to factors *outside ourselves* as the causes of our experience.<br>• Therefore, it is important to train our mind so it can be more useful for us.<br>• There are two different aspects of mind:<br>  * The busy, distracted aspect of mind<br>  * The clear, unobstructed quality of awareness that is the mind's true nature<br>• Daniel Kahneman calls these two aspects the *evaluating* mind and the *experiencing* mind. | |

- We can change our perspective from looking at the clouds from the point of view of the ground below, to looking from the point of view of the sky above.
- We need to develop a wish to change and then follow a step-by-step programme:
    - See stress clearly
    - Take it as an inspiration to change
    - Develop the wish to change
    - Take a step back
    - Develop self-awareness
    - Develop discernment
    - Take a fresh look at our habits from this new perspective
    - Choose a habit to start working on
- We can choose how we react to situations.
- We will learn more about our stress if we *lean into* it, rather than trying to avoid it, or distract ourselves from it.
- The new habits we want to establish will be supported by neuroplasticity.

## TIPS TO TAKE INTO EVERYDAY LIFE

- When you feel stressed, try to see when you are looking outside of yourself for the causes of the stress.
- Try looking into your stress and seeing which of your own habits has been triggered.
- From time to time, check in with yourself to see whether you are more with your experiencing mind, in the present, or if you are evaluating and judging your experience.

# 5 Developing a Peaceful Mind: The Basis of Compassionate Action

*With the practice of meditation we can develop this ability to more fully love ourselves and to more consistently love others.*

*Sharon Salzberg*[1]

What we are going to do in this chapter:

1. Look at why meditation is important as a basis for compassion
2. Explore the three elements of meditation: mindfulness, awareness and spaciousness
3. Try out different meditation techniques
4. See how to make meditation part of our life
5. Examine the benefits of a stable mind
6. Look at some of the scientific research

In the last chapter we looked at the mind that experiences stress and compassion and we saw that in order to use compassion to reduce our stress we need to work with how our mind is – in fact we need to begin to *train* our mind. Contemplative traditions over the last 2,500 years have found that the most effective way to train our minds is through meditation.

## A Checklist for What Meditation is Not

Although meditation has been practised in Asian cultures for hundreds of years, it is still relatively new to the West. It is easy to be unclear about what meditation is and how it works.

The left column states what meditation is *not*. The column on the right is for your comments and notes.

| | |
|---|---|
| **A religion**<br>Although it is possible to practise meditation as part of a religion or spiritual path, it is also of great benefit to people who simply wish to use it to help themselves in their lives and to better understand their minds.<br>**Something for people with special skills**<br>You don't need to be an especially quiet or contemplative person to learn meditation. It is useful for everyone. You do not need any special skills in order to start.<br>**A way of blocking out thoughts**<br>People will often say to me that they just cannot block their thoughts while meditating. This is an important misunderstanding – meditation is neither forcing, nor indulging thoughts, but simply allowing them to come and go without commentary, neither pushing them away nor chasing after them, just letting them rise and fade.<br>**A way of emptying the mind**<br>This is slightly different from the blocking thoughts. We can have the misunderstanding that meditation is about relinquishing control of the mind and allowing it to go into a blank, passive state – like being in a neutral gear, perhaps. Again, this is incorrect. Meditation is all about uncovering and working with the mind's natural dynamism and power, not about dumbing the mind down, or numbing it.<br>**Going into a dream, or zoning out**<br>Sometimes people will say that they already know how to relax the mind and when I ask how they do it, they describe how they may drive home from work and simply allow their mind to switch off from all the worries of the day and go into a pleasant dreamy state without any focus. Again, this is not meditation but a kind of daydreaming – a way of being on automatic pilot. It may have a short-term relaxing effect, but it does not help to train the mind. | |

## Getting to Know Yourself Through Meditation

Do you remember the Watching the Mind exercise (page 112) from the last chapter?

Did you notice:

- A whole range of thoughts, feelings, impressions, memories, projections and emotions racing through your mind?
- How your mind is pulled into replaying thoughts from the past and anticipating what you are going to do in the future?
- That our mind tends to engage in a running mental commentary detailing things we like and things we don't like; things we want and things we don't want – our hopes, fears and worries all endlessly playing themselves out?

It is this endless and often confused activity of the mind that needs training, because when our mind is chaotic like this it is not being as useful as it could be and, even worse, it can make us feel very stressed. Although, as we saw in the previous chapter, there are two aspects of mind and behind all these thoughts and emotions our essence of mind is naturally peaceful and clear, accessing these qualities often happens only momentarily. This makes it difficult to sustain a compassionate attitude either towards our self, or other people.

**Meditation is a way of accessing the essence of mind – the clarity and peace that lies hidden behind all the constant activity of our thoughts.**

The way that I was taught meditation emphasised that is has three elements: *mindfulness*, *awareness* and *spaciousness*. We will look at each in turn.

## 1. Mindfulness

*Mindfulness arises from paying attention on purpose, in the present moment, without judgement.*

Our never-ending mental activity means that we spend most of our time on automatic pilot going through tasks and events. Indeed, throughout most of our life we are only partially present and aware because so much of our attention is engaged elsewhere.

Have you ever driven home, and as you parked your car realised that you don't remember anything at all about the drive? Or gone around the supermarket and arrived at the checkout with a full trolley but no memory of putting anything in? Just think of all those moments of life we let pass us by. Big deal, you may say, what's so great about going shopping in the supermarket or driving along the motorway?

Which kinds of mindlessness do you recognise in yourself?

| Situations | Your comments |
|---|---|
| Not being present while doing routine tasks e.g. showering, chopping vegetables, ironing etc. | |
| Not listening fully to people because you are thinking how you want to reply | |
| Wandering mind – not thinking about what you are doing (as the Harvard research described) | |
| Allowing your evaluating aspect of mind to overrun your experiencing aspect of mind – trying to make your experiences into a continuous whole | |
| Wanting to 'switch off' and rest but instead letting your mind be hijacked by worrying and anxious thoughts | |

## *Switching off the automatic pilot*

Remember the analogy of the sky and the clouds in Chapter 4? We saw that although our minds are naturally flexible, spacious and aware, they easily become cluttered by all the activity of our thoughts and emotions. This makes the mind feel more cramped and limited than it actually is.

When we switch off our automatic pilot and allow ourselves to pay attention to what is happening for us in the present moment, we start to clear away this clutter, to quieten down the incessant noise coming from it. In this way, we begin to calm our mind down, to allow it to settle and discover its own peace and clarity. We can do this because these are the natural qualities of our mind; they are already there – we simply need to allow ourselves to get in touch with them.

A checklist for switching off the automatic pilot:

- Notice what you are doing in each moment
- Place your attention on what you are doing
- Notice when your attention slips away into the past, or the future
- Don't make a judgement – just notice
- Return your attention to what you are doing in the present moment

This will help you to:

- Have more stability of mind
- Engage all of your resources
- Make better choices
- Reduce stress
- Respond with compassion, rather than frustration

## *Ways to practise mindfulness*

So how do we begin? Fortunately, we have the most effective support for mindfulness with us all the time – our breath. We can use our breath to anchor our mindfulness at any time and in any place. While we are alive our breath is always there, sending us useful information about how we are and what is happening to us, but we are seldom mindful of it. Learning to tune in with the breath is a way to tune in with our moment-by-moment experience and therefore with ourselves.

Here is a very simple exercise we can start with:

*Exercise: Learning to pay attention to our breath*

It's helpful to learn to do this sitting down in a room by yourself for sessions of perhaps ten minutes or so, then in time you will feel confident enough to use it in lots of different situations to help you settle in yourself and become more present – for example, while waiting to start a meeting or while queuing up.

The good news is that trying this exercise out helps to create a new habit, and it will become easier over time.

Sit comfortably and straighten your back.

Take a few moments to settle and experience the quietness.

Become aware of your breathing.

Notice the rhythm of the breath entering and leaving your body.

Now rest your attention on your breathing – notice any changes in its rhythm.

When your mind wanders away notice that your focus is not on the breath, and simply bring it back.

Repeat this each time your attention wanders.

## TIPS

- When you first try to do this probably you will find your attention wanders a lot and you will need to keep bringing it back to the breath.

This is *completely* normal.

- If thoughts come up like, 'I should be watching my breath! Oh, how can I control stress if I can't even do that!' just notice these thoughts arising as being natural and normal, and bring your attention back to the task at hand (i.e. the breath).

*Do this over and over again.*

- You may find yourself judging how your mindfulness practice is going and keeping up a kind of self-assessment of whether or not you are getting it right.

*Just treat this like any other thought – drop it and come back to your breath.*

Having learned to steady our attention in this way, we can extend our attention to different points – the body, physical sensations, our thoughts and how our senses experience the world around us. Below is a more elaborate mindfulness exercise you can try using these additional steps.

### *Exercise: Extending mindfulness*[2]

Spend a few moments settling down by doing the simple breathing exercise above and then add one or more of the additional steps below, depending on how much time you have. It works best to go from one step to another rather than jumping around.

### *Body and sensations*

Allow your attention to extend to include your body.

Notice what you're sitting on.

Be aware of your hands at rest.

Notice the feeling of your body at rest.

Slowly scan your body from the top of your head to the tips of your toes, noticing any changes in your attention as it travels down your body. Take time to do this slowly and patiently, allowing yourself to notice each part of your body in turn.

Be aware of all the sensations you experience in your body.

Return to the breath.

### *Thoughts*

Allow your attention to extend to include your thoughts.

Simply notice the thoughts coming and going in your mind.

Don't dwell on them.

Don't judge them.

Just let them come and go.

Return to the breath.

*Repeat*

*Experiencing the world*

Allow your attention to extend to include the information coming to you through your senses.

Notice the sounds coming into your ears but don't follow after them.

Perhaps you can hear traffic outside in the street, or children playing. Just notice the noise but do not get into a commentary about it: 'There's too much traffic on my street.' 'Why don't those children's parents take them indoors . . .'

Just hear the noise and drop the rest.

Now continue with your other senses in the same way.

Notice what your eyes are seeing but don't get lost in it.

Notice all the sensations of touch on the surface of your body.

Notice the scents surrounding you.

Notice the taste in your mouth at this moment.

Let your attention rest lightly, without analysis or opinion.

Return to the breath.

When trying out each of these steps, there are a few things to note:

## TIPS

- Notice the occasions when you label sensations, thoughts or experiences as **something you want, or you don't want, or you are indifferent to**. Keep in mind that judgemental thoughts about liking or disliking will be stimulating parts of your brain that might not be helpful when trying to work with stress. It's not so much whether we experience something as likeable or dislikeable – we are bound to do that – it's more that we start *thinking* about how and why we dislike it, and how we can stop it, rather than just being with it and noticing the feeling of dislike.

- Notice when your mind drifts off into memories or starts projecting into the future.
- Notice the times when your mind starts to dwell on something that is worrying you – and this is likely to happen if you are feeling stressed, as we saw when we discussed the loops that our mind gets caught up in.
- Notice when your mind has wandered off into fantasy, imagination and daydreaming. Although this may seem harmless, at these times we can be avoiding something that causes us stress. Letting the mind roam in this way increases our habit of mind-wandering.

Each of these patterns represents a common way in which we get pulled away from the present moment, and all of them can make us feel stressed. It's often when things are not going the way we want them to that we feel stressed – we don't want to feel that twinge of backache that keeps bothering us; we do not want to keep worrying about our weight; and we hate it when we are running late. Of course, if you have a pain in your back it could be a good idea to get it checked out in case there is damage, or you need some kind of treatment.

Mindfulness is not about doing *nothing*; rather with mindfulness we just *notice* the back pain in the first instance, rather than allowing our mind to run away with itself and get into all kinds of stories as to why we have the pain.

Like Sister Helena, the 102-year-old nun whom we met in Chapter 3, we are just accepting what is coming to us in the present moment. We are not trying to protect ourselves, or avoid leaning into the sharp edges of situations and allowing ourselves to feel any discomfort that is there.

Worrying about the row we had last night with our teenage son or dreading the family reunion for an important birthday that is taking place next weekend will not help us with the problem. Instead, endlessly going over and over events will cause us stress. So, again, we can just notice that we are thinking of the row or the party and then return to mindfulness.

When we dwell on something that is worrying us – our job, a friend in difficulty or money troubles – we are causing ourselves more stress and yet not addressing the issue. Again, we can simply notice the worry and return to mindfulness. Of course, we will need to give these matters our attention, but by being mindful we can choose when to do so and how we want to go about it, rather than having our preoccupation spill out over everything we are doing.

It is a good idea to practise mindfulness exercises regularly, sitting in a chair in a quiet space, in order to get used to them and make them feel natural, but it is equally important to integrate them into your everyday activities as much as possible. Being mindful when carrying out routine activities can be a good support for your practice – such as mindful walking, mindful eating, mindful drinking and so on. Using the things, you do over and over again helps train us in mindfulness. In this way our mind becomes more capable of extending mindfulness to more complex experiences – it's easier to be mindful of, say, a mechanical activity like walking than it is to be mindful of one's thoughts.

Try out this exercise when you next have a cup of coffee.

### *Exercise: A mindful cup of coffee*

Instead of drinking the coffee at the same time as doing something else – reading, working, talking or watching TV – just allow yourself to take the time to simply drink the coffee.

Sit comfortably and then pick up the cup.

Notice the shape and texture of the cup and feel the warmth of the coffee.

Look at the coffee.

Notice the colour, the bubbles of foam, and the steam rising from the liquid.

Smell the coffee.

Breathe in the aroma.

As you take your first sip notice the changes in how you hold the cup, how the liquid flows in the cup and how it feels against your lips.

Let the coffee stay on your tongue for a moment and savour the taste, then slowly swallow it and feel it going down your throat.

The chances are you will be amazed at how rich the experience of having an ordinary cup of coffee has become! This experience is always available to us, but we miss it by not paying attention.

TIPS

**More mindfulness opportunities**

Taking a shower

Washing up

Vacuuming

Cleaning your teeth

Chopping vegetables

Ironing

In a workshop I held for managers in the UK, people were sharing experiences of practising mindfulness between sessions. One busy manager shared how he had continued his daily habit of taking a short morning walk before starting off for work, but now he was trying to take his walk mindfully and be fully present, rather than thinking about the work ahead of him for the day. He realised that now that he was trying to practise mindfulness, he could hear the birds singing – they had been singing all along, but he hadn't noticed. He said it made him realise how much he had been missing.

This illustrates an important effect of mindfulness – it enables us to move from just 'doing' all the time to include 'being'. So much of the time we are so focused on getting things done and accomplishing tasks that we rarely stop to think about how we are while we're doing them. The manager in question was accustomed to 'doing' his walk and never gave a thought to how he was 'being' while he did it. When he walked mindfully, he was able to relax and 'be' the person walking. Then he was able to appreciate the experience fully. When he reached his office, he felt refreshed and ready for the day, instead of already weighed down by all the worries he had tried to deal with on the walk in to work.

## *Applying mindfulness practice*

Let's think of a stressful scenario in which we could apply what we have learned about mindfulness. Perhaps your ten-year-old daughter comes down with a nasty case of flu and has to go to bed. Both you and your partner work full-time, but one of you will need to stay at home and take care of her. Your partner has an important series of meetings coming up and cannot take time off, so it falls to you. Your boss is not happy about you having to take time off but is slightly appeased when you tell him you'll take work home. So, there you are at home with a sick child and a load of paperwork – not to mention shopping, cleaning, cooking and so on. You feel a bit overwhelmed. Your habit could be to charge into all the things that need to be done, while worrying about how you will cope with it all and trying to make plans to keep everything ticking over.

Let's see how you could try something different.

### *Exercise: Applying mindfulness to a life situation*

#### Step 1: Take care of priorities

The priority is to see your daughter is settled comfortably. You can already try to be mindful of how you talk to her, stroke her and move around her bedroom. You want her to feel that you are there for her, rather than worried about coping with everything else you need to attend to. You can use her as the object of your mindfulness.

#### Step 2: Take some time for yourself

Once your daughter is settled you could take ten minutes to do the Extending Mindfulness exercise on page 134.

The irony is that we usually think we don't have time to do something like this because we have to 'get on' with things. In fact, taking these ten minutes for yourself could be the investment that helps you do what you need to do without getting stressed and overtired.

### Step 3: Mindfully work through your tasks

Having done the Extending Mindfulness exercise and taken stock of how you are feeling, hopefully you feel in better shape to get started on all the things that need taking care of. As you work through the list try to come back to what you are doing in each moment (rather than letting your mind roam over the next few days and keep asking what will happen about this and that, how this or that will get done). Just be mindful of each task as it comes and pay attention to that. Gently bring your mind back from anticipating problems that have not happened.

### Step 4: Take regular deep breaths

Set your phone to remind you each hour. When it pings, stop what you are doing and take three deep, slow breaths. In those few seconds, try to drop everything that is going on in your mind.

Make notes for yourself as to how this went. Note any adjustments that were helpful and that you want to remember.

## 2. Awareness

*The knowing quality of mind*

*Mindfulness* comes in keeping our attention on the meditation method, or on the task we are undertaking. It is supported by an *awareness* that sees when we have lost our mindfulness and gently reminds us to bring our attention back. As we have seen, mindfulness is about focus, but we need to combine this with awareness.

Think of a footballer expertly handling the ball, his attention focused mindfully on how he strikes the ball but lacking an awareness of the whole pitch and the pattern of the game, so that when there is a chance to make a skilful pass to a teammate at a crucial moment, he does not see it and misses the opportunity.

Another illustration of how mindfulness and awareness work together that I like very much is the example of carrying a full cup of coffee across a room.[3]

You need **mindfulness** to pay attention to the surface of the coffee and to make sure it does not spill over, but you also need to be **aware** of the room you are passing through in order to take care not to bump into anything or trip up, which would also cause the coffee to spill. *The mindfulness is focused attention and the awareness is a more all-inclusive attention that sees the whole picture.* Meditation includes mindfulness, but also incorporates unobstructed awareness, so that the mind is exquisitely balanced between being focused – seeing the coffee in the cup – and being aware of the context of the object of focus – the room as you walk across it.

## 3. Spaciousness

Remember the metaphor of the sky and the clouds that was introduced in the last chapter? If we think of the sky, we immediately get a sense of its vast expanse – its quality of spaciousness. We need to bring this quality to our meditation. In order for us to settle into meditation, we need to relax.

It's so easy to have all kinds of goals about what we want meditation to do for us, and ideas of how it should be. We need to let all that go and simply allow ourselves to deeply relax and our minds to settle. Remember, there is no race here, no big goal. We are just taking time to relax and enjoy being quietly with our own mind. In fact, most of our attention should be concerned with maintaining this attitude of *spaciousness and ease* – neither trying too hard and getting tight, nor zoning out and becoming too loose.

Our mind is naturally uncluttered, limitless and spacious like a clear blue sky. Its qualities of clarity and awareness are represented by the sun shining unobstructed. If we follow this metaphor further, we could say that the rays of the sun are like our natural compassion, shining as a natural expression of emptiness and clarity.

As we have seen, these three elements – mindfulness, awareness and spaciousness – work together to hold the meditation. We've seen that the advice is to give most of our attention to the third quality of spaciousness, with 25 per cent of our attention on mindfulness and another 25 per cent on awareness.

**How you can adjust the percentages according to your mood, or your personality**

If you are someone who is highly organised and result-orientated – increase spaciousness to 70 per cent and pay 15 per cent attention to each of mindfulness and awareness.

If you tend to daydream – increase mindfulness and awareness to 40 per cent and pay 20 per cent attention to spaciousness.

If you get worried about how you are meditating and feel you are not doing it well – increase spaciousness to 60 per cent and reduce mindfulness and awareness to 20 per cent.

## Meditation as a Means of Having Natural Control

In meditation we are uncovering the mind's natural qualities by allowing it to rest and its activity to calm down and settle. When we are able to do this, we realise that *in this actual moment of meditation* we are not so stressed, and even if the feeling of stress returns after the meditation session, we may be able to see it a bit differently. To begin with, meditation gives us a possibility of interrupting our stress and giving us a respite from it. If we continue to work with our meditation it can help us to develop a different perspective on our stress, which will help to dilute its impact.

Meditation is a way of getting to know yourself and then to make friends with yourself as you are – the basis of self-compassion. We could say it is a way of coming home to ourselves because we are learning to become familiar with what goes on in our minds and the nature of our experience. This helps us to become more aware of our emotional triggers and what causes us to feel stressed.

As well as becoming more aware of ourselves, meditation also helps us to become more aware of other people and what is happening around us. We gently open to a compassionate perspective. This enables us to choose whether or not we want to act, as well as *how* we want to act, instead of just responding in our habitual way.

Stress is often difficult to handle because we cannot predict when it will happen, and this can leave us feeling helpless and not in control. Because meditation enables us to see both ourselves and our environment more clearly, it becomes more possible for us to see things as they actually are, and to recognise that everything is interconnected and changing. As this understanding grows, we can see that stress and the suffering it can cause us is simply part of life and that it is inevitable that there will be times in our lives when we will feel stressed. Again, this insight deepens our compassionate instinct as we realise this is the same for everyone.

We come to accept the suffering caused by stress and become less destabilised when it happens – in a way we learn to *expect* stress to be unpredictable. Because we are learning to work with our minds and train them to be more useful, we have more natural control over our reactions to events. Things will still happen to us that we have no control over – we cannot stop the strike at the airport that spoils our holiday, nor can we prevent the cost of petrol increasing, but we can learn to notice our reactions and then begin to make choices about what to do about them.

As we become more familiar with meditation, it becomes a little easier to react from a place of stability rather than giving a knee-jerk response. This can help to break the cycle of feeling unable to cope or helpless in the face of difficulties. It cuts through the cycle of stress. Meditation can go directly to the root of the psychological habits that can make stress worse.

Think of a situation that is causing you stress right now.

Try to see it clearly without judgement:

- Who is involved?
- Where is the interconnection?
- How is the situation changing?
- How much of the situation is beyond your control?

---

Now look at your reaction:

- Is it helping you?
- Is it decreasing, or increasing the levels of stress?
- Where is your choice here?
- Are there changes you can make?

---

## Methods of Meditation

Here are two methods of meditation which use an object as a support for the meditation – the first uses the breath, in a similar way to the exercise we did on page 133, the second a candle.

Later on, when we look at compassion meditations, we will use visualisation and repetition of slogans as objects for our meditation.

### *Exercise: How to meditate using the breath*

Sit upright and keep your spine straight but not rigid.

Relax your shoulders while aiming to keep them flat, so that the chest is open.

Rest your hands lightly on your knees or fold them in your lap.

Keep your eyes open and the gaze soft. Angle your gaze at about 45 degrees – neither looking straight ahead or down at the floor, but halfway in between.

If you feel sleepy, lift the gaze.

If you feel stirred up, lower the gaze.

Breathe mainly through the mouth, with the lips slightly apart.

Rest your attention lightly on the out-breath.

Whenever your attention wanders, simply notice it has wandered and return to mindfulness of the breath.

| | |
|---|---|
| Why do we keep our eyes open? | On a practical level, if our eyes are open we are less likely to fall asleep which is very easy to do when we first start to meditate. With our eyes open, it is less likely that we withdraw and sink into some kind of detached dreamy state.<br><br>Meditation is about being at ease with ourselves, and with the world – this is demonstrated by keeping the eyes open.<br><br>If it helps to begin a session with closing the eyes for a few moments then that is fine, just open them as soon as you feel settled. |
| Why do we breathe through the mouth, rather than the nose? | Breathing mostly through the mouth helps calm the mind and slows down the stream of thoughts. Because it feels unfamiliar to breathe through the mouth, you may notice that your lips get dry or it feels uncomfortable. That's no problem – just take a moment to moisten your lips, swallow and then continue. |

### *Exercise: Meditation using a candle*

*People who suffer from asthma may like to try using an object instead of the breath.*

Sit upright and keep your spine straight but not rigid.

Relax your shoulders while aiming to keep them flat, so that the chest is open.

Rest your hands lightly on your knees or fold them in your lap.

Keep your eyes open and the gaze soft. Angle your gaze at about 45 degrees – neither looking straight ahead, or down at the floor, but halfway in between.

If you feel sleepy, lift the gaze.

If you feel stirred up, lower the gaze.

Rest your gaze lightly on the candle flame.

Keep your focus relaxed with just enough attention to hold your awareness of the candle. (There's no need to get involved in the details of colour, shape and so on.)

When your mind drifts away, just bring it back.

You could also use a flower, a crystal, or an inspiring photo.

## Thoughts and Emotions During Meditation

Staying with the analogy of the clouds and the sky, we saw that just as the sky is always limitless and spacious even when obscured by clouds, the essence of our mind is spacious, aware and unaffected by the thoughts and emotions that pass through it.

The more we can leave our mind alone and not stir it up, the more useful it can be for us. It is our thoughts and emotions that cause us stress – the activity of our mind, not the mind itself. If we can begin to understand our thoughts and emotions more clearly and work with them more effectively, we will be working directly to reduce our stress.

With meditation we can begin to work with the thoughts themselves and to see them for what they are – passing movements of our mind that come and go just like the clouds crossing the sky, or the debris that gets stirred up in a lake during a storm. The trouble is that our usual habit as soon as a thought comes into our mind is to take it as real and worry about it, turning it into something bigger and more substantial than it really is, adding to it with layer upon layer of additional thoughts.

To begin with we might find it quite hard to see them as passing and transient, but if we can manage it even for a few seconds it will make a big difference. With meditation we are changing our habit of looking at the clouds from the perspective of the ground to looking at them from the perspective of the sky. In this way, instead of them seeming to bear down on us and obscuring our vision, we can see them as simply passing by, without affecting the sky. Clouds do not change the sky; they simply cover it over – the sky does not become the clouds. In just the same way, thoughts and emotions do not alter our mind; they just obscure its natural spaciousness and awareness – we do not *become* our thoughts and emotions. We do not need to block anything or manipulate anything.

It is a matter of learning to distinguish between our mind and its contents – to be able to see our thoughts and emotions as mental events that come and go. This enables us to be aware of what we are thinking as well as the stories we create about our thoughts. It does not mean that we stop having thoughts – not at all, we need to be able to apply our intelligence – but rather that we can choose whether or not we want to act on them, because we can see them in perspective. We do not have to feel bad about some thoughts and good about others. We do not have to beat ourselves up about thoughts we feel embarrassed by. We can simply be forgiving towards ourselves. This will help to undermine our stress reactions at their very root.

I have a friend who is highly intelligent and quite intellectual. He tried meditation in the first place because he got completely fed up with trying to cope with all the activity going on in his mind. I always remember him describing to me how tiring his mind was for him – how his endless stream of thoughts could seem quite a burden at times – and how meditation has made a considerable difference to how he sees and interacts with these thoughts. He said that when he first started meditating, he noticed for the first time that in fact his thoughts were not continuous at all. Between each thought was a space – maybe only a very small space but enough to give the impression of the thought surrounded by space rather than by more and more thoughts. This gave him a sense of tremendous relief. Now he has been meditating for many years and is able to experience the space more strongly than the thought and view the thought as a passing experience within the space of his mind. This is learning to view our thoughts from the perspective of the sky, rather than from the perspective of the ground.

### *Exercise: Seeing thoughts from the perspective of the sky*

You can do this exercise either sitting by a window where you can see the sky, or even outside if you can find a quiet place.

Sit comfortably and straighten your back.

Spend a few moments watching your breath.

Look at the sky for a few moments and watch the clouds.

Ask yourself if the clouds are good or bad. (If you are hoping for a sunny day for an outing, perhaps the clouds seem to be a nuisance, whereas if you are hoping for some rain for the garden, perhaps they seem like a good idea.)

Think about how other people might view the clouds, depending on their own likes and dislikes.

Notice how these labels have no effect on the clouds.

Notice how the clouds move and change and, whatever you do, you cannot make them stay in one place.

Now spend a few moments watching your thoughts as they come and go in your mind.

Try not to follow one thought for too long, just allow your thoughts to come and go.

Notice how quickly you label your thoughts as good, bad, pleasant, unpleasant.

Try to realise that when you label them this way you are seeing them as solid and real, like trying to hold a cloud in one place in the sky.

Look again at the sky and notice how although the clouds move and change, the space around them – the sky – does not change at all.

Now try to apply this to your thoughts as they come and go in your mind.

Notice that the space around the thoughts does not change, only the thoughts.

Try to let your mind rest in this feeling of spaciousness for a few moments.

The process of looking at our emotions is similar.

Because our minds are calmed down during meditation, we have more possibility to recognise emotions as they arise, before they grab us and we start to react to them. If we can recognise our emotions as they start to form in our minds, then we can try to accept them without judgement. This gives us a chance to investigate each emotion and understand where it has come from. In order to do that, we need to be able to separate the emotion from its object.

For example, if I am frustrated by an email that I receive and then snap at a colleague who just happens to be nearby, the emotion that I am feeling clearly has nothing to do with my poor colleague! Our tendency, however, is often to justify our reaction by apportioning blame. So, in this case I may feel justified in letting off steam at my colleague who did nothing wrong, because I am frustrated by my email. In fact, my reaction – apportioning blame to someone who is blameless – could become a potential source of conflict and stress. It could lead to an argument with my colleague when in fact the frustration is nothing to do with them. When our minds are calmed down by meditation it is much easier to see what is really happening and take responsibility for our reactions.

In the final instance, it is important not to *identify* with the emotion. Just because you feel frustration, or irritation, it does not mean that is who you are. Just because you feel stressed, it is not *who you are*.

## Making Meditation Part of Your Life

Although meditation is relatively easy to learn, most of us are not familiar with it. Many of the ideas and techniques we have been discussing may be new to you and will take some time to get used to. It is possible to feel quite self-conscious at the beginning and to spend a meditation session waiting for something to happen. Meditation is so simple it can be almost a surprise. However, we can have such unrealistic expectations and be looking for such big experiences and instant results that we miss the quiet simplicity of the experience. It is not unusual in a group meditation session for someone who is new to it to become overwhelmed by giggles, or to be unable to stop fidgeting. At the other end of the scale, some people find themselves falling fast asleep. All these things are absolutely fine – they are just part of the process of getting used to meditation. The main thing is not to judge yourself or your meditation. There is no such thing as a bad meditation.

In fact, sometimes when we begin to meditate it can seem as if our minds have become even busier and that our thoughts and emotions are out of control. In Buddhist instructions on meditation this process has been likened to a waterfall rushing down a steep gorge and marks the beginning of us becoming aware of how our minds are. In fact, it is not that they have got busier – it's just that with meditation we can start to notice all that activity. Sometimes people find this depressing, but it shouldn't be – it is an important step to see directly how busy the mind is. Gradually, with practice, the stream of thoughts will slow down and will begin to feel more like a great river meandering through a valley. When the mind learns to settle it becomes like a great ocean, with the waves gently ruffling the surface of the water but not disturbing its depths in any way. So, we can see that there is no good or bad practice, no getting it right or wrong, but simply getting used to observing the movements of our minds.

The best way to get used to meditation is by actually doing it. As soon as we can make it a daily habit, it will be easier to become accustomed to it. Let's look at some practical points that will help us to do this.

| | |
|---|---|
| When should I meditate? | People often find it helps to get the day off to a good start if they do a session of meditation in the morning, but it is really up to you. There are no hard and fast rules. The best thing is to look at your schedule and see where it is easiest to make changes to include meditation. |
| How long should I meditate for? | Again, there are no rules – except to say the more you can do the more helpful you will find it! If you are a beginner, it might be a good idea to build up slowly over a period of a few weeks. Start with a session of sitting meditation for five minutes every day. After two weeks you could try increasing it to ten minutes and then fifteen, and so on. It is better to start small and build up, rather than planning to sit for an hour every day and feeling disappointed when you cannot keep it up. When your sessions do get longer you could always do half the session in the morning and the other half in the evening. That enables you to do more meditation without having to plan a really long session. |

| | |
|---|---|
| Where should I meditate? | The answer here is, wherever you can! Sometimes people like to have a special place that is their meditation spot. This is nice but will depend on the size of your home and who you share it with. Beware of making a meditation space that is just so special you never actually use it. I always remember two friends of mine showing me round their new apartment and proudly opening the door to their meditation room. When I commented on how pristine it looked they said it was because they never used it in case they dirtied it! |
| Are there any special props that I need? | It is helpful not to wear tight clothing – or for women, a short skirt – just because you are likely to find it uncomfortable. Other than that, it is up to you. You need a good cushion, or a straight-backed chair. Some people like to wrap themselves in a shawl to keep warm. You might want to set your mobile phone to time how long you want your session to be, but you could also use an egg timer. Sometimes people like to ring a bell, or singing bowl, to start their session. Generally speaking, try to keep it simple and flexible. |
| What do I do when I don't feel like doing my session? | When this happens – and it will happen – the best thing is to try to do it anyway because the more often you manage to do your session the more you are establishing a habit. We don't leave out cleaning our teeth, whatever happens. It helps to try to think of meditation as just another part of our routine. Of course, you should not force yourself if you really cannot face it – we need to have some humour as we try to fit meditation into our schedules. I know of someone who promised himself to meditate six days out of every seven and give himself a day off every week. By giving himself this 'holiday' each week he was able to maintain a much more regular practice routine than if he had forced himself to do it every day. |

### *Stop Moments*

Think of these as very short meditation sessions – perhaps just one or two moments long – that act as breathing spaces in the day. One of my favourite times for a Stop Moment is when I need to go to the lavatory. It is something that we all need to do several times in a day, and we can do it behind a locked door, where no one can disturb us. Just take an extra moment to straighten your back and watch your breath for a minute or so.

Nicki, a social worker, has this to say about using this particular strategy:

> During a very intense team meeting I excused myself and went to the loo to do some meditation practice to calm myself down as I could feel myself getting really stressed – my tension was rising, and I could see that the meeting wasn't going anywhere . . . it was stuck. This took me away from the situation and I could return fresher and less stressed. The meeting didn't get any better but at least I was in a better position to handle the outcome.

Having pauses like this during the day will increase the benefits of your daily session on the cushion or chair.

#### TIPS

**When Stop Moments can work well**

When you have to stop at a red light in traffic

Entering a supermarket

Standing in a queue

Waiting for the kettle to boil

Standing at the photocopy machine

Waiting for your computer to boot up

Here is Nicki again:

> After difficult situations with a family, I spend some time sitting in my car for a few moments watching my breath. This enables me to gather my resources so I can be fully available for the next family I see. However, this is only really effective when I have spent some more time focused on meditation in the morning and so have a base to build upon.

## The Benefits of a Stable Mind

As we learn to meditate, we learn to become more of a friend to ourselves, and to be more at home with ourselves. We find ourselves more in tune with life as it is, with its continual change, the inevitability of stress and suffering, and how we are all dependent on and connected to each other.

> In Buddhist instructions on meditation, the untamed mind is likened to a wild elephant, rampaging, bellowing and stamping all around. An elephant has tremendous power and strength, but if it is not channelled well it can cause damage to itself, to others and to its surroundings.

As we have seen, it is the same with the mind. If we allow our thoughts and emotions to pull us this way and that, then we have as little self-control as the elephant. We use an enormous amount of effort in keeping up an endless score of how well, or badly, we think we are doing, and how the world and everyone in it is treating us – what we like, and what we don't like; what we hope for and what we fear. It is chaotic, reactive and damaging, and as we have seen, a means by which we put ourselves under stress.

> Just as the wild elephant slowly calms down with patient care and discipline, so the mind is calmed and settled through meditation.

As the mind becomes more stable and we can discern more clearly how our thoughts and emotions arise, we can begin the process of unravelling the way we use our mind that causes us stress. In time, we can disarm the ways in which our reactions to stress cause us harm and begin to find peace with ourselves and with our world.

This does not mean that suddenly everything will start to go our way – all of our personal sharp edges and uncomfortable places are still there, the difficulties we need to deal with remain, but with this kind of stability of mind we can allow ourselves to become open to what needs addressing, rather than distracting ourselves from it. We will start to feel a certain confidence that we will not be so easily thrown off – we won't be dismayed by our own behaviour, nor that of others. This confidence enables us to be accepting of everything as it happens without needing to protect ourselves, and so it has the capacity to transform our reactions to stress.

Inner peace is the heart of the attitude of contentment that was discussed in Chapter 3. With contentment as our basis we can learn to use our discernment in weighing up which actions will bring us lasting happiness, and which will lead to suffering. In this way we can identify our habits.

Meditation is the key to the whole compassionate attitude that we are exploring in this book and an important element in developing lasting happiness. It doesn't miraculously remove all our problems or stress, but by strengthening the mind it gives us a new perspective in understanding them and a sustainable means to work with the challenges they bring.

*In the last chapter, we looked at a 'Formula for Change'. Let's now look at the part meditation plays in that formula.*

In beginning to train ourselves in reducing our stress, it is clear that to begin with **we need to *want* to change**. Meditation gives us a glimpse of what our mind can be like if we are able to train it properly, and so reinforces our wish to change our perspective and the way our mind reacts to stress.

Because we are learning to see our thoughts and emotions for what they are, we are no longer so likely to just react out of habit, but rather to **take a step back** in order to see what is going on with us.

Meditation helps us to develop **self-awareness** by accessing the peace, clarity and spaciousness of our mind and to **change our perspective** from the ground to the sky.

With this **fresh perspective** we are able to examine our habits with more clarity and kindness instead of self-criticism. We can therefore work out **which habits cause us more harm than good, and which are helpful.** This enables us to see where we want to begin with our process of change and how we want to go about doing it.

## Scientific Research into the Effects of Mindfulness and Meditation

Contemplative traditions such as Buddhism have recognised the crucial importance of meditation for more than 2,000 years, and now current neuroscientific research is providing scientific endorsement of this point of view. In November 2004, the first of a series of papers describing the impact of long-term meditation on the brain was published in the prestigious scientific journal *Proceedings of the National Academy of Sciences*.[4] It was the first time meditation had been described in scientific terminology.

Among its authors were Richard Davidson, his colleague Antoine Lutz and Matthieu Ricard. We have mentioned Davidson and Lutz already when we described the partnership between the Dalai Lama and Western science in the Introduction. Matthieu Ricard is a Westerner who has been a Buddhist monk for many years and who has acted as a guinea pig for research into the effects of meditation on the brain. Previously, meditation had been considered to be something beyond objective study, and something that could not be measured, but Davidson and his team have been able to translate meditation experiences into the language of high-frequency gamma rays and brain coordination.

To do this they have used two powerful tools for measuring brain function:

- The fMRI: functional magnetic resonance imaging – this measures brain function, rather than structure, by measuring the blood flow connected with emotional changes in the brain. Local blood flow is related to the amount of activity between neurons. It has only been possible to measure this with fMRI since about 1996 and it has greatly aided neuroplasticity research.

- EEG: electroencephalogram, or brain electrical activity – this is a way of showing the electrical activity caused by nerve cells firing. It is useful for picking up particular brain signals but can only give a rough approximation of where it arises, whereas the fMRI can pinpoint the exact location.

Davidson has worked on establishing an index for the brain's set points for moods. Through the use of fMRI, he found that when people experience difficult emotions such as depression, fear or anxiety there is more activity in the amygdala and the right pre-frontal cortex of the brain (see pages 17 and 71), an area connected with hyper-vigilance of the kind a person experiencing stress may engage in. When people experience enthusiasm, inspiration and positivity, these areas are quiet, but the left pre-frontal cortex is activated. In fact, gauging the activity of the pre-frontal cortexes proved to be a quick way to measure a person's mood.

Of the people Davidson tested, the majority were in a middle range, experiencing both good and bad emotions, and so activity alternated between the pre-frontal lobes: people who would be described as clinically depressed came out as highly active in the right pre-frontal cortex, whereas people who are content and happy with their lives to a high degree showed higher activity on the left side. The highly experienced meditation practitioners – many of them Tibetan Buddhist monks with thousands of hours of meditation experience – who came to Davidson's lab for testing all fitted decisively into this latter group. The kind of refined coordination of neurons demonstrated by the monks had been associated with mental activities such as focus, memory and learning in previous studies. Their brains also showed the kind of intense gamma wave activity connected to heightened awareness. This research confirmed that the brain can be trained to an extent science had not realised before.

What can we take from this? It is unlikely that many of us will ever manage to achieve ten thousand hours of meditation, so does this mean that our brain is not trainable in the same way as those people Davidson tested? The answer is that everyone's brain can be trained in just this way. Whenever we begin the training, change is immediately put in motion. Davidson began his research with what he calls the Olympic athletes of meditation – monks like Matthieu Ricard who had done thousands of hours of practice – because with them the results are clear and easier to detect, but he was also interested in widening the field.

In order to look at the effects of meditation on beginners, Davidson took part in a research project with staff at a cutting-edge bio-technology company in Madison, USA who were reporting stress at work.

For three hours a week over a period of two months one group of staff was given a course in meditation practice, while a control group was not.

Testing before the meditation course started showed that all participants' brain activity tipped more towards the right – the area of the brain that registers anxiety and worry – but by the end of the course all the participants showed a significant shift to left-pre-frontal cortex activity. People described themselves as having more energy and experiencing less pressure and stress.

As a subsidiary study, participants were given a flu shot. The immune system of those who had received meditation training caused an increase of antibodies in the blood by 20 per cent.

A comparable study was carried out with a pilot group of schoolteachers in 2002–3, with similar findings.

Since this research began, the number of studies of the effects of meditation on the brain and on health generally have grown significantly. The work of Jon Kabat-Zinn has been instrumental in bringing mindfulness meditation into the mainstream of medicine through his mindfulness-based stress-reduction programme. He is Professor of Medicine Emeritus at the University of Massachusetts Medical School, where he founded the stress reduction clinic in 1979. The clinic and its research have shown that it is possible to achieve long-lasting improvements in both physical and psychological symptoms, as well as major positive changes in health attitudes and behaviours, such as the management of physical pain.

So impressive are the results that the MBSR (Mindfulness-Based Stress Reduction) model has now been adopted in more than 200 medical institutions throughout the world. It was initially developed to treat people with chronic pain and stress-related disorders, but research has continued with studies involving its effects on women with breast cancer and men with prostate cancer; with prison inmates and prison staff, and in various corporate settings. A study conducted with patients suffering from the skin disease known as psoriasis showed that when they were given a mindfulness meditation exercise to do while receiving photo-therapy treatment, they healed four times faster than people not taking part in the exercise.

Research into the effects of meditation practice on the brain, on health and on wellbeing are in their early stages and there is much more work to be done, but the signs are compelling and give encouragement to the experience that any meditator can vouch for – that meditation helps in one's life. Davidson's work demonstrates that the trained mind, or brain, is physically different from the untrained one.[5] Any meditator can begin to experience a trained mind that is more workable, more stable, more equipped to deal with the inevitable challenges, joys and sufferings that life brings than an untrained one. The more the mind is trained, the deeper that experience.

Meditation is currently being used in a variety of institutions, such as schools, hospitals and prisons. It is even finding its way into the corporate world, with companies such as Apple, Google, Starbucks, Walt Disney and IBM using it as part of their support programmes for staff.

## Applying Meditation Practice

Let us look at an imaginary scenario to see how we could use meditation in a life situation.

You are due to attend a family gathering at your husband's parents' house. You enjoy visiting your husband's family and get on well with his parents and his brother. However, you find his brother's wife intimidating. She has a high-powered job as a human rights lawyer and is quite bookish and political. She's also very attractive.

You trained as a primary school teacher and now work part-time in a local school so you can be home for your children when they get back from school. Juggling work and the family means you often feel like you have not enough time for yourself and certainly do not have the means to spend a lot of money on your appearance.

Your sister-in-law decided not to have a family in order to pursue her career and is always immaculately turned out. She is always polite and friendly to you, but you suffer from feelings of inadequacy around her, and feel frumpy and out of touch. You even worry you are letting your husband down. You get either tongue-tied or over-talkative from nerves. You find the whole thing quite stressful and feel you dislike your sister-in-law.

How can meditation help with this? Let's run through a few ways in which it could make a difference.

In the first place, the experience of meditation will help assuage the feeling of running to catch up. By spending some quiet time each day simply watching your breath and training your mind you will help create space and ease in your day – however busy it is. This provides a more reliable basis for dealing with challenging circumstances.

Secondly, it will provide a space to look at your feelings of 'not being good enough' and allow you to see them for what they are – just fears that have no real basis and just rise and fall in your mind. You have a chance to notice they are only there when you think of your sister-in-law. They are not there when you are working in the school, caring for your children or with your husband.

You may even remember a time, perhaps from your own schooldays, when one of the older girls put you down for not wearing the right kind of shoes and not being cool, and realise that this old hurt is triggered by your sister-in-law but actually has nothing to do with her.

You are able to create a distance between the thoughts and feelings you have when you see her from how things actually are. As you do this you may even feel a slight sense of amusement at the games your mind has been playing, but instead of chiding yourself for being so silly, you acknowledge what has been going on and resolve to let it go and enjoy the family visits more in the future.

With meditation the whole situation has more ease, more space and an increased capacity for healing and reducing stress.

<table>
<tr><th>What we have learned in this chapter</th><th>Your reflections</th></tr>
<tr><td><ul>
<li>Meditation is important because it is an effective way of training the mind, which will help us to develop compassion and reduce our stress levels.</li>
<li>The mind as it is now is like a wild elephant – powerful but out of control. We need to calm it down in order to harness its natural potential.</li>
<li>Learning to become more mindful will help us to switch off the automatic pilot in our mind and enable us to be more present to our activity. This will release our energy and resources and help directly with stress.</li>
<li>Meditation is a way of coming to know yourself and making friends with yourself.</li>
<li>It can be said to have three elements: mindfulness, awareness and spaciousness.</li>
<li>The point is not to block our thoughts and emotions but to see them like clouds crossing the sky – they come and go and make no lasting impression.</li>
<li>Meditation enables us to be more in tune with life as it actually is, with its continual change, the inevitability of stress and suffering, and interconnectedness.</li>
<li>Current scientific research is endorsing the experience of meditators by showing that it has positive effects on our health and wellbeing.</li>
</ul></td><td></td></tr>
</table>

## TIPS TO TAKE INTO EVERYDAY LIFE

1. Try to create a regular practice of meditation, where you do some each day.
2. It is better to do short sessions regularly than a long session occasionally.
3. Remember to pay attention to routine activities that you take for granted – like drinking coffee, chopping vegetables, taking a shower.
4. Choose one activity to make your mindfulness-in-action practice for a week. Then try another the following week.
5. Try to include as many Stop Moments in your day as you can.

# 6 Identifying Our Unhelpful Habits

*Most people are afraid of suffering, but suffering is a kind of mud to help the lotus flower grow. There cannot be a lotus flower without the mud.*

*Thich Nhat Hanh*[1]

What we are going to do in this chapter:

1. Look into different levels of stress
2. Explore some psychological aspects of stress
3. Consider how we try to deal with stress
4. Look at habits that increase stress
5. Identify some habits that we want to get rid of

We have looked at how the mind works and how, through mindfulness and meditation, we can train it to be more effective for us. This provides the basis for beginning to become aware of and work with our habits. We can make a start by turning our attention to our unhelpful habits – the ones we need to change in order to reduce our stress. In Chapter 3 we looked at some basic causes of our suffering, such as our tendency to live as if we were independent, permanent and unchanging even though all the evidence of life shows us that this is not how things are. The effort we put into trying to feel secure and avoiding what makes us feel uncomfortable limits our view of life, causing us to develop a range of unhelpful habits.

It is these habits that determine how we cope with and respond to stress. As we have already discussed, taking the time to become familiar with our habits is an important first step but, as we have discussed, our tendency is rather to try and *avoid* suffering. Accepting that stress is a symptom of suffering can help us to try and find out more about why we get stressed and how we behave when we are feeling it – in other words, stress can have something to tell us about ourselves. This puts us in a more effective position to apply new, helpful habits such as compassionate mind techniques. We will start to explore how to do that in the next chapter.

## Layers of Stress

When we get up each morning it is likely that we are dealing with several layers of potential stress – stress that may stay as a distant murmur on our personal radar, or land decisively in our field of vision demanding a response. Understanding how these layers operate can help us to see more clearly what a potential stressor for us is. We can also get an idea of the times when we are especially vulnerable to stress, as well as how we react to it. Some of the outer layers may remain at low levels of worry, but taken together they can add up to a kind of sludge of potential stress that we carry around with us, which is probably already taxing our resources. Often, we do not even notice this continual low-level activity and can be surprised when we boil over at a relatively small provocation.

### *Identifying our layers of stress – the outer layer*

Take some time to think about how and when your own buttons get pushed, because you will almost certainly find that those are the places that get rubbed repeatedly, making you vulnerable in a way that can undermine you at the most unexpected times.

## Conditions of society

Maybe you need to fly when there has been a recent plane crash or terrorist threat.

Perhaps the economic news is weighing heavily on your mind.

You are feeling sad because of a recent hurricane or flood that has featured heavily in the news.

The news provides an ongoing display of painful events that may not impact on us directly but which, nevertheless, affect us as human beings and colour our outlook.

______________________________

______________________________

______________________________

______________________________

## Tone of our culture

Perhaps there has been a recent change in government that you do not agree with and you are constantly troubled by policies that seem short-sighted.

Maybe you worry about the rise of religious fundamentalism, or the far right.

Many people are worried about climate change.

Then there is the hold that technology has on many aspects of our lives.

______________________________

______________________________

______________________________

______________________________

## Consumerism

In his book *The Age of Absurdity*, Michael Foley writes:[2]

> *Shopping is no longer so much about the gratification of desire as the thrill of the desire itself, which must be constantly renewed.*

Oliver James takes this further in his study of what he calls the Affluenza Virus:[3]

> *A set of values which increase our vulnerability to emotional distress. It entails placing a high value on acquiring money and possessions, looking good in the eyes of others and wanting to be famous.*
>
> *. . . the Affluenza Virus increases your susceptibility to the commonest emotional distresses: depression, anxiety, substance abuse and personality disorder.*

He sees the Affluenza Virus as a product of what he calls 'selfish capitalism', a system geared towards profit at all costs that he believes has affected almost all aspects of modern life.

Consider the high level of personal debt many people are carrying in the UK.

Reflect on the use of the term, 'retail therapy'.

______________________________________________

______________________________________________

## Layers of Stress to Do With Our Own World

Closer to home are the layers of potential stress that have to do with our own environment – our neighbourhood, family and friends.

I have an example of my own that illustrates this kind of stress. My partner and I live in a very attractive area of Amsterdam. Previously the old dockland area, it is skilfully planned in order to maximise access to the water with lots of trees specially planted. We pay quite high charges for street cleaning, rubbish and recycling collection but the service we receive is excellent.

Unfortunately, however, not everyone keeps to the simple rules of placing household waste into the large bins provided and putting out oversize items on Thursday evenings for collection on Friday. Time after time we see small children stagger to the bins with large plastic sacks that they are not strong enough to lift into the bins and so leave them beside the bins to pile up. Often, just after all the large items have been removed on a Friday morning, someone will discard perhaps an old cupboard or chair and leave it by the bins, knowing it will be several days before anyone will collect it and, in the meantime, it will be kicked around the street.

Even though it happens on a regular basis, it unfortunately never fails to irritate me. I can easily find myself holding forth on how antisocial people can be, though, of course, no one hears except my poor partner! It does me no good at all and just leaves me feeling stirred up, but it is so hard to just accept that this is the way things are. Unless I catch myself, it can act as an uncomfortable irritant, a minor source of stress.

Events in our extended family life or the lives of our friends can occupy our minds in a similar way – we can find ourselves fruitlessly questioning why a certain member of the family cannot make a relationship work, or why our friend is having trouble at work once more. We can find ourselves going over the same ground again and again, worrying about a problem without reaching any solution – it's those mental loops again. It has not yet become a full-blown stressor, but it has the potential for wearing us down and reducing our resilience against stress when it does occur. The more of these kinds of worries we dwell on the more seriously we wear ourselves out.

Take a few moments to check in with yourself and see if you can identify any of this kind of nagging stress going on in your own life just now.

________________________________________

________________________________________

________________________________________

________________________________________

________________________________________

## Immediate Stress

For each of us, the most active layer of stress is what is happening for us directly in the course of each day, but this can take many different forms.

You may be struggling to communicate with your teenage son, or you may be caring for a parent who has dementia. Your partner may be suffering from ill health, or your neighbours might be noisy and antisocial. Many people live with continual low-grade pain and discomfort such as arthritis or back injuries. At a workshop that I gave recently, two of the participants had just been made redundant, and another had had six migraines in three months due to the stress she was experiencing at work.

Indeed, for many of us work is a major source of stress as we find ourselves trying to cope with situations that seem beyond our control.

A friend of mine is a family resource worker, which means she is assigned to families whose children are experiencing difficulties in school. She has to deal with all kinds of human suffering – including child abuse, truancy, underage pregnancy, alcoholism and domestic violence. Her caseload, and that of all members of her team, is enormous, and her power to actually bring any solution to the families' problems is limited. As a responsible and caring person this is a source of tremendous worry to her. She told me of a recent dream in which she became aware of a crowd of people gathered around the entrance to a multi-storey car park, shaped a bit like a giant filing cabinet. As she approached to see what the commotion was all about, she became aware of an awful stench coming out from the car park and a cloud of bluebottles rising up from the ground. She threaded her way through the crowd to see that they were all gathered around the decomposing bodies of one of the families that had been assigned to her and that she had not yet had the time to visit. The dramatic image in her dream sends a clear message of overload, and yet she does not have the luxury of changing her work conditions. She is thrown back on her own strategies for coping and has no choice but to examine her habits in relation to stress.

It is rare to find anyone who is not coping with one or more sources of stress in their daily life, and this is not taking into account the random unexpected events that can happen to us, such as bereavement, sickness or loss of a relationship. These are the things we always hope we will not have to face and spend quite a bit of time quietly dreading at the back of our minds. Strangely, when they actually happen, they tend to draw on reserves of courage and strength we hardly knew we had, and we get through them somehow – we are stronger and more resilient than we think.

On top of this, there is the constant wear and tear of everyday life.

Perhaps you are familiar with Charles M. Schulz's cartoon character Charlie Brown? For me, one of the most poignant descriptions of leaving behind the security of childhood and becoming an adult is when Charlie Brown becomes aware that he is now too old to fall asleep in the back of the car on the way home from a family outing and have his parents carry him indoors and put him to bed. He realises that if he falls asleep, he'll need to wake up and sort himself out when the family gets home, and it is his younger brother who gets carried in to bed. It sums up for me the moment when it all comes down to you: however many people you have who care about you, it is basically up to you to take care of yourself.

## Some Psychological Factors Affecting Stress

Let's take a look at three psychological factors affecting stress: predictability, control and learned helplessness.

### *Predictability*

Research shows that when stress is unpredicted its impact tends to be worse than when we are expecting it. Likewise, when we are experiencing stress if we have an idea of how long we are going to have to deal with it, we find it easier to cope than if we have little or no idea when it is going to end.

> This was demonstrated when London was bombed during the Second World War. Londoners knew to expect bombing every night for a protracted period of time, whereas the suburbs were hit more sporadically. Research on people suffering from ulcers showed that more people in the suburbs suffered from ulcers than in the much more severely hit areas of London. Furthermore, the increase in ulcers only lasted for three months. By the end of that period of time, people in the suburbs expected sporadic attacks, meaning they were less unpredictable.[4]

If we understand that stress of all kinds is an inevitable part of life, then it is possible to have a different take on the whole idea of predictability. Without being pessimistic, or anticipating difficulties which may not even happen, we can learn to become familiar with the different layers of stress that each of us deal with on a daily basis, so that we are prepared to cope with them. Too often stressful events can seem as if they have fallen from the sky and just landed on us, and then it can be hard to get things in perspective. If we can learn to expect and, most importantly, to *accept* that there will be stress in our lives, then rather than fighting this idea, we will find it easier to deal with stress when it does come our way.

### *Control*

When we believe that we are in control we tend to experience less stress than when we feel that we have none. Air travel is safer than driving and yet because when we fly, we are not in control of the plane, more people are afraid of flying than are afraid of driving. Even things we enjoy doing lose their attraction if we are told we *have* to do them, because we are no longer exercising control over whether or not we wish to take part. Raising teenagers can be a stressful time when children that we thought we knew and understood seem to turn into partial strangers, often with different agendas from our own. Our family may no longer feel within our control. This can also be a major factor in workplace stress, where workers feel that they have little control over what happens to them in their jobs.

---

> *At work, people may see little variation in how to do their tasks, but they still have other kinds of choices in terms of their attitudes – how they interact with their co-workers, whether they utilize certain inner qualities or spiritual strengths to change their attitudes at work.*

---

The quote above, which comes from *The Art of Happiness at Work,*[5] is referring to work life but in fact holds true for all aspects of our lives. We can have control over and change how we react to the stress that life throws our way by understanding and working with how our mind is. Rather than fighting the stress, trying to get rid of it completely or wishing it wasn't happening, we've seen that instead we can work with how our mind is and thereby reduce the negative impact that stress can have on our lives. This is the take-home message of this book.

## *Learned helplessness*

'Learned helplessness' is a condition that was discovered by accident by psychologists Martin Seligman (who we came across when we talked about positive psychology in Chapter 3) and Steven F. Maier.[6] It is a state that we can get into when we have been subjected to repeated, unpredictable and uncontrollable stress, and it is characterised by a sense of giving up on being able to manage a particular aspect of your life. For example, if you are told often enough as a child that you cannot sing, it is going to be hard for you to find the confidence to try out your voice later on, and much more likely that you will agree with the verdict and try to restrict your singing to the privacy of the shower. During my years of teaching I met many children who had been treated as second-rate learners for much of their school life and were subsequently failing. Fortunately, in most cases this was reversible once their self-confidence was boosted. Sadly, though, all too often the degree of stress that someone has been subjected to can lead them always to expect the worst outcome from whatever they attempt. With their perception clouded by past experience they lack the clarity to see when things are actually going quite well for them.

> This condition of learned helplessness is something that I see from time to time in workshops that I give for people at work. Highly stressed people can become so battered by their experience that they become almost deaf and blind to any support that is offered to them and seem to be almost afraid to believe that change is possible. Indeed, many of us feel this way from time to time. Maybe we're going through a particularly stressful time at work or are looking after someone who has been ill for a while. It is easy to lose sight of the fact that things won't necessarily stay the same for ever.

The best way to approach this feeling of being battered and slightly helpless is to spend time identifying what *is* working well and use that as a starting point for building our courage. If we can do that it becomes easier to identify the particular stressors that are causing us the most worry. It is important to pick out individual threads from the general sense of helplessness and then work out what to do about each one. For example, things might be tough at work but perhaps the shared worry has brought you closer to a work colleague and the strengthened relationship provides support. Maybe you realise you have isolated yourself too much and need to work on building closer relationships. This gives you an attainable goal in a challenging situation and helps you feel a sense of control. Be prepared for it to be a slow process, but the good news is that as soon as you make even a small start, things begin to feel different.

| **Psychological factors** | **Note where you experience this** | **What can you do about it** |
|---|---|---|
| • predictability | | |
| • control | | |
| • learned helplessness | | |

## Survival Mechanisms to Deal with Stress

When we looked at how our body reacts to stress in Chapter 2, we saw that these reactions were designed to help us to escape from hostile circumstances and to survive danger. We also saw that in modern times most of our stress is not caused by life-threatening situations at all. For example, we are capable of raising our blood pressure by recalling an argument we had several years ago, anticipating how a difficult boss will respond to our request for an early holiday, or leaping to the defence of a friend who's being criticised. Given that our potential stressors have become so varied and numerous it is not surprising that we then find ourselves trying to protect ourselves from the results of our own stress. Unfortunately, many of the ways we try to do this not only do not help us manage the stress in a more effective way – they can actually make things worse.

Let's look at some examples:

| Some survival mechanisms | Possible results | Relevance to my own coping strategies |
|---|---|---|
| 1. Comfort e.g. An extra glass of wine, smoking, chocolate | Not a long-term solution, not good for our health | |
| 2. Distraction e.g. Cinema, Netflix, social media | Problems are still there afterwards | |
| 3. Shutting ourselves away and not wanting to see people | We are not spreading our stress around, but we are depriving ourselves of one of the most effective means of support – talking things through with people who care for us. | |

| | | |
|---|---|---|
| 4. Suppressing our emotions as a means of retaining control | Increased feeling of isolation | |
| 5. Establishing boundaries and setting limits | It is as if we close an inner door in our heart that in fact shuts us off both from our own capacity for caring and self-nurture as well as any feeling of empathy for other people. We may be trying to cope, but it is a short-term strategy that will not help us to understand and look after ourselves over time. | |

Let's consider the story of Lynn.

Lynn was the CEO of a third sector organisation in the UK[7]. Her organisation was experiencing severe cutbacks. She had come along to a workshop that I was running because she wanted to find a way of managing her working life differently. **Her stress level was beginning to affect her health and she was concerned as to where she was heading.**

She was an intelligent, articulate woman, obviously dedicated to her job, but she came across as someone under siege. Although she was drawn to the idea of developing mindfulness and empathy skills, she had great difficulty in applying them to her own situation. Each time we came to talk about it she would present her case as being especially challenging, or herself as being less able to apply the techniques we were learning than the rest of the group. After a while I saw that **she was quite skilled in deflecting the very help that**

**she was seeking and thereby maintaining the circumstances she claimed she wanted to change.**

We discussed how to integrate a short session of meditation at the beginning of the working day and I asked her to describe her early-morning routine to the group. Lynn shared that she woke up to the news on her radio, and then turned on the TV so she could watch the news while she dressed and ate breakfast. **She did not allow herself one moment of quietness from the moment she woke up until she went to bed at night.**

We talked through how she could change her alarm call to music and keep the news off while she got ready for work. Somewhere between dressing and eating breakfast she would try five minutes of sitting meditation. Her breakthrough moment came with a very simple mindfulness exercise, similar to the one presented in Chapter 5, on page 133, which meant that for a few moments she just stopped and watched her breath. The ease of this almost shocked her and enabled her to see how effective silence and attention can be in cutting through habits of stress – in her case, the habit of having noise and activity going on all the time.

Up until the point where she had a direct experience of the power of mindfulness techniques, **Lynn demonstrated how easy it can be to justify unhelpful coping patterns to ourselves based on a misperception of our capacity to change.** Even when we feel like our back is against the wall and our health is threatened, we can still find ourselves clinging to the way we always do things and believing it's the only option available. So, for each of us it is not only important to recognise where we are vulnerable to stress and what is likely to cause it, but also the coping styles we bring to bear in trying to manage our stress.

Which of Lynn's survival mechanisms seem especially relevant to your own behaviour?

______________________________________________

______________________________________________

______________________________________________

______________________________________________

______________________________________________

## Habits that Increase our Stress

We have seen that the ways in which we try to cope with the insecurities of life can mean that we are limiting our view of ourselves and the world we live in. Although our intention is to try and maintain a feeling of security – and to be happy – the events life repeatedly puts in our way demonstrates that this limited view does not serves us very well. In fact, it causes us suffering and stress. Let's consider five of the habits we can develop that increase our stress.

### *1. The habit of not paying attention in the present moment*

> *If we sum up all the missed moments, inattention can actually consume our whole life and colour virtually everything we do and every choice we make or fail to make.*
>
> *on Kabat-Zinn*[8]

| What does this look like? | Is this something you do? |
|---|---|
| • Thinking ahead to what will happen in the future.<br>• Going over what has already happened in the past.<br>• Listening to someone talking and thinking about something else.<br>• Not being mindful of routine activities.<br>• Not noticing when our stress is triggered until it is too late. | |

*Exercise: Make a list of your stress triggers so you know what to look out for*

### *2. The habit of hoping for what we want and fearing what we don't want*

| EVENT | HOPE | FEAR |
|---|---|---|
| Going on holiday | Have a good time | Flight delays, bad weather, poor hotel |
| Holding a dinner party | Everyone enjoys the food | Someone won't like the cooking |
| Making a work presentation | Please our boss | He/she won't like it |
| Give some examples of how hope and fear work in your life<br>____________________<br>____________________<br>____________________<br>____________________<br>____________________ | | |

## Summary

There's nothing wrong in principle with wanting things to turn out well. It is part of our human make-up to strive to improve our lives and to increase our wellbeing. We know that everyone wants to be happy and avoid unhappiness. The problem here is the way we grasp so strongly on to our hope that things will go well and at the same time try to shut out the possibility that they may not go exactly as we would wish. Right there we are setting up a range of circumstances that can become possible stressors for us. Instead of accepting the natural movement of life – the ebb and flow of situations and events, the inevitability of some disappointment and loss – we try to impose our wish for happiness as if the harder we focus the more chance we have of success. Deep down we know that life just does not work like that, indeed experience shows us this repeatedly, and yet we continue to hope that this time things will be different.

Next time you make a plan try to reflect on all the factors involved in the plan working out.

Bring to mind other plans that you have made that turned out differently to how you expected.

Try to be open to the idea that your plan could come to fruition in a variety of ways – you don't have to cling to a fixed idea of a good outcome.

Accept that things could go wrong and that is just how life is – it's not personal.

## *3. Our emotional habits*

### A metaphor for turbulent emotions

Imagine a freshwater lake on a sunny day – the water is calm and so clear that you can see the stones and plants on the bottom of the lake. Then a storm comes, and the water is whipped up and disturbed, so grey and muddy that you cannot see anything – until the storm passes and everything becomes calm and clear again. Our mind is like the water of the lake – in itself it is clear and calm but when it is full of emotion it takes on the colour and intensity of the emotion itself. Emotions come and go, they are not who we are, but strong emotion changes our perception, and prevents us from seeing things clearly. This is particularly true of destructive emotions – the kind that undermine our peace from within, such as anger, worry and frustration. Love and forgiveness, on the other hand, are expressions of our intelligence and enhance our peace of mind.

## TIPS

Our emotions can be powerful weapons, and many of our reactions to stress are expressed through our emotions. Think about your own reactions to stress – when you're under a lot of stress, how do you feel? Short-tempered? Anxious? On edge? Upset? Frustrated? Downhearted?

Once we have begun with meditation, it is possible to find the space to see what is going on when emotions like these arise:

- Notice the emotion building.
- Don't try to suppress it but don't let it run away with you either.
- Catch it before it causes hurt to you, or to another person.
- Remember the metaphor of the lake and that whatever emotion you are feeling will pass, it is not solid or real.
- Use your discernment to see whether the emotion you are feeling will add to your wellbeing and the wellbeing of others – or detract from it.
- Ask yourself how you would feel if someone was expressing this emotion towards you.

Remember the Golden Rule: Treat others as you would wish to be treated yourself.

## *4. The habit of addiction to stress*

As I mentioned before, my professional training was as a schoolteacher. Although I have not taught for many years, I enjoyed my time in the classroom very much. Most of my teaching career was in inner London schools with tough kids who had bags of energy and faced lots of challenges. It was certainly a potentially stressful environment, but it was exhilarating too, with a great deal of interesting, innovative and creative work.

One of the reasons I eventually stopped teaching was not the pressure from the children but the culture of stress among the staff. It got to the point where if you were enjoying your work rather than complaining about it all the time, it was thought that somehow you were not taking things seriously enough and missing just what a tough time everyone was having. I met some wonderful people who were teaching, but sadly most of them subscribed to the 'them and us' attitude – 'them' being the government, the parents and the head teacher. If you did not join in this siege mentality, laced with a heavy dose of cynicism, then it was hard not to be seen as eccentric.

I sometimes come across a similar attitude in my workshops – people who are suffering from various sources of stress related to their work and their attitude to it but who feel safer clinging to the way they have always done things, rather than risk trying something new. It's a case of better the devil you know – in this case sticking with stress. It may be eating up their energy, undermining their private life and leeching the joy from their work, and yet it is familiar, and they feel they are just about able to manage it.

This addiction can be quite a subtle process, affecting people who have high levels of responsibility and commitment to their work but who take that sense of responsibility to extremes and place themselves in the role of a saviour for the situation – indispensable, always available and ready to pick up the pieces.

In Chapter 1, we looked at how the repeated activation of the stress response can have all kinds of negative consequences. The habit of addiction to stress can be one result of living in a constant state of what the author Rick Hanson calls 'simmer'[9] – an ongoing low-level stress response. Because of the impact this has on the amygdala and hippocampus, it can mean that our tendencies to be anxious, or even depressed, are increased. The higher levels of adrenaline coursing through our body keep us on a permanent state of high alert, which can be very hard to switch off. This is one reason why stress can become so endemic in certain situations.

Over the next few days observe how you are in relation to stress.

- Do you find yourself in a constant simmer state?

How do you talk about your stress?

- Do you exaggerate in any way?

## *5. Evolutionary habits*

If we think back to our predecessors living on the savannah all those thousands of years ago, it is not hard to see that it would have been negative experiences that taught them the rules for survival rather than the positive ones. We already touched on this in Chapter 1.

For example, failing to understand that it is better to run away from a sabre-toothed tiger rather than to try to stroke it could have resulted in instant death – so the fight-or-flight response was developed. Whereas, if our ancestors had a positive experience, like finding something new to eat, but did not have time to investigate it right then, it could always be sampled the next day – our brains didn't need to learn to respond immediately to the positive.

Because of the advantages of being more alert to bad things happening to us than to positive things, our brain is more geared to keeping an eye out for the negative and, in fact, this has become a habitual response – in other words, a habit, and part of our threat and protection system.

Our brain is constantly on the lookout for threats because that is how it needed to be in order to protect us from attack in the past, and the brain carries on doing it today even when it is no longer so necessary. Although this has some advantages, the downside is that it can leave us with a continual low-grade feeling of unspecified anxiety – the experience of 'simmer' that we just mentioned – which we cannot quite find a focus for.

---

Similarly, our brain detects negative information more quickly than positive information and tends to remember it for a much longer time.

---

We cannot do a lot about this in the short term, but we can learn to be aware of these tendencies and learn to be ready to balance them out, rather than simply react to them. Over time we can learn to begin to override them with more helpful habits.

## The Stress Response and the Stories We Create

If I feel that what is going on around me is demanding more of me than I feel I have the resources to cope with, then I am experiencing stress. How we *respond* to stress will determine how it affects us – not everyone reacts in the same way. We all know people who are thrown into a tailspin if they break a nail, and others who experience constant challenges with the minimum of fuss.

Recently, a work colleague was sharing with me the difficulty his parents were experiencing with some new neighbours who were turning out to be very noisy. He described how he had gone round to see his parents and his mother was talking on and on about the noise and its effect on her. He said he suddenly realised that at that particular moment the neighbours were being completely quiet, and yet his mother continued to fill all the space with her anxiety about the situation. This story demonstrated for me how much we add to our stress by the way we react to it.

My colleague's mother was certainly in an unpleasant situation, but she added to her suffering by talking about it all the time. How many of us find ourselves doing this? We end up talking about the potential cause of stress, often to the extent that we make ourselves feel more stressed.

---

I need to fly quite a bit for my work and one of my stress triggers is going through the security check. I always want to get through quickly and settle down to do some work in an airport café before my flight. Inevitably I find myself in the slowest-moving line, with people taking ages to unpack their bags, take off their shoes, repack their bags and move through. If I am not paying attention, I can find myself getting quite irritated by the people ahead of me as well as the over-zealous security guards. When I catch myself, I feel awful for harbouring resentment towards someone innocently wanting to get on their way, just as I do.

So, when I get stressed in this situation, I am adding at least two more layers of stress – firstly, my feelings of irritation, and secondly, by my feeling bad about feeling irritation.

Fortunately, when I am working, I am usually travelling alone, or else there could well be a fourth layer in which I share my feelings with my companion!

---

My airport story is an example of how something fairly minor can cause us stress and we can make it worse by the way we react to it. Exactly the same process applies to more serious sources of stress. Perhaps you know of a friend or relative who, on being made redundant, decided to make the career change they had always wanted to make but had been afraid to. Another person faced with the same situation might slip into depression and feel like a failure. A major health scare can leave us with tremendous fear for the future, or it may leave us feeling determined to use our time really well. Divorce certainly marks the end of an important phase in our lives, but it does not have to signal the end to any hopes of happiness. The stories we tell ourselves about the situations we find ourselves in can help us to either cope in a healthy, long-term way, or they can undermine our confidence and sense of wellbeing. If we are aware of what our stress triggers are, and the habits we have for dealing with them, it will provide us with considerable support in cutting down on the extra layers of stress our reactions can create. We will look at this in more detail in Part 3. For now, here is an exercise which will help you look at how you react to stress and identify any habits you fall into.

### *Exercise: Reflecting on how you react to stress*

Sit for a few moments and watch your breath.

Remember an occasion recently when you were feeling stressed. Take time to remember the situation clearly.

**Now take time to identify:**

What happened.

What your thoughts were about what happened.

What your feelings were about what happened.

How would you describe your reaction to the stressful event?

Have you responded to stressful situations in this way before?

Can you identify any habits you fell into here?

Take responsibility for your thoughts and feelings at the time but don't judge them.

**Now consider these questions as you remember this incident:**

Did you take time to calm down with mindfulness or meditation?

Were you able to separate your feelings from your behaviour?

Can you identify any additional layers of stress that you added to the situation?

Did you spread your stress to others by how you behaved?

Did you behave in a way that you yourself would like to be treated?

On reflection, is there anything you would like to have done differently?

Sit again.

## Stress Pollution

In Chapter 2 we looked at how the discovery of mirror neurons has extended our understanding of how we communicate and showed how connected to each other (interdependent) we are. Mirror neurons are cells in the brain that fire when an individual performs an action, as well as when he/she observes a similar action performed by someone else. When this connection is helping to spread compassion, it promotes a sharing of healthy feelings, but when it works in terms of stress it adds to an already tense atmosphere. We can transmit our feelings of stress in myriad ways – through our body language, our mood, through the words we choose to express ourselves with, and by how accessible we are to other people. Some people cope with stress by sharing their feelings with everyone around them, not always realising the impact it has on those who have to listen.

At the other end of the scale, it is easy to pick up on the stress of people we work or live with and to become affected by it. A bad-tempered boss will cause a ripple of unease to spread through a whole office, even reaching people who do not come into direct contact with them. In Japan there is a phenomenon known as *karoshi* – which means 'death from overwork'. There are support groups devoted to supporting the widows of men who have died from it. Here is an extreme example of a culture of working hard spilling over into one of intolerable stress. We can see how the poor people who fall victim to *karoshi* are not just highly stressed in themselves but operating in a culture where everyone's stress is allowed to infect others.

We call this 'stress pollution' and it happens when we are not paying attention to the present moment and have become focused on our own feelings and reactions to things. When it takes hold of an environment it can seem self-perpetuating, limiting the chances for that environment to change. It can happen in small ways almost before we realise it, which is where paying attention comes in.

It is not hard to see that without this kind of awareness, stress pollution can spread through a family or workplace, with corrosive results. Naturally there are times when it is important to talk about things that are bothering us, and to discuss our stress, but it is better to do that when we are feeling calm and able to have a productive discussion. Stress pollution starts with a person allowing their stress to spill over in an uncontrolled way, which is difficult for them and for the people around them.

When discussing this during a workshop, one of the participants, Margaret, had an example close to home that she shared with the group. She has to travel quite a bit for work. Both she and her husband have a well-balanced view of this and enjoy the time they spend apart engaged in separate projects. They communicate frequently by Skype and text messaging when they are apart and look forward to being reunited when the trip is over.

Whenever he can, Margaret's husband picks her up from the airport on her return and has supper ready at home. Margaret described her feelings of often being tired after the trip, longing for the supportive environment of her home, and looking forward to exchanging news and stories with her husband. She says by the time she arrives home she can find herself feeling quite vulnerable as she makes the shift in mood from the work trip to her quieter home rhythm.

This can make her oversensitive to anything that does not go smoothly. For example, if she finds that her husband has not kept their apartment as tidy as she likes, she can find herself getting irritable over a few unwashed lunch dishes or some unwatered houseplants. Quite rightly, her husband may feel he is doing all he can to ensure a pleasant homecoming and that she is being unappreciative.

She laughed as she described how they have both tried to work with this dynamic where her stress from her work trip and journey can spill over and spoil a happily anticipated homecoming. She said the trick was to recognise her own patterns of behaviour before they took hold and to pay attention to her reactions while she is feeling very tired. If she does not notice in time her husband finds a way of gently pointing it out to her.

| What we have learned in this chapter | Your reflections |
|---|---|
| • We have already begun to put some tools in place to help us work with stress.<br>• Most people try to manage several different layers of stress of different intensity at the same time, the most challenging being the immediate stress of each day.<br>• Psychological factors affecting stress:<br>  * Predictability: understanding stress is part of life<br>  * Control: we have control over how we react in any given situation<br>  * Learned helplessness: a result of too much stress<br>• Unlike animals, humans can feel stress about events that happened long ago, events that may never happen or events that just exist in their imagination.<br>• Unhelpful strategies:<br>  * Distracting ourselves from the pain of stress<br>  * Shutting ourselves off from support<br>  * Becoming rigid about being in control<br>  * Putting up limits and boundaries<br>• It is important to recognise where we are vulnerable to stress and the way in which we try and cope with it.<br>• It is very helpful to become familiar with what our own habits are when faced with stress, so we can spot them when they become active and try and change them into something more helpful. Typical habits are: | |

  * Not paying attention
  * Getting caught up in hope and fear
  * Emotional habits
  * Becoming addicted to stress
  * Evolutionary habits
- We cannot avoid stress in our lives, but we do have a choice in how we react to it. Cutting down the negative stories we tell ourselves about the situations we are working with will help us to be more effective in managing our stress.
- When we are not paying attention, we can spread our stress around in an unhelpful way, as well as picking up the fallout from other people's.

## TIPS TO TAKE INTO EVERYDAY LIFE

1. Try to be aware of what your stress triggers are.
2. Which are your default coping mechanisms when it comes to stress?
3. Which are your main habits to do with stress?
4. Is there one that you feel ready to take on and work with?
5. Be aware of when you exaggerate your stress.
6. Take care to notice if you are spreading your stress around.

# 7 Adopting Beneficial Habits

*Compassion automatically invites you to relate with people because you no longer regard people as a drain on your energy.*

*Chögyam Trungpa*[1]

What we are going to do in this chapter:

1. Establish the basis for working with compassion as an antidote to stress
2. Examine some basic principles that will help us with this
3. Look into two of our 'unhelpful habits' we identified in the last chapter to see how compassion can help
4. Consider some recent compassion research findings

## Basic Principles

In this second section of this book we are trying to become aware of our habits, gathering as much understanding of them as we can, and deciding what we want to do about them. So far, we have examined the habits that may increase our stress – the unhelpful habits we need to learn to let go of. Generally, these are habits that we have acquired to try and make sense of what is happening around us and to us – something that is not always easy to do. In fact, as we have seen, many of the habits we use when faced with stress are exhausting. They tend to make the problem worse and actually increase our stress levels.

## TIPS

The challenge is:

- To learn to understand what compassionate habits are.
- How we can develop them.
- To put them into practice so that they become our default way of responding to stress, rather than our habitual less helpful reactions.

*1. Among the beneficial habits we can learn to help us reduce our stress are habits to do with developing compassion for ourselves and for other people.*

- The instinct for compassion, as we have seen in Chapter 2, comes from a very different place than our stress responses.
- The potential for compassion exists in all of us as part of our human make-up – it does not have to be contrived or forced.
- Habits based in compassion have the potential to nourish us as well as other people – we can start to be less harsh with ourselves and develop kindness instead of anger in our dealings with other people.
- Stress tends to reduce our possibilities for action. It is as if our room to manoeuvre is shut down. When we pitch our strength against a perceived threat, we tend to see the possibilities for action as more limited than they actually are.
- Because compassion is about appreciating things as they really are, it creates possibilities and opens up space for movement – there is nothing to struggle against, so we are able to relax and look at the situation calmly.
- This enables us to engage with the two aspects of compassion as described by Professor Paul Gilbert and covered in Chapter 2. You will remember that the first aspect is *the ability to engage with and stay with suffering* – the wish that all people could be free from suffering – and the second aspect is *the willingness to help bring this about.*

> **TIP**
>
> Compassion could be said to open an inner door in our heart, whereas stress closes it.

**Take a few moments to re-read the points covered so far.**

*Ask yourself:*

- Do they resonate with my experience?
- Can I see the potential for using compassion to work with stress?

## *2. The importance of reflecting on interdependence as part of this process*

Chapter 2 introduced the importance of understanding interdependence in relation to compassion, whereas in Chapter 3 we considered how being unaware of interdependence leads to stress. Interdependence is a way of describing the interconnectedness of life and the interrelationship between people.

---

> *It really boils down to this: that all life is interrelated. We are all caught in an inescapable network of mutuality, tied together into a single garment of destiny. Whatever affects one directly, affects all indirectly. We are made to live together because of the interrelated structure of reality. Before you finish eating breakfast in the morning, you've depended on more than half the world. This is the way our universe is structured; this is its interrelated quality. We aren't going to have peace on Earth until we recognize the basic fact of the interrelated structure of all reality*
>
> *Martin Luther King*[2]

---

**To help bring this quote into your experience, spend some time thinking about your breakfast in the ways King implies.**

*Maybe you have cereal, toast, fruit and coffee or tea, or perhaps you go for something more elaborate?*

*Whatever your breakfast choices, think of just one item – your cereal perhaps – and ask yourself who helped get it from the field where it grew into your bowl.*

*There are the farmers who grew the grain, the people who picked it, the packers and transport people, but there are also their families and the people who made the clothes they were wearing as they worked. Then there are the people who brought it by plane or truck to the distribution centre, and through several steps into the local supermarket – so by now we can include all the people who built the plane or truck, and the supermarket, the designers of the packets, and the advertising agencies who convinced you to buy this kind of cereal – and their families too.*

*Even then we are not covering everyone.*

*If we start again with the milk that goes with it, or the bowl itself, we include more huge groups of people who have been involved in your breakfast as you sit in your kitchen at home.*

*This is how interdependence works – we can see that it has an impact on all aspects of our lives.*

You can do similar exercises with showering, dressing, travelling to work . . .

Training our mind to bring this understanding of the inter-relatedness of all aspects of life into the forefront of our thinking is an essential and helpful habit to acquire in terms of developing compassion. It helps us to develop awareness of other people and to realise how much we all depend on each other.

### *3. Everything is changing all the time*

Another way in which we misperceive the world we live in and so cause ourselves stress is by clinging to the idea that things are permanent and continuous; in other words, things are here to stay and will carry on as they always have.

*Very simply put, everything in our experience is always changing. The world around us, our bodies, our thoughts and feelings – even our thoughts about our thoughts and feelings – are in constant flux, a progressive and ceaseless interplay of causes and conditions that create certain effects, which themselves become the causes and conditions that give rise to still other effects.*

*Yongey Mingyur Rinpoche*[3]

There are aspects of this that are easy to understand, but others may be more challenging. It is not so hard to accept that everything is changing and moving all the time – although we often choose to ignore it. It is harder to see how one thing leads to another – if I grab the last carton of milk on the supermarket shelf, it could mean that you need to go and buy some milk in the late-night shop on the corner because you need milk to make a sauce for the dinner party you are hosting. While buying the milk, some teenage boys rush into the shop and steal your purse. All the resulting upset means you are late home to prepare the meal for your friends. You're a bit shaky and the cooking does not go well, so you end up needing to get a takeaway and spending more than you intended. We can see in this way that one small incident is in fact part of a much bigger web of events and they are all connected.

## Ways in which change happens – fill in examples from your own experience

A few months back I visited a town in the Netherlands where we used to have family. My partner and I remembered a café we visited a few times, and looked forward to having our favourite dish for lunch, but when we reached the place the café was closed and boarded up. So was the one across the road – in fact the whole street had gone downhill a bit and it was hard to remember what it was that we had enjoyed about it. The changes that had happened made it a different place from the one we remembered and spoilt our pleasure in revisiting it.

It is annoying when your local supermarket stops stocking the brand of shampoo that you always buy, or your neighbours move away and are replaced by ones you don't find as easy to get along with.

These are the more obvious changes that happen in our lives, but there are more subtle kinds of change also happening all the time, which are harder to notice. Do you know the surprise you feel when you see the children of friends or family that you have not seen for a while, and are taken aback by how much the children have grown? We rarely apply the same passing of time to ourselves and reflect how we too have changed as we have grown older.

Consider the changes in our body as blood is pumped around our system and we digest our latest meal. Our body is constantly getting rid of old cells and replacing them with new ones.

Of course, it is not just in our body that molecules, atoms and subatomic particles shift and change – the wood of my desk where I am writing is undergoing the same process, as is my computer and the very room I am sitting in.

Think about the thoughts and feelings that course through the mind – none of them last for very long before they are replaced by the next wave and yet we bundle the whole lot together and refer to it as 'me'.

This 'me' is not the same as it was yesterday, let alone five, ten, fifteen years ago, and yet we treat it as if it is.

### *Exercise: Reflection on the changes in your body*

Sit comfortably with your back straight and breathe naturally through your nose.

As you do so, pay attention to the changes in your body as you breathe:

The movement in your lungs.

The rise and fall of the muscles in your belly.

If your mind wanders away, don't worry, just come back to awareness of your breathing and the changes in your body.

Stop after a few moments.

Review what you noticed.

Perhaps you were aware of the breath flowing in and out of your nostrils, or your thoughts and sensations as you sat. All this is fine – we are just taking time to observe the constant small changes that happen all the time in our body.

Learning to be aware of the state of flux we live in, to recognise that everything is changing, is another beneficial habit to adopt in terms of understanding compassion. It helps us to realise that nothing lasts for ever and encourages us to appreciate the good things in our lives while we have them, while understanding that the difficult things will also pass.

> **TIP**
>
> Although these habits are a natural expression of our human nature, they are not easy to establish, and it requires sustained effort over a period of time to replace less helpful habits with new ones. Think how hard it is to establish helpful habits such as losing weight, exercising, or giving up smoking. In relinquishing our ingrained habits of stress, we will need to overcome our conditioning.

## *4. Evolutionary factors that can get in the way*

Evolution has provided us with survival strategies that enable the human race to survive but which are not always in tune with the bigger picture.

| Survival Strategies | Examples you think illustrate this |
|---|---|
| a) For example, our brain has been programmed to separate the world into what belongs to 'me' and what belongs to the 'other'. Our ancestors needed to learn to do this in order to protect their own tribe and keep out of the way of other possibly hostile tribes. However, as we have seen, everything is inter-related and interdependent, so it is not possible to make such neat distinctions. | |
| b) Our brain has been programmed to maintain stability in order to keep things in balance and provide the right environment for bringing up | |

| | |
|---|---|
| children. But in fact, everything keeps changing and stability is only ever temporary. | |
| c) The way we have evolved as a species makes us approach opportunities and avoid perceived threats in order to protect ourselves and escape from situations that threaten our survival. However, life shows us that not all opportunities turn out to be beneficial, and not all threats can be avoided. | |
| d) Our ancestors learned quickly that banding together in tribes increased their chances of survival and so it was a natural progression to want to care for and nurture other members of the tribe. This is still the prevalent attitude in most societies today – showing kindness and compassion to our family and friends is relatively easy but reaching out further than that small circle is much harder. | |

## Something to Think About

When we do manage to show compassion for people outside the circle of our friends and family, we can find that we have preferences for the kind of people we find it easy to show compassion for – it is often easier to have compassion for poor people than it is for rich ones, and the victims of crime and misfortune tend to receive more compassion than the perpetrators. So, if we are interested in learning to develop our compassionate minds we will need to move beyond this social and cultural conditioning that favours people we know and like, or feel more kindly disposed towards. Biased compassion of this sort is limited because it does not include people outside this circle. It means that we are evaluating the object of our compassion to judge whether or not they are worthy recipients. Once they disappoint us or annoy us in some way it becomes much harder to continue to be compassionate. In a similar way, if our compassion for others is driven by the hope of getting something in return, or the desire to get a good name for ourselves, then it is also limited because it has more to do with our own interests than the interests of the other person.

> **TIP**
>
> The best way to address these issues is to bring to mind over and over again that, just like us, everyone wishes to be happy and to avoid pain and suffering. Thinking in this way extends the circle of compassion beyond our immediate family and friends and moves beyond any preference for one group or another because it touches on a universal human truth. If we take it a step further and remember that, in spite of this aspiration, everyone encounters pain and suffering as an inevitable part of life, then we touch a deep tenderness in ourselves, which is like a seed for compassion.

## Compassionate Reasoning

Let's take some time to consider what we mean by a seed of compassion.

Each of us has experience of situations that touch us deeply, and the corresponding feeling of openness, warmth and softness that can arise – looking after someone when they are ill or seeing the love of a mother for her child could affect us in this way. This is like the first spark of compassion in our hearts, but along with this there often comes a feeling of sadness.

> I remember that when the shootings happened in Mumbai in November 2008 among those killed were a father and his daughter who had travelled from the US for a meditation retreat in India. The whole incident touched me deeply as the stories of people's ordeals came out, but this story seemed very close to home, and brought a deeper layer of sadness, as I reflected on how easily that could have been two people close to me. As this thought came to mind, it was closely followed by the realisation that, of course, these two people were close to all kinds of other people who would be in great pain.

Feelings like this can leave us feeling vulnerable and exposed. Perhaps we are afraid of showing such feelings and prefer to keep them hidden and ourselves well defended. Compassion requires the cultivation of a daring heart – one that is capable of cherishing itself, other people and life itself. Developing this kind of daring is another important habit of compassion.

Along with developing this courage, however, it is also necessary to have some sense of acceptance – acceptance that suffering is part of life but also acceptance for yourself as you are. Compassion is not about being perfect, nor is it about being able to be perfectly compassionate. In order to show compassion for others we need to draw on all our own experience of suffering, fear and making mistakes.

Remember how we talked about learning to *lean into* our suffering so that we can fully understand it and engage with it as a means to awaken compassionate feelings for ourselves and others? Without knowing our own suffering, how can our feelings for other people who are in pain and afraid be genuine? In choosing to develop our compassionate mind we are also choosing to change our own unhelpful habits.

This is one reason why developing a compassionate mind is so effective in helping to reduce stress. In order for it to work we need to pay attention to all our habits to do with stress, to recognise that we hold them in common with many other people. This makes us realise that as we work with our own habits, our understanding of other people deepens. As that happens, we become more able to address our own stress.

Compassion is not pity, it is not about condescension – nor is it a relationship between the healer and those to be healed. It is simply a question of starting with what we have, attempting to learn from our mistakes and pain, and then relating our struggle to the struggles that every other human has.

It is all too easy to judge ourselves continuously as getting things 'right' or 'wrong'. As we develop compassion, we try instead to just stay alert and open to our experience, without judgement, and to then extend this same attitude to others.

Try this exercise when you are watching the news and see if you can apply the kind of compassionate reasoning we have been talking about.

### *Exercise: Watching the news*

Try to watch the news a few times over the coming week.

Just sit down and watch it without engaging in any other tasks at the same time.

Notice any feelings of warmth, openness and softness that you feel in response to some of the news items.

Notice any feelings of revulsion or pain that you feel in response to other news items.

Notice any feelings of vulnerability that arise in you, along with the wish to protect yourself from unpleasant news.

Can you relate any of the news items to your own experience?

Try to view all of your reactions – both positive and negative – as part of the process of working to develop compassionate habits and remember it is not about you being perfect.

## *The logic of compassion*

As we work to develop compassion, we will engage in emotions such as **love, patience, tolerance and forgiveness**. All of these qualities will help us to develop lasting happiness and so bring benefit to ourselves as we try to benefit others. Here is another clue as to how compassion can help with stress – as we cultivate compassion, we are also cultivating the very qualities that will support us in dealing with our own stress. For example, recent research[4] has indicated that as we practise showing compassion to others, we open ourselves up to receiving support ourselves. Social support – the support of friends, family and so on – is an effective means of developing resilience to stress. Developing compassion can be likened to practising non-violence, because it is not possible to truly refrain from being harsh to others if we continue to punish ourselves. By showing compassion to others we inevitably learn how to show compassion for ourselves. We can learn to recognise ourselves in other people and be willing to take on the challenge of compassion. As social beings we are more at ease when we acknowledge our connection with other people and try to act in accordance with it.

| How the logic of compassion works | How this logic works for me |
|---|---|
| As we develop compassion, we develop emotions such as patience, tolerance and forgiveness | |
| Cultivating compassion enables us to open up to social support | |
| It is not possible to truly practise non-violence if we are harsh with ourselves | |
| We are more at ease when we recognise social connection | |

An amazing aspect of compassion is that helping others helps us too.

Research on the impact of volunteering brings home this point very convincingly. In the book that he co-wrote with Peggy Payne, *The Healing Power of Doing Good,*[5] Allan Luks gives a fascinating account of the beneficial effects of helping others.

During 1997 and 1998, he conducted a survey of 3,300 volunteers in more than 20 organisations in the USA that covered a wide range of volunteer activity. This was the first study to analyse the experience of helping and to demonstrate that a certain kind of helping could lead to measurably better health for the helpers themselves. Since then his findings have been confirmed by other studies.

The majority of volunteers reported experiencing what Luks has termed **'a helper's high'** – an immediate physical feel-good sensation, along with feelings of warmth and euphoria. This feeling is a sign of a decrease in stress in the body.

After this initial reaction comes **a second, longer-lasting, phase,** characterised by a sense of calmness, along with increased feelings of self-worth and relaxation.

**Eight out of ten volunteers** described how this sense of wellbeing could reoccur whenever they **remembered** helping out.

**Ninety-five per cent of helpers** reported improvements in their health, ranging from a reduction in the effects of stress, less awareness and experience of pain, and improvements in immune-system functioning.

It seems that these health benefits were more likely to occur in helpers who volunteered on a weekly basis rather than, say, once a year.

Another factor that improved volunteers' health was personal contact with the people being helped, as was the importance of helping people who were not family or friends.

These findings are in keeping with what we learned about compassion in Chapter 2. When we focus too fixedly on our own concerns, we can lose perspective and see our problems as overwhelming. Connecting with the suffering of others helps us to see our own situation differently and also to develop our natural capacity for empathy. When we place ourselves in the service of other people, we open ourselves up to considering their problems as being as worthy of attention as our own. If we can help them, then we feel useful and our sense of self-worth increases. The social contact that volunteering provides is also nourishing in itself and provides us with support in return.

Luks includes this quote from physician David Sobel and psychologist Robert Ornstein:[6]

> *The greatest surprise of human evolution may be that the highest form of selfishness is selflessness.*

As we learned earlier, compassion starts with where we are right now. We do not have to wait to become more capable of compassion than we are *at this moment*. All that we need in order to practise compassion right now lies in our current experience and capacity to work with our unhelpful habits. Recognising that helping others actually helps ourselves gives us a wider range of tools to start to address these habits. It is a helpful motivator to put in the work that is needed to truly develop compassion. As we understand more about compassion, we can learn to extend the natural concern we have for our own wellbeing to include the wellbeing of others.

## Habits Based on Compassion as Antidotes to the Habits that Increase our Stress

In Chapter 6 we talked about a number of habits that play a large part in the extent to which we are affected by stress. Now that we have explored some compassionate habits it's useful to look at how these work in relation to stress. To begin with, let's look specifically at two habits that have a particularly big impact:

- The habit of not paying attention.
- The habit of hoping for what we want and fearing what we don't want.
- The more specific habits we mentioned in Chapter 4 will be picked up in Part 3.

### *Habit 1: Not paying attention*

As we have already discussed, we all tend to spend a considerable amount of time thinking about the past or the future, and subsequently miss a lot of what's happening in the present moment. This is a shame, because if we think about it carefully, we realise that the present moment is all that we have to work with. The past has gone, and the future is uncertain – however much attention we give to it we cannot change that.

---

*Thich Nhat Hanh, meditation teacher and Nobel Prize nominee: You have an appointment with life, an appointment that is in the here and now.*[7]

---

| The Habit | The Compassionate Antidote | Our Experience – Your Insights |
|---|---|---|
| Our tendency to spend the present moment with all these thoughts about the past and the future tends to tire us out and means we are rarely bringing our full attention to bear on what is right in front of us. Even more serious is our habit of filling in the gaps in our attention in order to reassure ourselves that we are in touch with what is going on. This is why we can all have such different memories of the same event – each of us will have filled in the gaps in our attention with details from our own experience of the situation. | As we have seen, we behave as if we are independent units that just carry on with our own concerns when, in fact, we are part of a deeply interdependent world – one that is constantly moving and changing. As we train ourselves to adopt a compassionate mind, we are becoming more aware of the interconnectedness of all aspects of life, as well as seeing that it is in perpetual motion. This helps us to pay attention to how things actually *are*, rather than as we would *like them to be*. Learning to pay attention is the basis of awareness – self-awareness in the first instance, and then awareness of others. It is in itself an act of compassion for us and for other people because it reduces the extent to which we misperceive our life, and so decreases how stressed we feel. | |

*Habit 2: Hoping for what we want and fearing what we don't want*

| The Habit | The Compassionate Antidote | Our Experience – Your Insights |
|---|---|---|
| Many of us put so much effort into trying to organise our lives to fit with the expectations that we have developed as we have grown up and that are now part of our worldview. As a means of trying to fulfil our wish for happiness, there is nothing wrong with this approach if we can combine it with the understanding that things do not always work out as we wish – if we learn to be more accepting of what life throws at us. Unfortunately, this is something that many of us do not do and so we end up experiencing the repeated stress of trying harder, planning more carefully and still facing disappointment. | Compassion for ourselves begins when we notice this cycle and realise that instead of enabling us to achieve our goals, it is making us stressed and exhausted. If we can see our own suffering clearly then it becomes a springboard for being able to see the suffering of others and to want to do something about it. Compassion for other people begins when we see that just as we are caught in this cycle of stress, so are most other people. This touches us so deeply that we want to do something about it. Reflecting in this way reduces our focus on our own stress and so helps us to approach it in a more useful way. Training in compassion reduces the intensity of one's own problems because it helps us to see that our problems are not unique, or a special punishment for us, but are simply part of the inevitable ups and downs of life. | |

## Research Findings on Compassion

I mentioned the Dalai Lama's collaboration with Western science and the work of the Mind and Life Institute in the Introduction. The field of neuroscience – the study of the nervous system – has proved to be an especially fertile area for exploration and exchange between Buddhist scholars and Western scientists. We have already mentioned the important role of neuroplasticity – the discovery that the brain changes in response to experience – in this collaboration. One of the earliest studies into neuroplasticity was carried out on violinists whose brains were found to devote more space to the region that controls the digits of the hand that they use to manipulate the strings of the violin. Other studies have suggested that even simply thinking in a certain way can lead to changes in the brain.

Sharon Begley, science columnist for the *Wall Street Journal* writes:[8]:

> *Something as seemingly insubstantial as a thought has the ability to act back on the very stuff of the brain, altering neuronal connections in a way that can lead to recovery from mental illness and perhaps to a greater capacity for empathy and compassion.*

The discovery that our habits are not hardwired into our brain – that new connections between neurons can be formed, old ones fall away, and even completely new neurons develop – gives an interesting scientific perspective on the Buddhist view of the importance of training the mind. Buddhist training emphasises the need to train the mind in order to become free from suffering and to be able to help other people become free from suffering. Neuroplasticity demonstrates that by training our minds we can change our brain and support new, helpful habits.

Sharon Begley continues:[9]

> *Because the science is so new, the limits of neuroplasticity are largely unmapped. But there is no question that the emerging science of neuroplasticity has the potential to bring radical changes, to both individuals and the world, raising the possibility that we could train ourselves to be kinder, more compassionate, less defensive, less self-centred, less aggressive, less warlike.*

In terms of the impact for training in compassion, we have already discussed Richard Davidson's work with highly experienced meditators. Here are some findings from Davidson's studies on meditations on compassion that are very relevant to the areas of stress and compassion (we will be learning some of these meditations in the last section of the book):

- During compassion meditations, the brain regions that deal with what is self and what is the other became quieter as if the meditators' focus had shifted to include other people.
- The experienced meditators displayed increased activity in the brain regions connected to empathy and maternal love.
- When the experienced meditators were meditating on compassion, the part of the brain to do with planned movement showed an increase in activity – it showed a readiness to go and act to help others immediately.
- While the meditators were generating feelings of compassion, activity in the left prefrontal cortex (the site of activity that indicates happiness) swamped activity in the right prefrontal (associated with negative moods).[10]
- The rate of gamma wave activity in the brain is associated with perception, problem-solving and consciousness. The experienced meditators showed a higher rate of gamma activity than had ever been recorded before. Even more impressive was that the gamma activity continued to be higher than usual even when the experienced meditators were not meditating. This shows that meditating on compassion leaves an imprint on the brain that lasts beyond the actual meditation session.

From this we can see that meditating on compassion can change the way the brain functions: changes that are beneficial for us.[11].

What does this mean for us in terms of using compassion to change how we experience stress? In simple terms, it means that everything is malleable – nothing is fixed. The habits that lead to stress and deal with stress are not hardwired into our brain but can be replaced with more healthy ones, such as habits based on compassion. By applying ourselves we can unlearn old habits and learn new ones that will help change the way our brain functions. The bonus is that changing the way our brain functions will actually support these new habits further. As we have seen, through practising compassion, activity in the parts of our brain associated with depression and anxiety is reduced while activity in the parts of the brain to do with happiness and wellbeing is increased. Developing a compassionate mind enables us to create the conditions for a greater sense of wellbeing that will help us as we work to reduce our stress.

| What we have learned in this chapter | Your reflections |
|---|---|
| • Stress tends to reduce our possibilities for action, whereas compassion creates space and room for movement. Compassion could be said to open an inner door in our heart, whereas stress closes it.<br>• Training our mind to really understand the inter-relatedness of all aspects of life is an essential and helpful habit to acquire in terms of developing compassion.<br>• Learning to be aware and to recognise that everything is changing and nothing stays the same is another good habit to adopt in terms of understanding compassion.<br>• In order to work with compassion, we will need to overcome conditioning from our evolutionary history and our social circumstances. We can do this by remembering that everyone is looking for happiness.<br>• Compassion requires the cultivation of a daring heart – one that is capable of cherishing itself, other people and life itself.<br>• Compassion is not about being perfect, nor is it about being able to be perfectly compassionate. In order to show compassion for others we need to draw on all our own experience of suffering, fear and making mistakes.<br>• Helping others will also help us. | |

| | |
|---|---|
| • Training in compassion reduces the intensity of one's own problems because it allows us to see that our problems are not unique but part of the inevitable ups and downs of life.<br>• The idea of neuroplasticity – the idea that the brain changes in response to experience – underpins the idea that we can change our habits for the better and so reduce our stress levels. | |

## TIPS TO TAKE INTO EVERYDAY LIFE

1. Look for as many ways as possible to play the inter-connection game.
2. When you are people-gazing remember how, just like you, everyone wants to be happy and live a good life.
3. Try to find a volunteering opportunity.
4. Remember – everything is fluid and workable.

# Conclusion to Part 2

In terms of our five steps, we have been working with steps 2–4 in Part 2 of the workbook.

**STEP 2 Taking a step back in order to see what is really going on**

**STEP 3 Trying out a fresh perspective**

**STEP 4 Examining our habits to see which ones help us and which ones don't**

We have gone quite thoroughly into how our habits affect us and the role they play in our stress. We took a step back by looking at how our minds work. The metaphor of the sky and the clouds introduced the possibility of trying out a new perspective – seeing our thoughts and emotions differently. The chapter on meditation helped to establish this idea more thoroughly. It provides a basis from which we can approach working with habits that are not helpful for us and developing ones that are.

So, a lot of important ground has been covered in these four chapters. It is worth going over them a few times to really get used to the ideas.

We have seen that changing how we react to stress is possible; in fact, the very make-up of our brain supports us to be able to change. However, as we know, even though we can change how we work with stress for the better, it is not easy to change our habits. We need to *want* to change them and the best way to develop this wish is by realising how our current habits are causing us suffering and that we would be better off without them. Not only that, but there are a whole of range of alternative strategies that we could use that would actually help us – the habits based in compassion. Once we understand this it becomes easier to develop the determination to take on our habits: to let go of the harmful ones and replace them with helpful ones.

# Part 3

# MAKING CHANGE HAPPEN

Having spent time understanding our starting points for both stress and compassion in Part 1, and looking at how our habits work, and what we can do about them in Part 2, we can now turn our attention to compassion as a skilful way of changing our experience of stress. In Part 3 we will take a detailed look at how to increase this compassion until it encompasses ourselves, other people, and the widest possible perspective by exploring compassion for ourselves, compassion for other people, and compassion with a big perspective. With each chapter the scope of the compassion we are talking about increases and we can explore how understanding and appreciating this can provide us with a rich set of resources to bring to reducing our stress.

In terms of our five steps, we come now to the last step:

**STEP 5 Taking action**

# 8 Compassion for Oneself – Peeling Away the Layers of the Heart

*Compassion isn't some kind of self-improvement project or ideal that we're trying to live up to. Having compassion starts and ends with having compassion for all those unwanted parts of ourselves, all those imperfections that we don't even want to look at.*

*Pema Chödrön*[1]

What we are going to do in this chapter:

1. Explore how self-compassion works
2. Look at the elements of self-compassion and how they can operate as antidotes to threat
3. Look into moving from self-criticism to compassionate self-correction
4. Establish the connection between meditation and self-compassion
5. Discover the places where self-compassion can really help
6. Consider possible misunderstandings of self-compassion

In Part 1 of this workbook we looked at how fundamentally our stress response is a response to threat – threat from our environment, from another person, but also from our own minds and emotions. In Part 2 we have looked quite thoroughly at how our habits can make our stress easier to cope with or make it much worse.

We saw clearly just how easy it can be to create threats to ourselves and that the habits of our upbringing and conditioning can have a big role in how that plays out. We also learned that we can define compassion as *the ability to feel another person's suffering as if it is your own, to wish for them to be free from it, and to be prepared to help them in that endeavour.*

With self-compassion, we apply this to ourselves – *we are trying to develop the ability to feel our own suffering, to wish ourselves free of it, and to be prepared to do something about it.*

When we start to look deeply into what causes us stress and how we are working with it, it can be shocking to see how little attention we give to caring for ourselves in a healthy way. If we feel low, maybe we binge on chocolate, or wallow in cruising through an entire series on Netflix, or allow ourselves to finish the bottle of wine at dinner. Perhaps we feel that we deserve a treat because things are tough.

The question is, why do we tend towards this kind of remedy rather than allowing ourselves the comfort, support and understanding that we would offer a good friend going through something difficult? For many of us, it is our conditioning that has left us with an uneasy feeling that if we apply the full range of compassionate skills to ourselves we are being indulgent, selfish, and really giving in to feeling sorry for ourselves.

Let us begin very simply. Ask yourself what you think the qualities of a good friend are. Take time to reflect carefully and then fill in the columns below.

| List all the qualities of a good friend | Tick the ones you demonstrate towards yourself<br>Put a cross next to the ones that you rarely apply to yourself |
|---|---|
| | |

What did you learn from this?

It helps to get a clear picture of the extent to which we might be withholding compassion from ourselves.

### TIPS

As we start to learn about showing compassion for ourselves, it is important not to tell ourselves off for not taking better care of ourselves. Remember, with compassion we are all on a learning curve.

## The View of Self-Compassion

Self-compassion is a wonderful resource in our journey to work with stress in a more creative way. We will see how it can show us how to change the way we respond to threat and to cut through our stories and conditioning that have limited us. We can take as our basis our natural capacity for wholeness that was described in Chapter 2 and use this as a foundation to build on. The metaphor of the sky and the clouds that we are working with in this workbook supports us in remembering our potential. Each time we do this we are showing compassion for ourselves. This gives us the courage to stop trying to avoid pain and instead to turn towards the difficulties that come our way. We can do this because with self-compassion we can see our difficulties as opportunities to learn and to grow, rather than as evidence of our shortcomings. It is a more beneficial and lasting way of fulfilling our innate wish for happiness than the simple seeking of pleasure.

## Understanding the Need for Self-Compassion

> *We can all suffer from a sense of shame. No-one goes through life without being criticized, doing things you later regret or having attributes you'd rather not have. It's part of the human condition.*
>
> *The Compassionate Mind, Paul Gilbert*

When we worry that we are not good enough, that other people will turn away from us because we are not worth their attention, then we are experiencing a sense of shame. If we feel these things about ourselves, then we are triggering a sense of internal shame. Instead of being a good friend to ourselves when things go wrong, we can feel disappointment, dismay and frustration. As we have seen, we become the target of these threat-focused feelings.

## TIPS

This would be a good moment to check back to Chapter 1: How Stress Works.

On page 21 we describe what Professor Gilbert calls the 'loops' we create in our minds to go over old worries. When we are ashamed of an aspect of ourselves, what Pema Chödrön calls an 'unwanted part of ourselves', we can find ourselves going over and over it in our minds and worrying endlessly.

On page 22 our main emotional systems are explained. This is helpful to review as we go into self-compassion.

At the conclusion of our look at our emotional systems, we stressed the need for balance between all three. However, we can see that in terms of self-compassion, if we are being very hard on ourselves then that will increase the amount of threat we experience. If we are pushing ourselves to be successful, we could be over-stimulating our drive system and causing ourselves stress. We can see that the soothing system has an important role to play here in terms of learning to comfort and nourish ourselves.

### *Exercise: Working with stress and anxiety*

This is a useful exercise in which we use our understanding of our fundamental wholeness to support us in difficult times. In fact, we can use it to stimulate our soothing system because this exercise is all about settling your anxieties.

For the purposes of the exercise you divide yourself into two parts – for simplicity we call them 'A' and 'B', but you could apply whichever labels work for you:

A – is the aspect of you that is well, relaxed, compassionate, self-aware, a true friend to you, always responsive and never judging.

B – is the aspect of you that feels stressed, frustrated, overwhelmed and misunderstood.

This exercise focuses on the breath and there is a different activity for the in-breath and the out-breath. On the in-breath, the A aspect takes away all the difficulties the B aspect is experiencing, and on the out-breath gives healing and nourishment.

This enables B to relax and find some relief.

Allow yourself to feel this happening.

*As you breathe in*, consider that A opens their heart completely and warmly and compassionately accepts and embraces all of the stress and frustration that B is experiencing.

Touched by this, B can relax and open their heart, so that their pain and suffering melts away.

*As you breathe out*, consider that A sends out to B all their understanding, healing, comfort, love and confidence.

Continue the exercise for several moments and then sit in meditation.

## Looking Further at the Stress Response and Self-compassion

In his study of self-compassion Christopher Germer[2] relates the fight-or-flight stress response to how we react when we feel under threat in the following way:

- *When we are faced with a so-called threat which comes from our own mind – our inner mental and emotional functioning – rather than an outside stressor, the 'fight' response can become self-criticism.*
- *The 'flight' response becomes self-isolation.*
- *And the 'freeze' response leads to us getting caught up in our own thoughts to the extent that we are not able to act and a tendency to become self-absorbed.*

| **How this might work in practice**<br><br>THE THREAT<br><br>Let's imagine that you have been made redundant and are out of work. The job was one you enjoyed very much and knew you were good at. You did not foresee the situation that would lead to you losing your job. | APPROACHING THE SITUATION WITH SELF-COMPASSION<br><br>To begin with, it is important to acknowledge to yourself the shock you have had in being made redundant, and to give yourself permission to feel the pain of your loss. |
|---|---|
| FIGHT RESPONSE = SELF-CRITICISM<br><br>In your initial reaction to the shock, you feel angry and frustrated with yourself for not having read the signs correctly and trying to do something about them. You beat yourself up for having been gullible and stupid, but in spite of this you push yourself to start looking for a new job, because naturally money is a factor and the bills still need to be paid. Your first couple of applications are unsuccessful and your sense of failure deepens. You are worried about the future and how you are going to manage to pay the bills. | INSTEAD OF SELF-CRITICISM TRY KINDNESS<br><br>Although our instinct will be to try and put it all right as soon as we can, we need time to gather our strength. If there is any way you can financially afford it, try to allow yourself an interim period before you start looking for a new job in which you give yourself some quality care – take some exercise, do some of the things you never had time for when you were working, do a little extra meditation. Gradually, as you feel up to it, you could spend some time updating your CV and reminding yourself of the skills you have. The idea is to try and create a feeling of space and support for yourself as you start to look for work, rather than feeling like a failure that needs to cover up the embarrassment as fast as you can. When self-criticism arises, just try to look at it in a detached way and check if there is anything for you to learn from the situation and take forward with you. |
| FLIGHT RESPONSE = SELF-ISOLATION<br><br>It becomes harder to talk about the situation with friends and you start to cut yourself off from the social support that is essential to help you through this. | INSTEAD OF SELF-ISOLATION TRY CONNECTION<br><br>Remember that you are not the only person ever to be made redundant and this is part of life that affects many people. You might even ring others in similar circumstances and check how they are doing. Talking through what happened can help to reduce your own worries and may even open up new possibilities. |

| FREEZE RESPONSE = SELF-ABSORPTION | INSTEAD OF SELF-ABSORPTION TRY MINDFULNESS |
|---|---|
| Because you are seeing fewer people you have more time to dwell on all the worries, anxieties and stories that are churning around in your mind. You forget that up until a couple of months ago you were holding down a good job successfully and happily, and you fear that you will never find work that you value again. | If you can work with these first two stages in this way, the chances are that you will avoid the third stage of becoming locked in your own fears and feeling frozen. Perhaps if you wake up in the night and lie awake for a while these worries may come, but then you can try and apply some mindfulness practice and simply transfer your attention to your breath until your thoughts settle. |

## TIPS

At last you have a job interview coming up – it's for a job that you know you could do well and have a good chance of getting, but your recent experience since losing your job has left your confidence at a low ebb and you are feeling very nervous and insecure.

*You could use the Working with Stress and Anxiety exercise on page 216 to prepare for the interview.*

The A aspect of yourself would be the one that knows it can do this job and is well-qualified for it, whereas the B aspect is the one whose confidence has been undermined by recent events.

The idea is that as you do the exercise, the A aspect does not change so much but the B aspect finds comfort and healing, and the stress and anxiety you have been feeling is eased.

You may need to do it several times but that is fine.

Once you have become familiar with it, then on the way to the interview you could do an informal version of just paying attention to your breathing and imagining your nerves settling.

None of this will make the problem go away, but by being a good friend to ourself we can use our resources to meet a stressful and painful period of our life with a higher degree of resilience and so reduce the stress we experience.

With this scenario we have built on Germer's responses to threat using the three core components in self-compassion[3]: as identified by Kristin Neff, an associate professor in human development at the University of Texas, and a pioneer in the field of self-compassion.

---

- *Self-kindness: being gentle and understanding with ourselves.*
- *Recognising our common humanity: feeling connected to others rather than isolated by our suffering and pain.*
- *Mindfulness: holding our experience with a balanced perspective, neither exaggerating our experience, nor avoiding it.*

---

In their work together, Germer and Neff relate the three core elements of self-compassion to the three kinds of response to threat in this way.

---

***Self-kindness*** *acts as an antidote to the* ***fight*** *response of self-criticism*

***Recognising our common humanity*** *is an antidote to the* ***flight*** *response of self-isolation*

***Mindfulness*** *is an antidote to* ***freezing****, becoming trapped in our fears and self-absorbed.*

---

## How the Antidotes Can Work

### *Self-criticism and self-kindness*

We can be successfully holding down a demanding job while raising a family and running a home and yet the whole time we can be feeling that we are not living up to our own and other people's expectations.

Each time a deadline approaches we fear we will not meet it. If the children get sick or do badly on a test, we may feel that we're failing them. We are convinced the house should look cleaner, smarter, better. We know that we could look younger, thinner, more interesting.

We talk about ourselves to ourselves in a much harsher way than we would talk to anyone else. In fact, if we were to say out loud to someone else the kind of things we say to ourselves we would probably be deeply shocked.

We push ourselves harder than we would push any work colleague, child or friend, and yet we still do not feel we are doing as well as we should. This can be because we carry memories from our childhood of being punished for getting things wrong with our parents or teachers, and this can leave us with a fear of being rejected in our adult life. This makes us try even harder to fit in and be good enough.

It's really only when *someone else* tells us we are doing well, or praises something we've done, that for a moment we feel some ease. Then the next thing happens, and our self-criticism starts up again. It's as if we do not believe in our own accomplishments unless another person confirms them for us.

This tendency can be seen as a misinterpretation of our wish to find happiness and avoid suffering – that we can only really be happy if things are just as we want them to be and everything is ticking over according to plan. If we experience pain and stress then we are letting in the possibility of unhappiness, which is not what we set out to achieve. We saw in Chapter 3 that as long as we have this attitude of believing we can hold stress away from us by effort and willpower, we will certainly suffer. It is only by recognising that stress and suffering are an inevitable part of life that we will find the strength to deal with them from a basis of self-compassion.

---

> *The problem is that humans feel threatened by the possibility of becoming marginalized, excluded or rejected. In fact, our brains are very attentive to that. Our ability to be supportive of and helpful to each other is the upside of evolution. The downside is that we become threatened if we can't create positive feelings in the minds of others, and so fear that the support and care of others might not be there if we need it.*
>
> *The Compassionate Mind, Paul Gilbert*

---

Let's take some time to examine the inner critic.

| How does your inner critic behave? | What does it tell you about what is going on? |
|---|---|
| When is your inner critic most active? | |
| What kind of things does it say to you? | |
| What tone of voice does it use? | |
| Does it remind you of anyone that you know now, or from your past? | |
| How does it make you feel? | |
| How do you respond to it? | |

Here is an exercise that you can use to engage more creatively with your inner critic – you will need your notebook.

Sit quietly and comfortably.

Take time to listen to your self-critic and the tone it takes in your mind.

Does it speak to you like a good friend, who is interested in your wellbeing?

Or does it use a harsh and judgemental tone?

If a friend, or colleague spoke to you that way would you find it helpful?

Would you talk to someone else using this kind of language?

Perhaps your own self-criticism is not as reliable as you first thought?

Take a piece of paper and make a list of all the ways in which your self-criticism is unhelpful and even harmful.

Note the threat that you experience when you engage with it.

See that the self-critic is always focused on the past and what has gone wrong.

Imagine how it would be if the approach was kinder, more understanding, less judgemental, and consider trying to use more of this kind of language when you review your behaviour.

[Adapted from *The Compassionate Mind*, Paul Gilbert, page 340]

Once you feel that this exercise is working for you, it is time to take the next step and actively look at how to move your critical voice to compassionate self-correction.

Here is an exercise to help with that.

| **The characteristics of compassionate self-correction** | **As an antidote to self-criticism** |
|---|---|
| • Focuses on your wish to improve | Instead of punishing and condemning |
| • Emphasises growth and development | Focuses on the positive |
| • Looks ahead | Instead of returning to past errors and frustrations |
| • Given with encouragement and kindness | Rather than anger and disappointment |
| • Builds on what you are good at | Instead of stressing your shortcomings |

| | |
|---|---|
| • Focuses on specific issues to work with | Instead of a global sense of self |
| • Encourages success | Rather than threatening failure |
| • Increases your wish to participate in learning | Rather than encouraging withdrawal and giving up |

Adapted from 'Distinguishing Between Shame-Based Self-Criticism and Compassionate Self-Correction', *The Compassionate Mind,* Paul Gilbert, page 328

In the next chapter we are going to be looking in detail at how to show compassion for other people. We will be doing a Loving Kindness Meditation, but we are going to have a preview here in this chapter. It is possible to take the first part of the meditation and do it as a short but powerful practice for yourself.

## *Loving kindness meditation for yourself*

Sit quietly and rest your attention on your breath.

When you feel settled, bring to mind a person who you feel embodies kindness (it could be your grandmother, the Dalai Lama, Desmond Tutu . . .).

Imagine them sitting in front of you smiling, warm and accessible.

Now feel their kindness emanating out from their heart like rays of light.

Let this light enter your heart, filling you with a feeling of being loved.

As the light pours into you, allow yourself to feel deeply well and happy.

Quietly repeat to yourself:

*May I be happy, may I be well*

*May I be happy, may I be well*

As you repeat the phrases, let the feeling settle deeply in your being.

When you are ready, return to your breath for a few moments.

This is a simple but powerful practice. Don't rush it. Take time to get used to the idea of taking in loving kindness for yourself. Notice what it brings up for you, if you have any resistance to it. For many of us, it will be a change of perspective.

**A note on kindness**

In the next chapter we will be looking at the Four Immeasurables, which are the ways in which we can warm up to meditation. The point has been made several times throughout this workbook that developing compassion does not happen all in one go – it takes time and courage. Kindness, according to Buddhist teachings, is the antidote to anger. Using it here as a skilful means to work with our harsh inner critic is part of our process of warming up to compassion.

## *Perfectionism*

Another way in which we can withhold kindness from ourselves is in trying to be perfect at all times, come what may.

There is nothing wrong with working towards being the best you can be and to want the most out of life. This whole workbook is about trying to find skilful ways to work with stress and to handle it better. It involves us looking inwards to understand more how we work and to learn new ways of working with what we find.

Perfectionism tends to focus on what other people think. In fact, it is propelled by an underlying fear that if we can't manage perfection, then people won't want us around and certainly won't want to nourish and care for us. Somewhere we believe that if we can make people approve of us, then they will be there for us when we need them. We hope to manage to avoid the pain of other peoples' judgement, or blame.

This can all be quite subtle. Maybe we don't view ourselves as a perfectionist, but it is still worth checking out how we react when we get something wrong or behave in ways we didn't plan. Are we able to embrace failure as a learning opportunity? Do we see it as an inevitable step in our growth?

Here is a quote from Kristin Neff's book, *Self-Compassion*,[4] which is one of my favourites.

*Everyone makes mistakes at one time or another, it's a fact of life. If you think about it, why should you expect anything different? Where is the written contract you signed before birth promising you would be perfect, that you'd never fail, and that your life would go absolutely the way you want it to.*

Struggling against all odds to be perfect actually robs us of the chance to be vulnerable. If you are anything like me, you would have been brought up thinking being vulnerable was for sissies. My mother always encouraged me to not let other people know how I was feeling in case they used it against me. My parents were loving in a no-nonsense kind of way – you got on with things and did not make a fuss. If things were hard you didn't complain but just dealt with them.

It's taken me a while to understand that allowing myself to be vulnerable is all part of the package of learning to know myself. How can I understand my stress, and see where I need to change my habits if I don't allow myself to see the parts of myself that I am not so happy with? If I brush over my own vulnerability, how can I recognise it in others?

### *Reflecting on perfectionism*

Think about the quote from Kristin Neff – does it apply to you at all?

When are the times that you feel yourself trying to be perfect?

What does it look like?

How do you work with it?

What is your main habit around vulnerability?

---

*We need to learn to love ourselves first, in all our glory and our imperfections. If we cannot love ourselves, we cannot fully open to our ability to love others.*

*John Lennon*

---

*If you search the whole world for someone more worthy of love than yourself, you will not find anyone*

*The Buddha*

---

## *Self-isolation and connection*

We all know the feeling of wanting to stay under the duvet and hide away when we have tough things to face. Feeling ashamed, under attack, or depressed can make us keep ourselves away from other people.

In Chapter 2, we looked into the idea of interdependence and how connected we all are – beyond our differences. In Chapter 3, we explored the basic premise that everyone we meet just wants to be happy and to avoid pain and suffering.

These are important ideas to bring into our understanding of self-compassion. Whatever is going on for us, we can be confident that something similar is going on for many other people in the world. There is no need for us to hide away – better to reach out and embrace our common humanity with understanding and compassion.

Social support is important for our health and wellbeing.[5] We need and benefit from loving relationships with other people. All the happiness research agrees that the happiest people are those with the most supportive social networks.[6] People seek relationships in order to be happy and happy people attract relationships. Sadly, our relationships beyond our close family circle can suffer from our tendency to drive ourselves too hard and we can often feel we have not enough time to include meeting with friends. Changing this attitude provides us with a way of coping with stress, as it provides us with people who care for us and are willing to offer us support – whether it is *practical*, such as babysitting our children if we need to go to the doctor; *emotional*, such as when you talk over a problem with a friend and benefit from their advice; or *informational*, such as giving us advice on which new computer to buy.[7] We tend to think that our friendships will take care of themselves and we can pick them up when we have time. We drive ourselves so hard that we think the 'fun' things can wait. All too often we allow so little time for seeing friends that we drift apart and lose touch. Making time for a morning coffee, an after-work drink, an occasional meal together is a good investment in our wellbeing.

Here is an exercise you could try when you are out and about – on public transport, in a busy café, or walking though the city.

### *Connecting with other people*

- Turn your attention to the people around you.
- Notice the people near to you.
- Take a few moments to scan the area you are in and to see as many of the other people as you can.
- Take note of the thoughts and emotions that pass through your mind as you do this:
  *notice if you make a comment in your mind about someone*
  *notice the people you feel drawn towards and the ones you do not like the look of*

- Try to imagine how they might see you as you sit, or stand alongside them.
- Take a moment to be aware that everyone around you wants their day to go well and to avoid any unpleasantness – just as you do
- Then realise that inevitably for some people things will go wrong during the day. Let that feeling touch you and help you to feel a common humanity with your fellow city dwellers.

## *Self-absorption and mindfulness*

We have dealt with meditation quite thoroughly in Chapter 5. We have seen that for almost half our waking hours we are distracted from what we are doing and are thinking about something else.

In terms of self-compassion, we can see that an ongoing process of rumination could be quite undermining.

It might go something like this:

- We have an idea of how we want things to be
- We compare that idea to how things are right now
- We note if there is a difference between these two
- If we detect a gap, we monitor our progress to see if we can close that gap
- We consider it a success when the gap has closed, and how we want things to be and how they are, are in alignment.

The gap between what we want and how things are can appear as a reflection on the kind of person we feel ourselves to be – somehow lacking and inadequate. Our minds go around and around the problem, which makes us feel worse. We find ourselves using phrases such as, 'have to', 'ought to' or 'need to'. Our basic feeling is one of unsatisfactoriness, along with a continual sense of checking up on ourselves. It means that our thoughts and emotions are mostly caught up in thinking about the past or future, and there is little sense of the present moment.

This is where we start to become so bogged down by our own concerns that we become quite self-absorbed and unable to see the bigger picture.

**With mindfulness meditation** the emphasis is on accepting and allowing things to be as they are, without an immediate need to change them. It is not goal-orientated and so there is no need to evaluate experience. Our attention is not narrowly focused, and we can access the present moment in all its richness. Thoughts and feelings can be experienced as passing events that come and go in the mind, so there is less pull into rumination. There is a sense of freshness and a freedom to dance with the possibilities of each moment as it arises.

Meditation has many benefits, but in terms of self-compassion two are particularly important.

| **Resilience**<br><br>As we have seen, our brains have evolved to notice negative events more quickly than positive ones and to remember them for longer. This makes sense when we think of our ancestors wanting to avoid danger – knowing where a predator is lurking becomes more important than sampling some juicy berries we have just come across. Furthermore, we need to remember the places the predator is likely to hang out, so we can avoid it in the future. However, for many of us in our daily lives this can mean that we focus on the bad stuff that happens to us at the expense of the good. Perhaps we have a lovely night out with friends – good food, lively conversation and lots of laughter – but then on the way home we get caught by a speeding camera. From then on we will remember the event as, 'that evening I got caught for speeding'! Once our brains have latched on to a negative thought, we tend to replay it over and over again. We call this rumination.<br><br>Being able to work with our thoughts and emotions in meditation helps us to build resilience. As we become more proficient at allowing our thoughts to come and go – like | **Make notes from your experience** |
|---|---|

clouds moving across the sky – something settles. We see our thoughts and emotions more clearly and are less entranced by them. We can allow ourselves to be in each moment without judgement and without wishing things were one way or another. Resilience is an important skill in working with stress.

**Accessing our soft spot**

Because in meditation we are not defending anything, it is easier to connect with our own soft spot, our capacity for love and kindness. This soft spot is the source for compassion for us, and for others. With meditation, we can peel away the layers that obscure our natural kindness, revealing a rich resource with which we can face life's difficulties. We are more in touch with our own tender heart, our innate gentleness. Accessing this part of ourselves is a tremendous boost to our ability to practise self-compassion. It can help to provide the alternative voice to our harsh inner critic.

Meditation is an effective way of taking care of oneself and establishing lasting happiness. It can be considered to be the basis for self-compassion because it enables us to connect with our sense of inner wholeness and deep wellbeing, and from that perspective develop a sense of acceptance of ourselves and of our world. For me, meditation is really the basis of self-compassion. What greater gift can we give ourselves than coming to know ourselves better and being more at home with ourselves? Practising meditation is a way of giving ourselves the best quality attention.

## How We React to Life's Challenges

There is a great story that is said to be from the time of the Buddha.[8] He asked a student if being hit by an arrow would hurt – naturally the student replied that it would. Then the

Buddha asked if being hit by a second arrow would also hurt and again the student said it would. The punchline of the story is that there is often not so much we can do about the first hit of the arrow. However, the Buddha said the second hit was our reaction to whatever is going on and that we can do something about.

Try this exercise to gather some clues about how you react when challenged.

> Do you try to ignore the fact that you are suffering and focus on fixing the problem?
>
> Or do you take some time to give yourself comfort?
>
> Do you get carried away by the drama and tend to make a big deal of what is happening?
>
> Or do you keep a balanced view of what is going on?
>
> Do you feel cut off from others when things go wrong and feel as if it is only happening to you?
>
> Or do you take some time to think of others in a similar situation?
>
> Do you see that the three elements of self-compassion are in this reflection?

## *Self-Compassion Stop Moment*

In Chapter 5 we looked at having Stop Moments throughout the day. One way to respond to the first element in this reflection is to have your own Self-Compassion Stop Moment. It will help to give some perspective on how you are reacting.

You might like to come up with a gesture that goes with this – holding a hand to your heart for example. Always take a couple of moments to watch your breathing to settle into the Stop Moment and give yourself another moment at the end.

The best strategy would be for you to design your own, using language you can feel comfortable with. Here is something that I use, just to give you an idea and spark your creativity.

Where I find myself now is stressful and challenging

Feeling like this some of the time is part of life

Many people in the world will be going through something similar

I want to be able to give myself the compassion that I need right now, so I can learn from this situation for the future.

This Stop Moment has the following elements:

- acknowledging the stress and leaning into it
- recognising that this is part of being human
- remembering common humanity
- trying for a compassionate response
- seeing that this is an opportunity to learn.

Sometimes, after I have done the Stop Moment several times, I choose one of the phrases to focus on as I go about my day. This can work as a sort of self-compassion mindfulness exercise.

Now have a go at designing your own Self-Compassion Stop Moment

### *Writing yourself a self-compassionate letter*

Another very useful tool for working with your reactions is to write yourself self-compassionate letters.

Sometimes in workshops I gather people's letters in and post them back to them a couple of weeks later. This can be very powerful.

Here are some guidelines for how you might set about writing such a letter to yourself.

Choose the topic that you wish to write about, perhaps something that is worrying you and making you feel bad – perhaps an occasion when you think you did not behave well, or one where you made mistakes.

Now take some time to sit quietly by yourself and compose a letter giving yourself advice. Write it from the point of view of a kind, wise friend who cares for you very much.

As you write, bear in mind that everyone has things about themselves that they are not happy with and would like to change. Think of all the people who are struggling with issues very like the one you are struggling with right now.

Think about events in your life and your conditioning which have contributed to this aspect of yourself that you are worrying about.

Quietly and kindly ask yourself whether there are things you could do to cope better with this aspect of yourself, or this situation. Focus on compassionate advice and constructive change. Avoid any judgement of yourself.

When you have finished the letter put it aside for a while and then come back to it later.

Does it help you? Does it give you any insights that could be useful to you?

If it does, keep it and come back to it again from time to time.

## Three Crunch Points Where Self-compassion Can be Very Useful

### *1. Pushing ourselves too hard*

A common way in which a lack of compassion for ourselves can manifest is how hard we drive ourselves. We tend to make greater demands on ourselves than on anyone else and feel guilty and frustrated when we cannot keep up these unrealistic expectations. The climate of individual achievement and the importance of success that is part of our society fuel this tendency in us. We are brought up to feel that anything is possible but, as life unfolds, if we feel we are not making it all happen as we wish, then we worry that we have let ourselves down.

This is something that can contribute to compassion fatigue, or even burn-out. If we think that our compassion is a finite resource that can become depleted and even exhausted, then it is only a matter of time before we feel that we are giving too much of it away.

We may be able to respond to the suffering and pain we see in others, but often, when faced with our own, we are more likely to tell ourselves not to indulge and to buck up our ideas. We can tell ourselves off about how we look, the way we do our job, the kind of parent we are, our level of competence in the world – this list is endless. One friend of mine often says she feels as if she is carrying her mother around on her shoulder, and she is engaged, all the time, in a running commentary of all the ways my friend should be doing better.

Take a look at four practical ways we can interrupt this cycle of pressure.

| | **How are you going to make it happen?** |
|---|---|
| **Taking exercise**<br>We all know that taking exercise is good for us, but few of us find the time to do much about it. The truth is that exercise helps us to feel better about ourselves – it helps to reduce anxiety and increases production of mood-enhancing hormones. Exercise also stimulates the production of dopamine, which is associated with pleasure, happiness, motivation and interest. When we do things we like, dopamine is released. However, from our teenage years onwards our brain's capacity | |

| | |
|---|---|
| to produce dopamine decreases – it's a case of 'use it or lose it'. Research has shown that low dopamine levels can be associated with various diseases – for example, one of the characteristics of Parkinson's Disease is low dopamine production. Neuroscientific research shows that stress can impair the brain's ability to create new neurons, whereas exercise can promote the growth of neurons.[9] We feel better about ourselves when we take control of our body and our health, instead of just fretting about it and wishing we were a few pounds lighter. | |
| **Making changes in your routine**<br><br>We can be so busy just keeping up with all that we have to do that we may suddenly find our lives have settled into a predictable routine that has lost some its freshness and excitement. If we pay attention to this, and instead of feeling trapped by routine decide to make some changes, then we can reconnect with the moment-by-moment quality of life and feel refreshed. We can do this by looking at our routines and reviewing which of them are necessary and helpful, and which are simply habits that we can change or cut out altogether. It can start with very small things – do you put out your clothes for the next day the night before, or do you wait to see how you feel in the morning and what you would like to wear? Do you always eat the same things for breakfast? Then you could tackle bigger things such as what you usually do at the weekend and where you normally go on holiday. Trying something completely different introduces us to new impressions and experiences that can inspire us. Sometimes our routines are just ways of trying to over-organise our lives and are not really necessary. We can get much more satisfaction from responding to how life is in the present moment. | |

| | |
|---|---|
| **Connecting with friends**<br><br>We discussed this already. Let's make a start by taking out our diaries and looking at the month ahead and seeing where we can fit in at least one social event each week with a friend. | |
| **Making room for gratitude**<br><br>Appreciating what you have in your life and expressing gratitude for it helps us to move from being a glass-is-half-empty kind of person, to a glass-is-half-full kind of person – with all the accompanying benefits to our wellbeing.[10] We can learn to do this by taking the time to notice the things in our lives that are working well and savouring them, rather than shrugging them off and focusing on the things that may not be going so well. Incidentally, research is showing that this helps to reduce our tendencies to adaptation and comparison, two of the ways in which we undermine our happiness that we looked at in Chapter 3. If we are grateful for what we have, it keeps it fresh and we are less likely to take it for granted (adaptation), and if we are happy and contented with what we have then we have no need to compare it to what others have (comparison).[11] | |

## *2. Coping with social media*

We already touched on the internet as a source of stress in Chapter 1. Here we will look at two aspects of social media which are proving to be quite tricky, and how self-compassion can help.

We will start with FOMO – Fear of Missing Out

---

> *Abbreviation for 'fear of missing out': a worried feeling that you may miss exciting events that other people are going to, especially caused by things you see on social media:*
>
> *Cambridge Dictionary (dictionary.cambridge.org, 2020)*

---

We know that as human beings we enjoy social interaction and connection. It matters to us. When we see our friends engaged in all kinds of fun activities, we can feel left out, or unwanted.

People tend to post their most compelling photos online, showing them in the best possible light. We might wonder if we look as good on our photos, or as impressive. No one wants to look at the posts of people feeling a bit down, or – horrors – lonely, so we keep our posts upbeat and 'happy'. This might not reflect how we are actually feeling.

---

> This can work in quite subtle ways. A couple of years back I did some work on stress with undergraduates at one of Amsterdam's international universities. The students were intelligent, motivated and engaged. Their social media posts from their vacations showed them taking part in numerous adventurous and socially aware projects. They shared with me during our sessions that they often felt inadequate about their own plans, after seeing what other people were doing.

---

The second phenomenon is social comparison.

The whole range of social media platforms have rating buttons where you can like, not like and comment on what people post. It is easy – especially for young people – to be affected by the response they get to their posts. If you put up pictures of your birthday celebrations and only get five 'likes' what does that say about your social network? What about your friend, sister-in-law, work colleague who gets eighty-five 'likes'? Does that mean people like her more than you, that she is a better person?

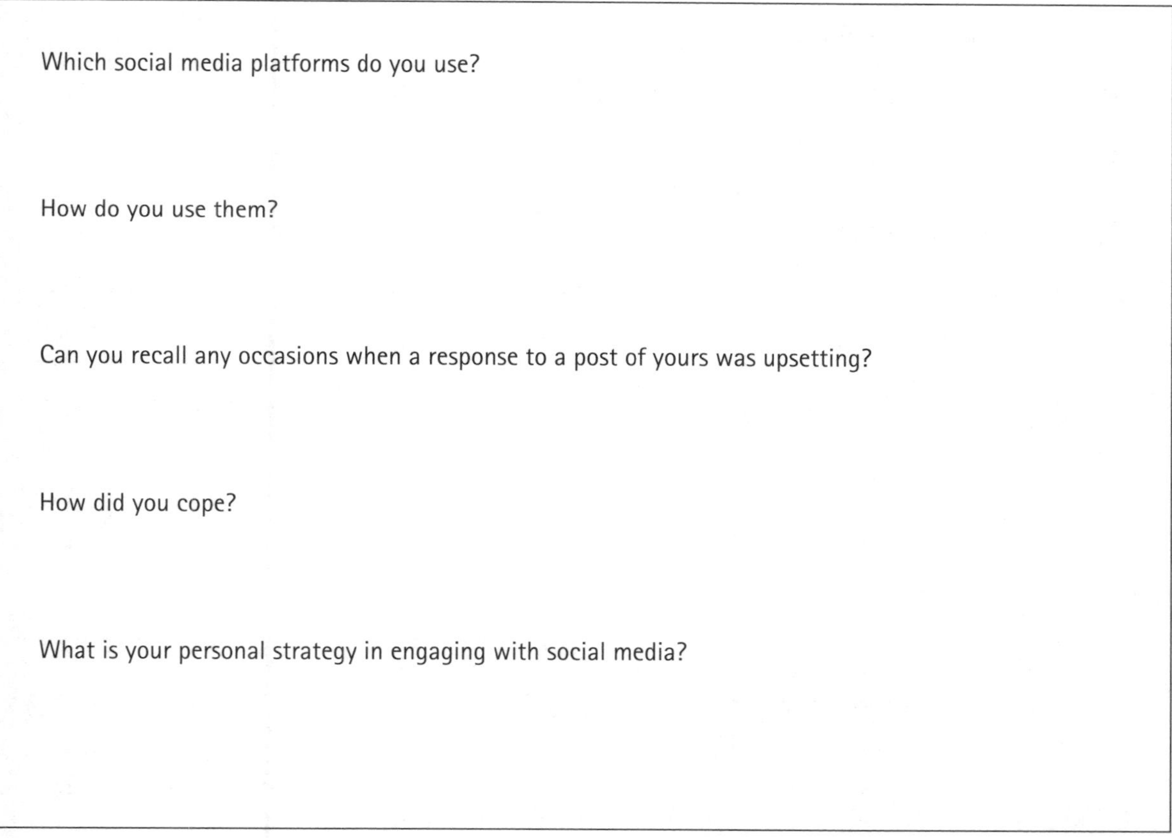

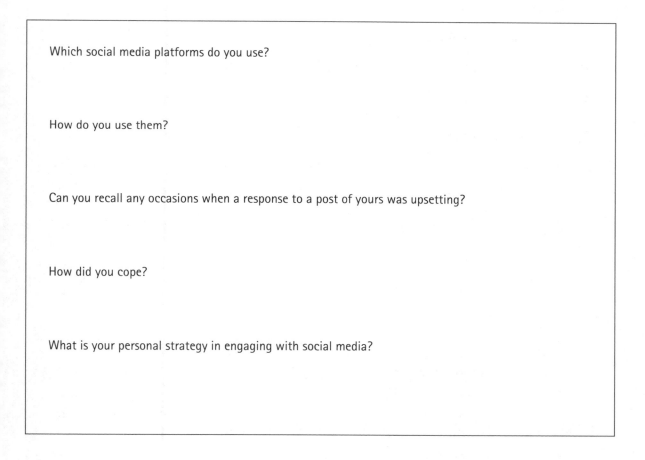

Which social media platforms do you use?

How do you use them?

Can you recall any occasions when a response to a post of yours was upsetting?

How did you cope?

What is your personal strategy in engaging with social media?

The internet is still relatively new and research into its effects is evolving. However, we can plainly see that if we are already feeling in any way low, or not good enough, this can be increased by our engagement with social media. Research shows that our urge to check our social media platforms is linked to a need to experience fast, short-term pleasure, along with dopamine production. (As we have seen, dopamine is a chemical in the brain associated with reward and pleasure.) If these needs are not met, or are thwarted in some way, this can cause us to feel lonely, anxious and dissatisfied.

### TIPS

Self-compassion can help us get this in perspective in the following ways:

- Self-Compassion Stop Moment
- Loving Kindness for ourselves
- Understanding that everyone feels this way some of the time
- Building our resilience

**What would you add?**

You might like to check out these guidelines, called Netiquette, for using the internet. Here is a link: https://www.carolefrancissmith.co.uk/diamondleaf-training/the-netiquette-revolution/

## *3. Handling our emotions*

It is easy to give emotions a bad press and blame them for getting us into trouble, but emotions are a natural part of our human make-up and necessary to help us survive.

For example, if we did not experience feelings of **desire and longing** at some level, we would not feel motivated to get up in the morning and do all the things necessary for our survival.

**Anger** can help us to avoid situations that threaten our safety.

**Pride** can give us the energy and inspiration we need to explore and create.

**It's not the emotions themselves that cause the problem but our reaction to them that can sometimes be excessive** – we just need to watch ourselves quietly cursing the driver who nips ahead of us into a coveted parking space, or the people in the long queue ahead of us in the post office, to realise we can get our emotional reactions out of all proportion.

*As part of our exploration of self-compassion we will look at some exercises to help us work with our emotions.*

### TIP

Knowing what triggers your negative emotions is a good way to give yourself space to prepare.

If we look closely at the times when we experience destructive emotions, we can see that the event can be divided into three stages:

- A *preparatory stage*, which takes place when our peace of mind is under threat.
- The *actual event*, which takes place when our peace of mind has been disturbed and we react.
- The *concluding event*, or the *consequence*, after we have acted from the place of a disturbed mind and things may need to be put right.

If we take an emotional event such as getting angry:

- The *preparatory stage* would be when we feel anger rising in our minds, but we are not yet angry.
- The *actual event* would be when we express our anger, with all that goes with it.
- The *concluding event* would be when we set about trying to sort out what happened and to apologise and heal where necessary.

*We will look at an exercise that we can use to work with each stage of an emotional event to try and stop it escalating to the next stage.*

### *Exercise: Don't go there – recognising what will undo your composure*

- This exercise emphasises the point that we have a choice when dealing with our emotions.
- It is good for working with the first stage of emotion: the preparatory stage.
- It is an effective way of avoiding responding to our emotional triggers by simply not giving them attention.

- One word of caution though – *this exercise is not about avoiding difficult emotions but rather choosing how you wish to react to them.* It is a way of cutting the loops that our mind can get into when we go over and over a problem.
- This is not about avoidance; we are not trying to avoid things because we are too frightened to deal with them, but instead choosing to focus the mind on what is helpful. It is similar to the way that we avoid high-fat foods – not because we are frightened of them, but because we know they are bad for us.

Take the time to identify a specific source of frustration:

It could be at work, for example a coffee machine that never works properly and always irritates you.

It could be in your neighbourhood, for example the noise made by teenagers hanging out late at night.

It could be in your family, for example your husband's habit of placing a new roll of lavatory paper on top of the old empty one instead of replacing it.

Reflect on it for a moment or two, to fix it in the mind.

Decide not to engage with it further – feel really determined about this.

Whenever you are faced with the thought pattern, or circumstances that upset you and cause you stress, say to yourself **'I'm not going there!'**

### TIP

You can also use this for a habit you are trying to break.

I have a friend who prevents herself from getting into gossiping by saying, 'Well, we don't need to go there', whenever the conversation verges on being catty about someone.

### *Exercise: Using the breath – for when our sense of calm is disturbed*

This is the exercise to use for the second stage – the actual event. The emotion has taken hold and our sense of calm is disturbed, but we can still try and not let things go too far.

We can use our breathing to settle the disturbance of the emotion.

The breath has a great capacity to calm and transform emotion and as it is always with us we can use it to good effect.

### *7/11 breathing*

1. Breathe in for a count of 7.
2. Breathe out for a count of 11.

Make sure that when you are breathing in, you are doing deep 'diaphragmatic breathing' (your diaphragm moves down and pushes your stomach out as you take in a breath) rather than shallower, higher lung breathing.

If you find that it's difficult to lengthen your breaths to a count of 11 or 7, then reduce the count to breathing in for 3 and out to 5, or whatever suits you best, **as long as the out-breath is longer than the in-breath.**

### *Exercise: Putting things right – for when you've lost it*

This last exercise is for the third stage when everything has gone wrong and we have made an emotional mess.

Perhaps we have got completely wound up and upset ourselves, or we have acted harshly towards others and caused them pain.

The aim of this exercise is to help you to process what happened, put right what needs to be put right and move on without holding on to negative feelings.

It enables us to forgive ourselves for behaving in a way we regret and to do all we can to learn from the experience.

The exercise uses the breath in the same way as the one earlier in this chapter for working with our stress and anxiety (page 216).

Imagine vividly a situation where you have acted badly; one about which you feel guilty – it's hard to even think about it.

Then, *as you breathe in*, accept total responsibility for your actions in that particular situation, without in any way trying to justify your behaviour. Acknowledge exactly what you have done wrong, and in your mind wholeheartedly ask the other people involved for forgiveness.

Now, *as you breathe out*, send out reconciliation, forgiveness, healing and understanding.

So, you breathe in regret, and breathe out the undoing of harm; you breathe in responsibility, breathe out healing, forgiveness and reconciliation.

We can cause ourselves a lot of unnecessary stress and waste a lot of time feeling bad about messy emotional situations. With this exercise we have a means to deal with all the difficult aspects that we would rather not face. When we do this, we are using compassion and kindness for ourselves to heal our pain and suffering, and, at the same time, enabling ourselves to put things right with the other people involved.

## TIPS

Try out all three of the exercises above.

See how they relate to the different stages of an emotion.

Experiment with using them throughout the day, in informal settings.

Which one works best for you?

## Some Concerns We Might Have About Self-compassion

- Self-compassion can be confused with self-pity. However, self-compassion is about helping us to grow, rather than just feeling sorry for ourselves. Because we no longer try to tune out the bad stuff, self-compassion can make us more willing to accept and acknowledge difficult feelings with kindness. That makes us less likely to get caught in self-pitying thoughts.
- Self-compassion can be confused with self-indulgence. There is nothing wrong with giving ourselves a treat from time to time but if we are focused on wellbeing for ourselves, then we can see that we do need a balance between trying our best and letting ourselves rest and relax.
- It can also be seen as selfish – if we are paying attention to ourselves, is someone else missing out? Ask yourself this: When you are engaged in harsh self-criticism, are you thinking of others at that time? Not really, is the likely answer – we tend to be pretty self-focused at such times. In fact, the compassion we cultivate for ourselves can directly transmit to others.
- Self-compassion can be seen as a way of making excuses for ourselves, a sign of weakness. When we are struggling, we can feel as if being tough and holding ourselves in is the only way to get through. In actual fact, because we see more clearly when we practise self-compassion, it is a safer and more effective way to motivate ourselves and to get the best from ourselves.
- We can worry that without self-criticism we will not be able to motivate ourselves to succeed. Unless we criticise and push ourselves, we are afraid we will get lazy and drop our standards. Remember that self-criticism is a fear-based response and can easily lead to depression, loss of confidence and just wanting to give up. When we give ourselves support and encouragement it actually strengthens and increases our confidence.
- An attachment to self-criticism gives us the illusion that we are in control of ourselves and events – erroneously we think it really is possible to be perfect!
- On the other hand, self-compassion focuses on self-acceptance rather than self-improvement. Contrary to our fears, this does not have to be passive or complacent. The paradox is that when we can fully accept ourselves as we are, then we are seeing ourselves clearly – rather than as we wish ourselves to be. It is when we see ourselves clearly, as we are, that change is truly possible.
- In fact, self-compassion provides a fully supportive environment for change.

## Some Benefits of Self-compassion

### *Increase in happiness*

It comes as no surprise to hear that practising self-compassion can lead to higher levels of happiness. As we have seen, practising compassion in any form will serve to lift the feeling of being locked into our challenges. Once we open to compassion, we open to a heightened sense of awareness of what is going on with others. Caring about other people opens a space in our thinking and turns us away from focusing solely on our difficulties. This broadening effect can help us to feel that there are more possibilities available to us than we thought and so increases our optimism and gratitude for what we have.

### *Decrease in stress*

Perhaps the fundamental reason that self-compassion leads to lower stress levels is that its driving force is love rather than fear. We may feel that the best way to spur ourselves on to achieve what we want is by giving ourselves a stern talking-to and telling ourselves off if we fall behind in our goals. However, as we have seen, the results of this approach are limited and not sustainable over the long term, because of the stress that we cause ourselves – even leading to anxiety and depression.

Self-compassion taps into our kind-heartedness and enables us to apply it to ourselves with greater effect. It does not mean that we no longer wish to achieve but rather that we are less concerned with self-esteem, performance goals and social approval. Instead the wish to achieve is rooted in our sense of personal growth and development. In fact, people who practise self-compassion are more likely to want to change aspects of their behaviour and to take the time to reflect on what those changes should be. Once we have freed ourselves from the tyranny of an unkind inner critic, we find we have more courage and determination to work with ourselves.

### *Deepening of wellbeing*

People who are self-compassionate tend to be less depressed, less anxious and have a more positive outlook. Because self-compassion is not based on social comparison but on the simple fact of being human, it is more stable and reliable when facing difficulties.

## *More engagement with the 'tend and befriend' response to threat*

We know that the neocortex area of the brain developed much later, with the arrival of mammals and the necessity for parents to protect and defend their offspring. Mammals developed a tend-and-befriend response to stress, which meant that they were willing to face danger themselves in order to protect their offspring. Imagine a female tiger fighting off a predator trying to attack her cubs.

In humans, the 'tend' aspect refers to a nurturing response to a child or a person in need. The 'befriend' aspect involves seeking social contact to assist in the tending process.

This response is linked to the hormone oxytocin, the effects of which are enhanced by the predominantly female hormone, oestrogen. Because of the role of these hormones, this response is more often linked with women than with men. Indeed, oxytocin is released when a mother breastfeeds her baby. However, it is also released when parents interact with their children, or if someone receives a tender caress.

When it is activated, we feel more empathy, connection and trust. We experience a greater sense of calmness and safety. Our fear centres are inhibited, and we feel more courageous. So, this response is able to override our basic instinct for survival and avoidance of harm. We need to be fearless at such times and to have the confidence that we can make a difference – otherwise we will not be able to protect those we are trying to help.

Although this system developed to enable us to protect others, it works just as well when we apply it to soothing our own stress, fears and anxieties – we know that thoughts and emotions have the same effect on our bodies whether we direct them towards others, or towards ourselves. So self-compassion could be a powerful trigger for the release of oxytocin, and we can learn to tend and befriend ourselves rather than attacking with self-criticism.

Current neurological research is showing evidence that self-kindness and self-criticism operate differently in the brain. Self-criticism is associated with areas of the brain associated with error-processing and problem-solving. Self-kindness is associated with areas of the brain associated with positive emotions and compassion. Instead of approaching ourselves as a problem to be sorted out, self-kindness encourages us to see ourselves as worthy of care and support.

| What we have learned in this chapter | Your reflections |
|---|---|
| • Meditation practice is the basis of self-compassion.<br>• Self-compassion is important because we can cause ourselves a lot of stress by being very hard on ourselves and beating ourselves up about any mistakes we may make.<br>• Becoming a true friend to ourselves means cutting through the stories that limit us and bring us down and building on our natural capacity for wholeness.<br>• Stress from within our own mind can mean that the fight-or-flight response manifests as self-criticism, self-isolation and getting caught in our own thoughts and feelings.<br>• Self-compassion includes self-kindness, recognising our common humanity and practising mindfulness.<br>• Observing how we interact on social media can give us good clues about how to integrate self-compassion.<br>• While we are working on developing the deeper aspects of self-compassion we can begin by not driving ourselves so hard and making time for activities that enhance our wellbeing.<br>• Working with our emotions will help reduce our stress levels by helping us to feel more in control.<br>• An emotional episode can be divided into three stages: the preparatory stage, the actual event and the consequences. There is something we can do at each stage. | |

## TIPS TO TAKE INTO EVERYDAY LIFE

1. Cultivate awareness of how your inner critic functions.
2. Experiment with simple ways to interrupt it.
3. Practise Self-Compassion Stop Moments.
4. Take on one of the four practical things you can do for each of the following four weeks.
5. Try out the three strategies for working with emotions while you go about your day.
6. Strengthen your meditation practice.

# 9 Compassion for Others – Removing Our Armour

*Compassion doesn't mean feeling sorry for people. It doesn't mean pity. It means putting yourself in the position of the other, learning about the other.*

*Karen Armstrong*[1]

---

What we are going to do in this chapter:

1. Explore how practising compassion for others helps us with our own stress levels
2. Ask ourselves when we cause harm
3. Look into melting our resistance to compassion
4. Learn meditations to help with this

---

When you think about it, engaging in compassion for others is the most effective way of ensuring a peaceful and stable world. If each of us took as our guiding principle that whatever action we take to benefit ourselves should also benefit others, we would have no need of police forces, armies or defence systems. Although this no doubt sounds idealistic, we can begin to work towards such a transformation right now by paying attention to how we relate to other people and benefiting from the effect this will have on all our lives.

We have said that compassion is having the wish that everyone becomes free of suffering, along with the willingness to help bring that about. So, compassion is based on our ability to identify with other people, as well as our willingness to help them in any way we can. When we are working with compassion for ourselves, we learn to accept ourselves as we are and try to offer ourselves kindness and understanding. It works in the same way when we engage in compassion for other people. Compassion is not dependent on whether or not people are shaping up to our expectations or standards but is a response to their suffering without judgement. It is not an easy process. It requires courage and daring as it goes against much of the way we have been conditioned and means we need to learn some new ways of relating to other people.

This is why the subtitle of this chapter is *removing our armour*. As we learn to develop compassion for other people, we will find that we need to undo many of the protective mechanisms we hold on to – such as fighting our corner or automatically putting our own point of view first. We do this in the mistaken belief that these strategies will help us and keep us safe. Defending and protecting ourselves takes a lot of effort and because it is impossible to do it effectively all the time, the effort we put into trying can become a source of stress. If we can replace this constant effort to defend ourselves with a sense of trust in our own fundamental wellness and capacity for thinking of others, then we have a more reliable basis from which to tackle stress because we are not forcing anything.

A few years ago, I gave a two-day training session on compassion fatigue and burnout for palliative care nurses in Majorca. They were wonderful people, dedicated to their work and deeply caring. They dealt with human suffering and pain on a daily basis and had stories to tell that were heartbreaking to hear. However, **they claimed that they coped with the obvious stresses of their jobs by making a separation between their work and the rest of their lives.**

One experienced nurse described this as like changing the chip in her mobile phone – one chip connected her phone at work, and the other connected her phone at home. She did not want the two to connect to each other because she did not want to take her concern for her patients home with her. She felt that would undermine her recovery period at home, intrude on her peace of mind and interfere with her family life. For her, compassion meant making a definite separation between what she needed and the needs of others.

What struck me was that she was setting herself up for compassion fatigue by seeing her compassion as a finite commodity, and her peace of mind as something that needed defending. As we will explore in this chapter, compassion shows us that we are stronger, happier and more able to work with our stress when we remove these limitations from our attitude and our actions.

> **TIP**
>
> Ask yourself how you feel about the nurses' attitude.
>
> Where are you at with being able to remove your armour from time to time?

In Chapter 2 we looked at how the development of compassion is a gradual process incorporating the following stages:

- Trying not to cause harm.
- Melting the ice in your heart.
- Seeing other people as just like you.
- Putting yourself in the other person's shoes.
- Seeing others as more important than yourself.

In the last chapter, we looked at not causing harm to ourselves by beating ourselves up and being harshly critical. We also went into detail about the importance of caring for oneself and showing kindness to oneself, and so melting the ice in our hearts. In this chapter, we will revisit both these stages in the light of compassion for other people, as well as going through the third stage: Seeing other people as just like you.

## How Will Developing Compassion for Other People Help Me Reduce My Levels of Stress?

Perhaps you are wondering how developing compassion for other people is going to help your stress levels – isn't it more likely to make them worse?

It is not common in our society to connect healing oneself with concern for others – in fact, when we are feeling stressed and over-stretched our tendency can be to turn inwards and focus more attention on our own situation. However, most of the time this does not help us to feel better. Instead it serves to intensify our problems.

Let's look at this a bit more closely.

| When we practise compassion | My insights |
|---|---|
| • When we try to engage with compassion, we are connecting with a part of our deepest nature – our fundamental wholeness and wellbeing. Automatically we tap into the richest and most effective parts of our self – so, as we work with others, we are working with ourselves at the same time.<br>• We have a natural capacity for compassion; it is part of who we are. As we learn to express this, it is as if an inner door in our heart opens and we can communicate more directly and effectively. Stress, on the other hand, can have the effect of closing this inner door as we seek to defeat any threat to our wellbeing, and we tighten up as we try to do so.<br>• We have seen that compassion involves using constructive emotions such as love, kindness, patience, tolerance and forgiveness. Constructive emotions, unlike destructive ones, enhance our peace of mind and contribute to the development of lasting happiness. So, by being compassionate we are engaging with behaviour that is *beneficial* to our wellbeing. By being willing to be available to others, we are automatically taking care of ourselves and behaving in ways that will reduce our own stress responses.<br>• When we can make the connection between our own difficulties and the difficulties of others, this allows us to recognise these difficulties as part of the human experience. When we show compassion, we are acting in accordance with our understanding of the deep interconnectedness between ourselves and other people and the knowledge that we all experience stress, suffering and pain at various times in our lives. This helps to reduce the intensity of our own feelings of stress and to see things from a wider perspective. | |

*Let's look at a possible scenario to try this out.*

If your boss at work stresses you out because she seems to be a bully who doesn't appreciate your efforts, you could well feel resentful, frustrated and even angry. All these emotions disturb your peace of mind and make you feel wretched.

Say you decide to turn this around by trying to practise patience instead of frustration and resentment, and by going out of your way to be friendly and cooperative instead of angry. When you do this, you are engaging with compassion for her and benefiting yourself in the process. By replacing painful emotions with compassionate ones, you can reduce your stress and feel more satisfaction with how you are handling the situation. You have taken matters into your own hands rather than simply reacting in a defensive way.

Furthermore, we can see this as a process of inner disarmament – the disarming of our destructive emotions – which in turn helps to disarm the outer situation we find ourselves in. It is like the practice of non-violence and it comes about by trying not to cause harm and instead showing compassion towards others.

It can also help to spare a thought for how her life is and why she may behave as she does. The chances are that she is just trying her best to do her job well and perhaps feels pressurised and anxious. Maybe you appear threatening to her and so she overreacts, so if you show more friendliness it will help soothe her fears. A compassionate attitude creates the space for this kind of reflection and gives us a choice as to how we wish to behave.

## The Science Backs this Up

We have already seen that the part of the brain called the **amygdala** is activated in response to a perceived threat, but research is now showing that the extent of this activity is modified when we can transform destructive emotions into constructive ones and engage in compassion.

A similar reaction has been detected in the case of **the hormone cortisol**, which is released during the fight-or-flight response. Cortisol has a natural daily cycle of production – peaking in the early morning with the sunrise and tapering off after sunset – which dictates when our body should be active and when it is time to rest. Anyone who has experienced jetlag will know how it feels when this cycle is disrupted. In people who are good at transforming destructive emotions, the natural low level of the hormone in the evening is especially low. This also indicates that they will be more effective in reducing stress – it suggests that if we can work with our own negativity, we can contribute to keeping our cortisol levels down. There is an area towards the front of the brain called the **ventromedial pre-frontal cortex**, which is involved in emotion regulation and decision-making. Not surprisingly, people with higher activity in this area of the brain also have a lower level of cortisol in the evening.[2]

All the evidence shows that practising compassion is good for us. By connecting us with our inner source of wellbeing it enables us to heal ourselves while being open to the feelings of others. Contrary to the popular belief that compassion is demanding for us and may cause us to deplete our resources, it is an opportunity to work with ourselves effectively from a sustainable basis. This is worth remembering when it seems hard to be compassionate – which it certainly does sometimes. We have seen that the development of compassion is a gradual process that starts from our current position and then increases step by step as we feel ready to take on more. If we feel inspired to practise compassion in the first place because it is good for us, this is called being **'wisely selfish'**. A lot of the time we are just selfish, but when we recognise that compassion will help us in reducing stress it represents a start in the development of compassion that can grow from strength to strength as we experience its benefits.

## Not Harming

Very few people would deliberately set out to cause another person harm and yet, in many small and unconscious ways, we sometimes do. We can be quite quick to strike out with our thoughts.

For example:

- Deciding we don't like someone we have just met
- Having angry thoughts about an inconsiderate driver
- Blaming a colleague for a work problem

We can be impatient in the supermarket when someone is slow in the queue. If someone annoys us, do we stop to allow them the benefit of the doubt?

Quite often we hardly realise that our behaviour can cause harm. Stress will make the tendency more pronounced and cloud our perception of how we react.

Read this story from Claire, a woman in her late forties who does volunteer work for a local charity. She is happy to do it, but from time to time the pressure of her other commitments becomes intense and she relies on good management from the team in order to maximise her time and contribution.

Recently, one of her routine jobs had come up at a time when her line manager was under a lot of pressure from another project and was less efficient than usual. Claire started on the task but halfway through got the feeling that she was duplicating work that had already been done. She asked her line manager for advice by email but got no response. She investigated further on her own initiative and found that she was right, and time was being wasted.

Claire confessed that at the time she was feeling quite stressed, as she had a lot on besides this volunteer job, and she felt badly let down by her manager. She said she felt justified in being frustrated and angry with her. She found herself being critical and annoyed, and felt put out and taken for granted. This went on for several days until she received an email from her line manager who shared her regret at what happened. Her line manager also confessed that she herself was finding her voluntary commitment too much but couldn't find anyone else to take it on. Claire said that hearing how things were just as difficult for her manager as for herself helped her to see she was being judgemental and critical. Once she saw this, she was able to drop the issue and immediately felt better. She ended up feeling grateful for the manager's attempt to take the blame for what was happening and so remove the harm from the situation. It enabled her to stop 'harming' her manager with criticism and so reduced her own stressful feelings.

*The pressure Claire was under made her more reactive to the disappointing behaviour of her line manager and reduced her resilience. If the situation had not been defused by her line manager's email,*

*she would have carried that stress forward to her next challenge and been at risk of reactin*
*strongly the next time.*

| Avoiding harming others | My insights |
|---|---|
| Think about any recent events in your life where you found yourself inadvertently causing harm. | |
| Ask yourself if you could have reacted in a different way. | |
| Did you remember that there is a choice to make between going with our stress reaction, or applying a bigger perspective such as seeing the annoyance as simply part of the challenges of life, or giving the person the benefit of the doubt? | |
| Did you ask yourself how you would feel if you were the 'other' person? As we understand the effects of suffering and pain more deeply, we want to avoid contributing to other people's pain. | |
| Were you able to trace the spiral of the stress you experienced from one situation to another? | |

## Melting the Ice in Your Heart

Trying to pay attention to whether or not we are causing harm to ourselves and other people helps us to bring into focus how we are expressing our capacity for compassion. As we learn to do this, our perspective opens up and the defensive measures we put in place to protect ourselves begin to seem less useful than we thought. When we try to practise compassion for other people, we can start by taking the natural concern we have for ourselves and extending it to include others. As we learn to treat ourselves with compassion it becomes easier to want to share a similar process with other people. *This process can be said to be like melting the ice in our heart that keeps our interests separate from the interests of others.*

As I mentioned in Chapter 2, in the Buddhist teachings on compassion there is a set of exercises called the **Four Immeasurables,** which are designed to help with exactly this process. These exercises have been tried and tested by meditators for more than 2,500 years and are a powerful way of helping us to transform our destructive emotions.

The Four Immeasurables are Immeasurable Loving Kindness, Immeasurable Compassion, Immeasurable Joy, and Immeasurable Equanimity (a sense of acceptance of how things are). There is an exercise to do for each one.

### TIPS

You will see that some of the exercises follow a formula:

They begin with developing the quality for yourself.

Then extending it to the people you love,

the people you are fond of,

people you do not have strong feelings for one way or the other

and people you have problems with.

After going through the sequence, the idea is to try and extend the practice as widely as you can.

As we have seen already, practising compassion is based on working with positive, constructive emotions that broaden our perspective, whereas negative, destructive emotions limit us and keep us focused on ourselves. So, these exercises enable us to work on a range of our difficult emotions while at the same time developing compassion for other people. They are a good example of how sharing compassion with other people brings benefit to us as well. Through developing the qualities of these exercises, we are learning to replace the unhelpful habits of destructive emotions with helpful habits of loving kindness, compassion, joy and equanimity. We saw this process is part of the formula for change presented in Chapter 4.

### TIPS

*Loving-kindness* overcomes anger and hatred.

*Compassion* overcomes craving and attachment.

*Joy* overcomes envy and jealousy.

*Equanimity* overcomes ignorance, pride and prejudice.

The exercises are known as 'immeasurable' because there is no limit in sharing them – the idea is to develop these qualities in order to benefit the greatest possible number of people.

We will go through the Immeasurables one by one.

Here is the formula we will use:

- Each section begins with a quote to illustrate the essence of the quality we want to develop.
- Then we will have a definition to clarify what we are talking about.
- We will go through the main elements of what it means to develop this quality.
- Then we will share a practice.
- After the practice we will unpack further advice on how to do it.
- There will be a story to illustrate how the immeasurable can work in everyday life.
- A chance to come up with a story from your own experience.
- Each section will finish with some practical tips to bring it into your activity.

## Immeasurable Equanimity

*A person is a person because he recognizes others as persons.*

*Archbishop Desmond Tutu*[3]

Equanimity is the ability to view other people and the circumstances we find ourselves in without bias – with a sense of acceptance of how things are, rather than according to our likes and dislikes.

It is all about taking a fresh look at our tendency to have preference for our loved ones or things we like to do and to avoid those people and situations that we are indifferent to or do not like.

**Developing equanimity gives us the opportunity to transform our habits of ignorance, pride and prejudice.**

**We could see this as ignorance of the interconnectedness both of how things are and between us and other people – one of the habits of stress we identified in Chapter 6.**

If we really take this to heart, how can we instantly like some people and feel only dislike for others?

**Pride comes when we favour our own country, our own friends, the people who agree with us and so on.**

**Prejudice is when we are not willing to listen to the needs of people outside our own circle.**

With equanimity we recognise ourselves and everybody else as a person worthy of attention and respect. We can learn to face the circumstances of life with more patience and detachment, which allows us to feel more at ease. This brings a corresponding reduction in our stress levels.

ASK YOURSELF: How do you get on with equanimity? Is it a quality that comes naturally to you, or is it something you need to work on?

### Exercise: Developing equanimity

Close your eyes.

Imagine you are sitting on a chair.

On your right side is a good friend.

On your left side is a person who is challenging for you.

Reflect on the following points:

*Your friend*

Have you always had the affection for this person you have now?

Does this person ever behave in a way that you don't like?

Can you imagine them doing something that would prevent you continuing as friends?

*Your challenging person*

Have you always experienced this person as challenging?

Does this person ever behave in a way that touches you?

Can you imagine them doing something that would enable you to become friends?

Make notes of what you discover.

This exercise is quite easy to do and helps us to question the assumptions we make about people. Even the people we love can behave in ways we do not like, and if we give them a chance, people we think we do not like can surprise us by behaving in a pleasant and friendly way.

Relationships can change, as anyone who has been through a divorce will know. At the very moment that someone agrees to marry another person and is full of love for them, the seeds can be there for the ultimate collapse of the relationship.

In the same way, first impressions can be misleading and if someone we thought we did not like shows us kindness then often our attitude towards them will change.

*Doing this simple exercise can help us to develop a greater awareness of how fluid relationships are and how no one is purely lovable, or purely unlovable.* If we can do it with one or two other people, it will help when we look at our prejudices on a wider scale – people who do not share our views, people we see as causing harm and so on.

Remembering the sequence that was just mentioned, we could try to develop equanimity for all our family members, then all our friends, then the people at work, then in our community – pushing the limits further and further out as we feel more confident. We don't have to rush it, just go at our own pace.

I am often reminded of my experience with a CEO of a voluntary organisation in the UK who attended a long training session I was involved in delivering. Let's call him Steve. In the early sessions of the training I found Steve quite exhausting – he had something to say at every stage of the day and seemed to have no idea about how much of the group time he took up. He would talk for ages about his own relationship to what we were discussing and whenever I managed to include someone else in the discussion he would come in again and respond to their comments as well!

It took me a few sessions to see that Steve was actually connecting deeply with the material and was moved and excited to the extent that he could not stop talking about it. He had no intention of dominating – he was simply thirsty for information and experience. Once I realised this it became easier to see how to handle his input because I could do it from a basis of understanding rather than irritation. The discipline required by my role as trainer ensured that Steve never knew I had ever felt any impatience with him, but in the cut and thrust of ordinary interaction we do not usually have those safeguards.

We need to learn to give people the benefit of the doubt and allow time for a good rapport to develop, instead of jumping to a position of like or dislike that we then defend and solidify.

Can you think of a story from your recent experience that brings this alive for you?

### TIPS

Defending people we like and dealing with people we do not like can cause us a lot of stress.

Equanimity can help us cut through our stress responses by enabling us to see people from a different, less threatening perspective.

## Immeasurable Loving Kindness

*Constant kindness can accomplish much. As the sun makes ice melt, kindness causes misunderstanding, mistrust, and hostility to evaporate.*

*Albert Schweitzer*[4]

Loving kindness is about wishing everyone to have happiness and all the causes of happiness.

Remember in Chapter 3 when we explored lasting happiness and its power to benefit those who experience it? When we focus on generating loving kindness for other people this is what we want to share with them.

**Not surprisingly, loving kindness is the antidote to anger and hatred – it is hard to wish someone lasting happiness and be angry with them at the same time.**

Here we have an opportunity to transform the habits of anger and hatred, which we have seen tend to cause us unhappiness, and replace them with loving kindness.

Research into the causes of heart disease show a correlation between hostility and heart disease.[5] In addition, research also shows that an attitude to life that is very focused on oneself and one's own interests contributes to stress and a greater likelihood of heart disease. People tested who used the terms *me* and *mine* frequently in their conversation had a greater tendency to anger and high blood pressure.[6]

The good news is that research is also showing that changes in behaviour that result in a reduction of hostility can help to reverse this process of deterioration in the heart.[7]

Behaviours such as consideration for others and showing kindness and love featured highly in this process.

Generating loving kindness can help us to soften our attitude and disarm our anger and hostility, thereby reducing our stress levels and increasing our sense of wellbeing.

ASK YOURSELF: How do you get on with loving kindness? Is it a quality that comes naturally to you, or is it something you need to work on?

We can see this clearly when we look at the importance of forgiveness. When we hold a grudge against someone because they have caused us pain, not only are we preventing them from making amends, but we are causing harm to ourselves at the same time. Research shows that when we just think of a person or group that we feel has treated us badly, our body responds with pent-up anger. Our system is flooded with stress hormones, and our blood pressure rises. Each time we feel this way, the same damaging response occurs. Forgiveness reverses this process and lowers our blood pressure, heart rate and levels of stress hormones.[8]

*In his extraordinary book, I Shall Not Hate,[9] Palestinian doctor Izzeldin Abuelaish recounts the story of his determination not to surrender to feelings of hatred after three of his daughters were killed in an Israeli airstrike on the Gaza strip where he lived with his family. He wanted to honour his daughters by transforming the tragedy of their deaths into an opportunity for dialogue and peace, rather than them simply becoming another statistic of anger and revenge.*

On his release from prison, Nelson Mandela in *Long Walk to Freedom*[10] expressed a similar wish to transform his anger and hatred in order to be free of it and to use his experience creatively:

> *As I walked out the door toward the gate that would lead to my freedom, I knew if I didn't leave my bitterness and hatred behind, I'd still be in prison.*

When we are unable to forgive, we deny the person or people who have hurt us the possibility of changing and reconciling with us. We also deny ourselves the benefits of forgiveness and reconciliation.

We give up our faith in the future of the relationship and maintain a painful division between friend and enemy. This locks us into a stressful, defensive position that keeps us in a prison of conflicting emotion.

Some years ago, a friend of mine suffered a painful and protracted divorce. Her husband had become emotionally unstable and developed an alcohol problem, which meant he often behaved in a way that was frightening for her and her daughters. When the divorce was finally over, my friend had no wish to hear news of her ex-husband – although she did not stop her daughters seeing him if they wished. She remained hurt and angry.

Recently her eldest daughter died tragically – an event that shook the whole family. My friend's ex-husband suffered a breakdown and could not attend the funeral.

Sometime later my friend told me that she was visiting her daughter's grave and her ex-husband turned up and joined her by the graveside. She said that seeing his grief close up softened her own heart and they sat together and talked for the first time in years about their time together, the children they had borne and their affection for each other.

My friend said that she felt a huge relief as her anger and resentment ebbed away and she could see her ex-husband as an ordinary man – sad and alone – rather than a monster. It took a terrible tragedy to help her drop her hostility, but when she was able to do so it brought her ease in the midst of her grief.

Here is the exercise we can do to help us develop loving kindness.

### *Exercise: Loving Kindness Meditation*

Settle your mind.

Think of a time when you have felt fully loved by someone or think of a person that symbolises love for you, for example Mother Teresa, the Dalai Lama, your grandmother, a favourite singer and so on. We can either use the memory of this feeling from the past to spark that feeling in us in the present, or we can use the inspiration of a compassionate figure.

Allow the memory, or inspiration, of this love to nourish you, so that you yourself feel full of love, worthy of love and able to offer love.

Connect with the feeling of gratitude for having known this love and the wish to share it with others, so that they can benefit also.

Say to yourself several times, 'May I be well and happy, may I be well and happy . . .' The key here is not just the words but trying to contact your heartfelt wish for this to happen; put as much kindness and warmth as you can into the words as you say them in your mind so that they are not just words but help to focus your compassion *feelings*.

Now think of someone that you love very much and imagine that the immeasurable love flowing from your own heart enters theirs and fills them with loving kindness.

Say to them, 'May you be well and happy, may you be well and happy . . .'

Now think of a friend that you are fond of and again imagine the immeasurable love flowing from your own heart enters theirs and fills them with loving kindness.

Say to them, 'May you be well and happy, may you be well and happy . . .'

Now, think of someone that you have neutral feelings towards, or to whom you are indifferent, and in the same way imagine the immeasurable love flowing from your own heart enters theirs and fills them with loving kindness.

Say to them, 'May you be well and happy, may you be well and happy . . .'

Now, think of someone that you find difficult and in exactly the same way imagine the immeasurable love flowing from your own heart enters theirs and fills them with loving kindness.

Say to them, 'May you be well and happy, may you be well and happy . . .'

Consider that the feelings of love in you continue to grow, so that you can wish happiness and wellbeing to all the people you have already brought to mind.

Try to extend this circle of love wider and wider . . .

Remember that the sun shines on everyone in the world, whoever they are, whatever they have done – our loving kindness is just like the sun in that it can touch anyone and everyone.

Drop the visualisation and sit with this feeling for a few moments.

A key thing to remember when you do this exercise is that the loving kindness you are generating in your heart is *immeasurable,* without limit – it will not get exhausted, or worn out.

We start with ourselves so we can get in touch with our natural capacity for love and kindness and really bring it out.

Then we can even direct it towards people we find challenging and eventually towards people we have not even met.

The phrases, 'May you be happy, may you be well', can be used to remind yourself of the practice in everyday life situations. I like to repeat them when I am among crowds at an airport or passing by lots of drivers on a motorway.

*This is how Matt, a primary school teacher, uses the phrases at work:*

When I'm in tense, stressful situations involving people being very angry and upset, I try to cope with it by reciting silently to myself, 'May you be happy, may you be well'. I find when I do this, I am more able to listen to their pain and hurt rather than taking it personally. This gives them space to air their issues and enables me to not react but instead to respond to them in a creative way. This approach I found helps de-escalate heightened emotions and therefore we can move forward in resolving the underlying issues.

We can see clearly here how by using the exercise even in a very simple way, Matt is able to defuse difficult interactions at work and at the same time reduce his own stress and increase his effectiveness. He can do this because it feels so much better to give love, rather than anger and resentment – when we are engaged in being kind and loving we are more well in ourselves and experience less stress. This enables us to attract more kindness and affection towards ourselves, so it becomes a mutually beneficial dynamic. We have seen that social support is a big factor in dealing with stress and that a strong friendship network is an important factor in our wellbeing. Having this kind of support nourishes us and reduces our tendency to offload our frustrations on others.

Can you think of a story from your recent experience that brings this alive for you?

In his book, *The Happiness Hypothesis,*[11] Jonathan Haidt, Professor of Psychology at the University of Virginia, has coined the term 'elevation' to describe the mutually enhancing beneficial effects of acts of love and kindness. Research has already shown that people who regularly engage in acts of kindness are happier, but Haidt claims that the effect goes further – we benefit from witnessing another person perform an act of kindness, or compassion, even if it is not directed at us. When this happens, our mood is 'elevated' with hope, inspiration and optimism – and this feeling is contagious, affecting anyone who comes into contact with us.

### TIPS

- Take this practice gently to begin with – you don't need to go through all the sections every time.
- Find as many opportunities as you can to use the phrases – that will help build a relationship with the practice.

## Immeasurable Compassion

*Until he extends his circle of compassion to include all living things, man will not himself find peace.*

*Albert Schweitzer*[12]

Immeasurable Compassion here is the wish for everyone to be free of suffering and pain.

You may be surprised to find the word compassion used here, as we have been using it in a larger sense than one specific context. Remember that the Buddhist approach to training in compassion goes step by step. So, at this stage of removing the ice in our hearts through practising the immeasurables, compassion features as one of the four.

**Immeasurable compassion is the antidote to craving and attachment** – so here we have an opportunity to transform these potential sources of stress and replace them with a helpful habit.

When we crave a person, or object or lifestyle, we tend to exaggerate its positive side and view it as essential for our happiness. This view is based on self-centredness, a narrow wish to have perfect circumstances for ourselves.

Even if we manage to obtain the goal of our craving, we rarely find the satisfaction we hoped for because possessing it brings its own problems – we fear that it may be taken away from us; it does not live up to our expectations and we are disappointed in it, or we feel we have to guard it jealously.

Generating immeasurable compassion and wishing people to be free from suffering reverses these tendencies. When we looked at the beneficial effects of volunteering in Chapter 7, we saw how helping other people with their problems helped the volunteers themselves.

Being able to connect with other people and their suffering makes us feel better about ourselves and counterbalances the stress we may incur by simply pursuing our own cravings. It softens our hearts, enabling us to care more deeply and so be less likely to cause harm to others.

This attitude is a basis for compassionate action – not only the wish for people to be free from suffering but the willingness to do something about it.

### *Exercise: Compassion meditation*

Here is an exercise for developing Immeasurable Compassion.

Settle your mind.

Allow yourself some time to connect with your own suffering and pain by thinking of a time in your life when you were having a difficult time.

Say to yourself, 'May I be free from suffering and pain, may I be free from suffering and pain . . .'

Think of someone you love who is dealing with suffering and pain.

Say to them, 'May you be free from suffering and pain, may you be free from suffering and pain . . .'

Think of someone close to you who is dealing with suffering or unhappiness – a friend, perhaps, or someone at work.

Say to them, 'May you be free from suffering and pain, may you be free from suffering and pain . . .'

Think of someone that you have neutral feelings towards, or who you are indifferent to and try to create the same wish that they may be free from suffering.

Say to them, 'May you be free from suffering and pain, may you be free from suffering and pain . . .'

Now think of a person that you find challenging and who is dealing with suffering and pain.

Say to them, 'May you be free from suffering and pain, may you be free from suffering and pain . . .'

Try to extend this circle of compassion wider and wider . . .

Drop the visualisation and sit with the feeling for a few moments

This is an exercise that I often do when I am watching the news. If you are like me, you may find the evening news an intense time of the day. It is easy to feel overwhelmed by the plight of some of the people we see on our TV screens. It is then that I find simply wishing that all the people involved in the news stories of the evening be free from suffering and pain at least helps me to feel a connection with what they go through and keeps my heart accessible, rather than becoming hidden behind a protective cover of cynicism.

Can you think of a story from your recent experience that brings this alive for you?

## TIPS

- It is good to do the whole practice, but you can also take a section that relates to a particular person or situation in your life and practise that section regularly.
- This is a great practice to do on your commute, or in an airport. Look for people who seem burdened and mentally practice this for them.

## Immeasurable Joy

*Find a place inside where there's joy, and the joy will burn out the pain.*

*Joseph Campbell*[13]

Immeasurable Joy is to rejoice in other people's happiness, good health, accomplishments and prosperity. There is a suggestion of seeing the good in others and learning to admire that.

**Generating joyfulness in the wellbeing of others is the antidote to jealousy – by developing joy in life both for our own situation and for the situation of others we can transform our unhelpful habits of jealousy.**

Being able to savour what we have in life, to express gratitude for our good fortune, and to appreciate the qualities of other people are all factors that can add to a sense of joy.

When we are feeling low or experiencing stress it is easy to feel a bit sorry for ourselves. Then hearing of another person's success, or good fortune can make us feel a bit envious. Immeasurable joy is about allowing ourselves the freedom to be happy for another person, without grasping at it for ourselves.

As we rejoice in another person's happiness, we can use it to wish the same for everyone – that this person's good fortune should spread to many other people.

We can find ourselves waiting for a successful outcome for a project we are working on, or looking forward to a holiday, or anticipating a new job – all of this can get in the way of simply connecting with the joy of the present moment. It helps to slow things down and take time to rejoice in a piece of good news we hear, or to enjoy the beauty of our surroundings – or even to appreciate our own good qualities.

An optimistic, joyful attitude to life in general can act as a buffer against stress arousal because a joyful person does not have the habit of perceiving every potentially stressful situation as a threat – their amygdala (see page 17) has not become hyperactive due to being constantly stimulated.

In Chapter 7, we looked into the evolutionary pattern of always seeing the negative side of a situation first and allowing its effect to last longer than any positive aspects – joyful people are at an advantage in dealing with this because of their less reactive amygdala.

Furthermore, when we have to deal with a difficult situation a joyful attitude can help us count our blessings even in the face of adversity. It enables us to reinterpret stressful situations positively so that we can adjust to them, and move on, learning what we can along the way.

Below is an exercise that aims to help you develop immeasurable joy. The point here is to focus on feeling delight in every kind of happiness that the people you bring to mind are enjoying. We can try to try to drop our habit of resenting someone else being happy, successful or well off and wishing it was us instead of them.

### *Exercise: Meditation on joy*

Sit quietly and settle your mind.

Bring to mind someone who is prosperous, powerful, intelligent and enjoys good health, with many friends, good circumstances and plenty of comfort and happiness – someone who in your opinion has a life other people would dream of.

Without any feeling of jealousy, or rivalry, wish them even more of all these good things.

Then reflect on how wonderful it would be if everyone could enjoy circumstances like these.

Firstly, imagine someone that you love enjoying all these benefits and allow yourself to feel joy for them.

Next do the same for a good friend and allow yourself to feel joy for them.

Now imagine someone you have no special feelings for enjoying all these benefits and allow yourself to feel joy for them.

Finally, imagine someone who is challenging for you enjoying all these benefits and allow yourself to feel joy for them.

Try to extend this circle of joy wider and wider . . .

Drop the visualisation and sit with the feeling for a few moments.

It is hard to feel this kind of joy for other people if we feel that their good fortune in some way encroaches on our territory – that somehow it should be us rather than them. Jealousy is like a combination of craving and hatred – we want good things for ourselves so badly that we feel negative towards anyone else who has them. We can undermine our jealousy by looking more closely at exactly what we are jealous of and by realising how fragile good fortune at times can be.

A close friend of mine was diagnosed with cancer a couple of years ago. He immediately had to undergo routine tests to see if the cancer was contained, or if it had spread. When he was told that there was no spreading, he said he experienced overwhelming joy, which seemed surprising when he still had all the surgery and treatment ahead of him. He explained that having some good news to rejoice in, gave him a lot of energy to face what lay ahead, and to examine his habits of pushing himself too hard, which he believed had contributed to his becoming ill.

Can you think of a story from your recent experience that brings this alive for you?

### TIPS

- As with the previous three immeasurables, we can focus on any one section of the practice to fit in with a person or situation we want to focus on.
- Try to remember this practice as you go about your day and see people who have the potential to inspire envy in you.

## Seeing Other People as Just Like You

*If we could read the secret history of our enemies we should find in each man's life sorrow and suffering enough to disarm all hostility.*

*Henry Wadsworth Longfellow*[14]

The basis of seeing people as just like you is remembering that everyone wants to be happy and to avoid pain and suffering. We could also add to this the essence of what we covered in Chapter 3 – that although we may wish for happiness, finding lasting happiness is not easy, and in the meantime, suffering and pain come along as an inevitable part of the difficulties of life. Just as we experience this in our own lives, so does every other person on the planet – so, in that sense, we can view other people as being 'just like us'.

This may seem relatively straightforward when we are dealing with friends and loved ones but becomes increasingly demanding as we widen the circle to include people we do not see eye to eye with and even dislike.

Greg, a social worker, tries to use this perspective in spite of the sometimes perplexing behaviour of his work colleagues:

> The approach to my work is the belief that everyone is doing their best given their set of circumstances. Their underlying wish is to be happy – even if the way they are going about it can be very dysfunctional. This enables me to be more compassionate towards them because they are just like me, just another me.

This is a sensible and pragmatic view – we can see that other people may not behave as we want them to but at the same time, we can recognise that their behaviour simply comes from wanting to be happy. We do not need to take it personally.

In fact, with a bit effort we can even imagine that our own behaviour can seem odd to other people on occasion and yet we know we are just trying our best!

The exercises of the Four Immeasurables create the basis for this attitude. By helping us connect with the wellspring of love, kindness, joy and compassion within us, our attitude becomes softer and more tolerant. The more we are able to extend that innate feeling and the more people we can embrace within it, the more possible it becomes to see other people as being just like us. Just as we try to include challenging people within the immeasurable exercises, so we can use the perspective of our basic similarity even with people we find difficult.

I had a small but interesting reminder of this recently. I have become hooked on a 'reality' singing competition on TV. As is usual with these sorts of programmes, my partner and I have our favourite singers and ones we don't like so much. When I watched an episode recently, one man that I had been finding quite irritating was facing going out of the competition. As I watched his face and listened to his interview about how he was feeling, it came to me so strongly that he was not irritating at all – he simply really wanted this to go well for him, just as I would have done if I were in his situation. It reminded me strongly of how easy it is to make a separation between oneself and others and how unhelpful that can be.

Even people we may think that we do not like are just like us underneath – sharing the same hopes and fears. As Longfellow says in the quote at the beginning of this section, remembering this can indeed help to disarm our hostility towards them.

The exercise below will help you to see another person as just another 'you'.

*Exercise: Seeing another person as just like you*

Sit for a few moments and settle your mind.

Consider how everyone wishes to have happiness and to avoid suffering.

Bring to mind someone you know and think about them in this context.

Reflect on how, just like you, they simply wish to be happy.

Reflect on how, just like you, they wish to avoid suffering.

Try to experience them as another 'you'.

Reflect on what effect this has on your perception of them.

Sit again.

Make a note of what you realise.

## Empathy

In Chapter 2 we talked about the recent discovery of what scientists call 'mirror neurons'. We saw that these neurons enable us to understand the meaning of the actions of other people, the intention behind those actions and the emotions they are feeling about them. Our brain is actually built to connect us to other people. This ability to 'feel with' another person is the basis of empathy. It is the impulse that moves us to respond and try to help when we hear a cry of pain or see someone else in trouble.

Empathy can be seen to have three forms:

- Cognitive empathy: *knowing* another person's feelings.
- Emotional empathy: *feeling* what they feel.
- Compassionate empathy: *responding compassionately* to their distress.[15]

Cognitive empathy can help in motivating people to make their best efforts, but if it is not combined with feeling what they feel it can be cold and detached. Politicians can read people's feelings and turn them to their own advantage while not really caring about them very much. So cognitive empathy alone is not enough – we need emotional empathy as well.

However, here again there can be problems – if we feel what is happening to another person too intensely, there is a danger of us becoming emotionally overwhelmed and distressed ourselves. This is why medical practitioners and rescue workers cultivate a positive detachment, so they do not fall apart while trying to help.

If we can turn our understanding of another person's feelings and our feeling for them into compassionate action, then we are combining all the elements of empathy in a constructive and practical way.

### *Obstacles to empathy*[16]

All through this workbook, we have made it a priority to see where our natural expression of compassion can be blocked. With regard to empathy, there are four fundamental social and political barriers:

| **Barriers** | **Antidotes** |
| --- | --- |
| PREJUDICE<br><br>This happens with stereotyping of all kinds – for example, racial, sexual orientation, nationality, social class and wealth. We form all kinds of opinions about the group of people we are encountering and act from those opinions, whether or not they are based on facts. | The antidote is to humanise the other person or persons and to see them as people just like you. |
| AUTHORITY<br><br>When people cite the orders that they have been given or their job description, they are taking refuge in an idea of authority that prevents them from making real contact with the other person. | The antidote is to discover what you share with the other person and what you don't share – to become more personal. |
| DISTANCE<br><br>The further we are from a tragedy or a need, the easier it becomes to block it from our minds. | Here there has been great work done on building empathy circles[17] and empathy cafés to get people of different views talking to each other. It is possible to understand someone else's point of view without agreeing with it. |
| DENIAL<br><br>This can happen as a result of compassion fatigue, or empathy fatigue. We allow ourselves to become immune to the need for compassion. | The antidote can be the practice of putting yourself in the other person's shoes. |

*Think of an example of each of these barriers that you see happening in your own life – show how you could work with the antidotes.*

Prejudice

Authority

Distance

Denial

The study that Army Brigadier General S.L.A. Marshall carried out at the end of the Second World War is a disturbing example of how some of these barriers can be manipulated.

Marshall was asked to set up a study on how soldiers conducted themselves during battle. Marshall was a US Army historian in the Pacific during the War. He had a team of historians working for him and together they carried out research based on individual and group interviews with thousands of soldiers from more than 400 infantry companies immediately after they had been in close combat with German or Japanese troops. The results were a revelation – they showed that only 15 to 20 per cent of American riflemen actually fired their weapons at the enemy. However, those who did not fire did not run away or hide. Instead they risked great danger to rescue comrades, get ammunition or run messages.

These findings were taken seriously by the American military and led to the institution of new training strategies that were designed to enable soldiers to overcome their natural reluctance to kill. These strategies include desensitisation conditioning and denial defence mechanisms. Desensitisation works by using language and images that dehumanise the troops of the opposing army, so it is harder to see them as other human beings and easier to view them as an 'enemy'. Troops are encouraged to see killing the enemy as part of their job and to view the enemy as less than human. Instead of learning to shoot using a static target, soldiers dressed in full combat gear stand in a foxhole and fire at human-shaped targets that pop up in front of them. In this way, the soldiers become more conditioned to the act of shooting to kill. Sometimes the targets are filled with red paint to make the experience of 'killing' them even more realistic. Bill Jordan, a career US Border Patrol officer, explains:[18]

*There is a natural disinclination to pull the trigger when your weapon is pointed at a human. To aid in overcoming this resistance it is helpful if you can will yourself to think of your opponent as a mere target and not as a human being. In this connection you should go further and pick a spot on your target. This will allow better concentration and further remove the human element from your thinking.*

He calls this process 'manufactured contempt' and it describes how denial defence mechanisms work.

Such methods did indeed serve to suppress soldiers' natural empathy towards their opponents, to the extent that by the Korean War 55 per cent of soldiers fired their rifles, and by the Vietnam War this proportion had reached 95 per cent. However, the story does not end there – it is well known now that many of the soldiers who returned from Vietnam were severely traumatised by their experiences, with between 28 and 54 per cent suffering from post-traumatic stress disorder (PTSD).

Modern warfare with its long-range, hands-off methods of killing presents other challenges as it offers even greater opportunity for desensitisation. Modern video games with their graphic on-screen violence could also serve as a kind of conditioning and denial mechanism as they tend to view the opponent as a target rather than a human being.

We can see that empathy is a particularly important skill in our technological age when it is theoretically possible to stay in one's apartment and conduct much of one's life online without ever having to actually meet another human being. We need to make the most of our opportunities to connect with other people and recognise our common humanity in order to maintain our wellbeing. Although we may think that compassion for others is all about helping other people, we have seen in this chapter that actually it helps us at the same time. Compassion for other people lifts us out of a preoccupation with our own affairs and at the same times provides us with ways of working with destructive emotions that cause us unhappiness.

| What we have learned in this chapter | Your reflections |
|---|---|
| • Engaging in compassion for others is the most effective way of ensuring a peaceful and stable world.<br>• It requires courage and daring as it goes against much of our conditioning and means we need to learn some new habits of relating to other people.<br>• We have seen that compassion involves using constructive emotions such as love, kindness, patience, tolerance and forgiveness, which enhance our peace of mind and contribute to the development of lasting happiness. So, by being compassionate we are engaging with behaviour that is beneficial to our wellbeing and will lessen our stress responses.<br>• All the evidence shows that practising compassion is good for us. By connecting us with our source of wellbeing it enables us to heal ourselves while being available for others.<br>• The first step in practising compassion for others is to try and avoid causing harm.<br>• The next stage is melting the ice in our hearts and here we can use the exercises of the Four Immeasurables:<br>  * Immeasurable Loving Kindness, the antidote to anger<br>  * Immeasurable Compassion, the antidote to craving and attachment<br>  * Immeasurable Joy, the antidote to jealousy<br>  * Immeasurable Equanimity, the antidote to ignorance, pride and prejudice<br>• The next stage is seeing others as just like you: remembering that everyone wants to be happy and to avoid pain and suffering.<br>• The basis of this is empathy. | |

## TIPS TO TAKE INTO EVERYDAY LIFE

1. Try to be aware of the times when you are unwittingly causing harm with your thoughts.
2. Check yourself to get a feel of how expressing compassion for others helps raise your own wellbeing levels.
3. Choose the Immeasurable that resonates with you most and try and do the whole exercise at least three times each week.
4. Play with the Four Immeasurables as you go about your day, using the phrases with people you come across.
5. Engage with the Golden Rule (see page 38) to support how you work with the obstacles to empathy.

# 10 Compassion with a Big Perspective – Removing our Blindfold

> *To serve the world out of dynamic union of wisdom and compassion would be to participate most effectively in the preservation of the planet.*
>
> *Sogyal Rinpoche*[1]

What we are going to do in this chapter:

1. Look at compassion from a big perspective
2. Try taking ourselves out of the centre of the action
3. Learn Tonglen practice
4. Take a look at universal responsibility

We have already covered the first three stages in training the mind in compassion, which are:

- Trying not to cause harm.
- Melting the ice in your heart.
- Seeing other people as just like you.

Now we can take a look at the final two stages:

- Putting yourself in the other person's shoes.
- Seeing others as more important than yourself.

We will look into these in this chapter as part of our exploration of compassion with a big perspective. Here, we build on the work we have already done on developing compassion for others and try to take it even further by being willing to actually put ourselves in the shoes of another person – to see things from their perspective. That is why we talk here of 'removing our blindfold' – the last barrier to being willing to understand the importance of seeing things from another person's point of view.

### TIPS

Although we talk of stages in training the mind in compassion, we might not maintain a steady forward momentum in our attempts to develop more compassion. There will be days when we feel low and will fall back. At times our stress might feel so intense that all our energy and courage goes into coping with it. This is completely natural and does not mean that we can't do it, or it is not working. It just means we are human.

Try to be aware of yourself during those times, and when you are feeling stronger, go back and ask yourself where you could have done things differently. Those occasions could turn out to be your most effective learning moments.

## Putting Yourself in the Other Person's Shoes

In the earlier stages of developing compassion, we were still using ourselves as a point of reference for our compassion for others. There is nothing wrong with this, but now, with putting ourselves in another person's shoes, we make a shift and become more willing to take ourselves out of the centre of the picture.

How does this work?

| | |
|---|---|
| When we are working on the earlier stages of developing compassion it is as if we are walking along in the rain with a big umbrella. We want to stay dry and to enable other people to stay dry, too, so we invite them to come under our umbrella. We are in the middle, holding the umbrella, and everyone else is crouching underneath as best they can. | When we put ourselves in the other person's shoes, we hand the umbrella over to someone else and we take our place with everyone else who is crouching underneath for shelter. |

| Can you relate this to situations in your own experience? | Can you relate this to situations in your own experience? |
|---|---|

For most of us this is not something that is easy to do on a daily basis. We have not been brought up to see things from another person's point of view, and society is not set up to support us doing so. It is understandable if we forget to do it from time to time. The thing is to understand *why* it is a good idea both for other people and as a way of reducing our own stress. Once we are clear about this, we will feel more inspired to experiment with it and to try to make a place for it in our dealings with people.

Let's hear from Tom, a middle manager responsible for a large team.

I often find myself in tense meetings with conflicting problems and pressures. What I notice is that when I hold strongly on to my own point of view, it quickly causes me to tighten up, physically fuelling a sense of frustration. But when I remind myself to mentally swap places with someone else – even for a couple of seconds – straight away I can feel something release, my awareness seems to expand and my frustration eases. I definitely hear what is being said more clearly, with more discernment, rather than with a heavy, loaded, judgemental mind. I also find I'm able to present my own point of view with more clarity. However, if I'm honest, I often forget this mental exchange very quickly, especially in a difficult meeting. But I do try and remind myself, again and again, to swap places in my mind. I have noticed when I do, the quality of my interactions with other people does improve, compromises become possible, and relationships with others develop in a more sustainable way.

Let's look at what Tom is actually saying here. Read through the points from his story and add your own observations from your experience.

| Tom's story | Your view |
|---|---|
| • Holding on tightly to his point of view causes him frustration and stress.<br>• It reduces his ability to express himself well in a meeting.<br>• When he can mentally change places with another person in the meeting and get a direct impression of how things are looking for that person, it enables him to better hear their point of view.<br>• Then he is able to express himself more effectively.<br>• He acknowledges that he often forgets to do this, but because he experiences the benefits – improved relationships and more cooperative working – he is inspired to keep trying to remember to work in this way. | |

Below is an exercise you can try which can give you a direct experience of the effectiveness of this kind of compassion. This can be quite a powerful exercise if you take the time to really feel that the other person is sitting there in a chair opposite you. It might be a good idea to try it out a few times before working with someone you find challenging. You could imagine your brother or sister sitting in the other chair and experiment with thinking about how they see you. Then move on to a work colleague and eventually get to your challenging person.

### *Exercise: Putting yourself in the other's shoes*

Arrange two chairs sitting opposite each other.

Start by sitting in 'your' chair.

Sit for a few moments.

Think of someone that you are challenged by.

Invite them to come and sit in the chair opposite to you.

Look at them carefully for several moments.

Think about:

How they want to be happy and they do not want to be unhappy.

How they are a human being with all the same kinds of hopes and fears as you.

Recall what you know about their personal life.

Take time to think about their life in general.

Reflect on what stress they may be suffering.

Sit for a few moments.

Change seats and sit in the 'other person's' chair.

Now imagine that you are the other person looking at you.

What do they see?

How do they experience you?

Have you caused them worry, or pain?

Sit for a few moments.

Go back to your own chair.

Look again at your guest.

Do you see anything differently?

Sit for a few moments.

Silently think to yourself, 'I forgive you any pain or frustration you have caused me.'

Sit again.

- It is helpful to give yourself at least fifteen minutes to do this exercise. You need plenty of time to really look at your chosen person and reflect about them in the first section – it will then be easier to make the shift to looking at yourself through their eyes.
- Allow yourself time to take in the information you receive about yourself when you see yourself from another person's point of view – it could give you some important clues as to how you come across in all your relationships.
- It is hard to accept that we may behave in ways that other people would not like, but it is useful information for us – seeing how we can be misunderstood will help us avoid similar situations in the future.
- Being able to get a sense of how other people may see us is a very effective way of putting ourselves in another person's shoes – it can help to avert all kinds of miscommunication and potential conflict.

On a recent return flight to Amsterdam from the UK I had an opportunity to observe a situation where putting yourself in the other person's shoes might have helped.

As the refreshment trolley came around, I overheard a fellow passenger giving a flight attendant a really hard time. It was hard to catch the full story from where I was sitting but it involved the passenger asking for hot water in a plastic see-through cup. Apparently cups of this sort are not safe to hold hot water and the only alternative was the purchase – for €3 – of a polystyrene cup. Not surprisingly the passenger found this rather excessive. What was more surprising was his response – he proceeded to cross-examine the flight attendant in an increasingly aggressive manner, applying the kind of ruthless logic that would not have been out of place in a courtroom.

The flight attendant did his best. He remained polite, consistent and managed not to react to the escalating tone of complaint and anger that he was subjected to. He had a kind of party line that he could fall back on: 'Sorry sir, this is company policy, I am not allowed to give you this cup', and so on. After some time, he managed to get away and push his trolley on to the next customer. As he came past me our eyes met and he gave me a rather desperate look.

Although unflinchingly professional, the flight attendant adopted the slightly world-weary attitude of someone who has seen and heard the full range of human unreasonableness in their time, and who feels that their job does not carry the appropriate reward in either status or payment to demonstrate an acceptable appreciation of what they suffer. It did not occur to him to put himself in the shoes of the disgruntled passenger.

I happened to be one of the last off the plane and exchanged a few words with the flight attendant. Remembering my look of sympathy, he asked me what I thought of the sort of thing they had to put up with. During our short conversation my earlier hunch was confirmed – when dealing with a stressful situation he relied on his determination to stay professional, rather than adopting any strategy to manage his stress. Instead of de-hyping the situation for himself and easing the strain he was feeling, he took up the burden as a way of demonstrating to himself how efficient he was at enduring one of the downsides of his job. The tension he was holding looked like it was heading towards a stiff drink and a good moan – not so bad in small doses but not a good long-term strategy for stress reduction.

Let's take a closer look at this story and compare it to Tom's experience earlier on.

| **Tom's story** | **Your view**<br><br>**Can you relate this to any experience of your own?** |
|---|---|
| • Tom was able to reduce his feelings of stress simply by seeing the situation from another person's point of view.<br>• The flight attendant's approach depended on his defending his position as a representative of the airline, and by so doing overcoming the objections of the passenger.<br>• It all relied on effort of will, rather than empathy. | |

| | |
|---|---|
| • Although he was not rude in any way, he made the passenger feel not heard and not understood by sticking so faithfully to the party line – which is probably why the passenger became more and more agitated.<br>• By trying to see the situation from the passenger's point of view, the flight attendant could have injected a little humour, and a little warmth, which would have given the passenger the sense of being a person being communicated to by another person.<br>• It would also have helped the flight attendant to relax and be less defensive, which would have meant he felt much less depleted by the whole exchange. | |

## Tonglen Practice

In Chapter 8 we looked at an exercise for reducing stress and anxiety in which we used the in-breath and out-breath as ways of working to absorb our stress and exchanging it with wellbeing and healing. We can use the same principle of exchange using the breath to do an exercise called *Tonglen,*[2] which literally means 'giving and receiving' and helps us to take another step in putting ourselves in another person's shoes.

### *Exercise: Tonglen*

Sit quietly for a few moments and watch your breath.

Remember that just as you want happiness, everyone wants happiness, and that just as you wish to be free from suffering, so does everyone else.

Give yourself some time to really feel the truth of this.

Then as you breathe out, consider that you are giving happiness to everyone – if it helps you can imagine it as a bright light shining out and touching everyone.

As you breathe in, consider that you are taking in or receiving everyone's suffering – if it helps you can consider it as a smoky cloud that dissolves into you.

Continue to do the exercise using the out-breath and in-breath in this way for several minutes.

Now think of one particular person. It could be someone who is having a lot of difficulties in their life. It could be someone you find challenging and want to understand better.

Do the breathing exercise in the same way but now focusing on this one person.

As you breathe out, give them happiness, wellbeing and joy.

As you breathe in, take in their suffering, stress and pain.

As you do so, imagine the person receiving all this wellbeing and being freed from their suffering, see them changing and becoming lighter.

After several minutes, drop the exercise and simply watch your breath.

- The thing to remember when doing this exercise is, just as with the Four Immeasurables exercises in Chapter 9, the good stuff never runs out.
- Your happiness will not decrease because you want to share it with other people; there will always be enough to go around.
- Also, taking in other people's suffering will not increase your own suffering – wishing to take it away from another person does not mean that it becomes yours.
- We are simply expressing the wish that the people we have in mind be free from suffering and we use this strong image to help make it feel real.
- The point of an exercise like this is that is helps us to open up our willingness to respond to other people's suffering and to develop the wish to help.
- This enables us to feel a sense of ease because instead of defending a position we are willing to be open to others. This sense of ease helps us to overcome our own stress and contributes to our peace of mind.

### TIP

However, do not push yourself to do this exercise. If doing it does not feel natural, leave it for a bit and continue with the exercises on the Four Immeasurables on pages 258–74. You can always come back to it later on. Remember, there is nothing to force with compassionate mind training. The most important thing is to be able to *feel* the spirit of the exercises and use that feeling as a basis from which to continue.

## Seeing Others as More Important Than Yourself

This is the last of the five stages in the Buddhist approach to training in compassion. It is included here for completeness and to show just how vast our compassion can become. Although we all have the potential for compassion in our minds and hearts, it is up to each of us as to how willing and able we are to develop that potential. We need to have a fully trained mind to be able to see other people as more important than ourselves from a healthy perspective without neurosis. Most of us have felt the wish to put our loved ones' interests before our own on certain occasions and frequently we hear stories of people performing acts of tremendous bravery for strangers – rescuing people from drowning, or fire, or natural disasters. The seed is there in all of us, but it takes time and practice to bring it to full maturity.

## Universal Responsibility

Universal responsibility is based on our concern for other people's wellbeing in that we see that if we wish to help other people, then feeling a concern for the world at large is an important part of that wish. All our actions have the potential to affect the world in a small way.

Learning to take responsibility for oneself in a healthy and sustainable way is already a big step. Taking this further to feeling responsibility for the wellbeing of others is an even bigger step. With universal compassion we aim to remove any boundaries to our compassion and to feel a responsibility for our world and all the people in it. At each step along our exploration of developing a compassionate mind we have seen that we can build on what we have learned to take our compassion further – once we have understood the importance of compassion for ourselves, we can learn to extend that to compassion for other people. By recognising this and trying to make it part of our lives we are engaging in compassion with a big perspective.

Let's take some time to get a feel of what that means for each of us.

Our world has become very complex – it is rare now for even small groups of people to be able to live independently of the rest of the world. Technology can make the world feel very small but can at the same time obscure precious and vital regional differences. Our political discourse has become more polarised and less inclusive. I read recently that younger people in the UK are admitting that they would not like a close friend or relative to marry a person on the opposing side of the Brexit debate.

Look at some of the big themes of our time: migration, climate change, distribution of resources, ethical disposal of waste materials. For many of us these all seem to be happening somewhere else, to other people, and yet each of us is affected as the situations play out.

Below you will find a series of worksheets exploring some aspects of Universal Responsibility. Each one has some facts or questions for you to consider and a space for you to add thoughts of your own.

## Worksheet 1: Food production

- As recently as 200 years ago, it is unlikely that people would have eaten any food that they did not know the origin and history of.
- People would have produced a range of foods themselves and then they would have probably known the butcher, baker or dairyman who supplied additional products.
- The choice of foods would have been much smaller than what is available to us now, but the knowledge of how it was produced would have been more detailed.
- Nowadays – at least in the West – we have a dazzling selection of food available to tempt us, but we have much less knowledge of where it comes from and how it gets from the point of origin to our plates. Supermarkets have made it possible to offer a wide choice but have tended to alienate us from its production.
- I remember clearly from my teaching days explaining to disbelieving nine-year-olds that their Big Mac started life as a cow!

## Worksheet 2: Supermarkets[3]

- An average supermarket will stock 20,000 items – 4,000 of these are chilled and will need to be replaced within three days; the remaining 16,000 will need restocking in two weeks.
- Half the contents of the warehouses that supply the supermarkets are always 72 hours away from being inedible.
- If there is disruption to road, rail and air travel, it only needs to last for three days and immediately large amounts of food will have to be thrown away.
- Consider how nowadays it is possible to buy strawberries all year round. They are imported from Spain in the spring, from Holland in early summer, from the UK in August, from California in the autumn, and Israel in the winter.
- The catch is that there are only 96 hours available from the moment the fruit is picked until it starts to mould, so all the transport has to be by air and as fast as possible.

## Worksheet 3: Compassion with a big perspective

- It is not that each of us is individually responsible for the wars, famines and squandering of resources that have such an effect on our world, but rather that we can be aware of each person's equal right to have happiness and avoid suffering.
- If we can see any opportunity to help others then we should try to take it, instead of remaining focused on our own interests alone. Helping others now can also mean helping our planet.
- If we can try to develop this kind of awareness in as many of our activities as possible it will help in the process of removing our metaphorical blindfold, enabling us to appreciate and be nourished by the big view of compassion.
- Looking down over a town or city from a plane can help to remind us that we are just one person going about our business among so many others. When we are on the ground it is easy to see our own problems and concerns as special and unique, whereas the chances are that there are probably many people having their own version of the same situation.

## Worksheet 4: Where does my electricity come from?

- As we aspire to have an attitude of universal responsibility, we can try to give thought to the numerous small daily actions that we rarely pay attention to. How often do we consider the immense amount of expertise and human effort behind the simple act of switching on an electric kettle, or turning on a cold-water tap in the kitchen? Numerous people have been involved in building the power stations that produce the electricity or laying the pipes to conduct the water to our taps. Each part of the kettle or the tap and all that goes along with it has been designed and made through human effort.
- These apparently simple actions are only possible because of an intricate series of interconnected actions performed by a wide variety of different people – people who, just like us, want to be happy and avoid suffering and pain.

## Worksheet 5: Aiming to be satisfied with what we have

- In general, our society is preoccupied with the acquisition of material gain. Our pursuit of material wealth seems to permeate all aspects of life and yet, as we saw in Chapter 3, it does not bring us lasting happiness.
- Developing a sense of contentment, an ability to savour what we have rather than thirsting for more, is in itself an aspect of universal responsibility.
- Our acquisitiveness, if left to itself, can never be satisfied and can lead to destructive competition and exploitation of natural resources as well as the populations of poorer nations.
- Unlike a householder switching on her kettle with no awareness of the bigger picture, we need to try to see our wish for a second car, increased air travel, or simply more choice in terms of its impact on other people beyond ourselves, as well as on future generations.

## Worksheet 6: How to deal with people with different views from your own?

1. Perspective-taking: do you pause to consider the person's point of view and where it comes from before challenging it?
2. Do you take time to inform yourself about an issue before entering a discussion about it?
3. How much do you rely on social media for your news?
4. Do you take time to consider the person's background and life situation when entering a discussion?
5. Are you aware of the development of Citizens' Assemblies for making policy recommendations?
6. Are you aware of the work being done on Empathy Circles and Empathy cafés?
7. Do you know of any local initiatives in your neighbourhood to encourage exchanges of views?
8. As Abraham Lincoln said, 'I don't like that man. I must get to know him better.'

Seeing how we fit into the big picture will help us to have the desire to ensure that it is a compassionate and beneficial one. Each one of us is helping to create the world that we are living in. It is so easy to feel that we have no say in how the world works, that there is too much suffering for us to have any effect on it at all. Worse still is to feel cynical and detached, as if it is all nothing to do with us anyway. Universal responsibility means that each one of us remains committed to trying our best to practise compassion within our own lives in the hope that its effect can reach as far as possible. We can begin by remembering that we are all the same in that we all want to be happy and to avoid pain and suffering. It makes sense to focus on our similarities rather than on our differences. If we can build bonds based on common understanding, then our individual differences can be seen as interesting and informative rather than a source of conflict. We can look to trying to create harmony rather than divisiveness. We all know people who are skilled at making people feel at ease and welcome, whereas there are others who easily get into gossiping and complaining and create an unfriendly atmosphere.

If we ask ourselves what impact developing a sense of universal responsibility will have on our stress levels the answer is clear. As we have seen throughout the book, activities such as recognising others as being the same as ourselves and focusing on harmony between people helps to dissolve stress. We feel much better when we are experiencing love, tolerance, patience and compassion than when we are feeling anger and hatred. Connecting ourselves with the bigger picture gives a sense of meaning and purpose to our lives, and helping others nourishes us at the same time. Contentment dissolves the stress of struggling to acquire more things, of becoming bored with what we already have and of envying what others have. There is a direct link between the satisfaction of using our energy in a beneficial way to society and experiencing a reduction in our own stress – and this link can become a spiral as we see more and more that our wellbeing and the wellbeing of each person on the planet is intricately connected.

| What we have learned in this chapter | Your reflections |
|---|---|
| • The last two stages in training the mind in compassion are:<br>* Putting yourself in the other person's shoes.<br>* Seeing others as more important than yourself<br>• Here, we build on the work we have already done on developing compassion for others and try to see things from their perspective<br>• We have not been brought up this way and society is not tuned to supporting us to continuously try to see things from another person's point of view, so it is understandable if we forget to do it from time to time. The thing is to understand *why* it is a good idea both for other people and as a way of reducing our own stress.<br>• Being able to get a sense of how other people may see us is a very effective way of putting ourselves in another person's shoes.<br>• Universal responsibility is based on our concern for other people's wellbeing in that we see that if we wish to help other people, then feeling a concern for the world at large is an important part of that wish.<br>• It is not that each of us is individually responsible for the wars, famines and squandering of resources that have such an effect on our world, but rather that we can be aware of each person's equal right to have happiness and avoid suffering.<br>• If we can see any opportunity to help others then we should take it, instead of remaining focused on our own interests alone. | |

- Seeing how we fit into the big picture will help us to want to ensure that it is a compassionate and beneficial one.
- Universal responsibility means that each one of us remains committed to trying our best to practise compassion within our own lives in the hope that its effect can reach as far as possible.
- We can begin by remembering that we are all the same in that we all want to be happy and to avoid pain and suffering. We can remember this by:
  - Focusing on our similarities rather than our differences
  - Seeking harmony rather than divisiveness
  - Developing contentment as an antidote to greed
- There is a direct link between the satisfaction of using our energy in a beneficial way and experiencing a reduction in our own stress.

## TIPS TO TAKE INTO EVERYDAY LIFE

1. As you go about your day, choose people at random and mentally try to put yourself in their shoes.
2. Do the chairs exercise (page 287) a few times over the next month.
3. Try out Tonglen practice to see how you get on with it.
4. Try being aware of how things work in your environment.
5. Try to see your actions in terms of Universal Responsibility.

# Conclusion: Making this Approach to Reducing Stress Part of Our Lives

Changing our habits is not easy. Most of us have experience of trying to give up something – like chocolate or cigarettes – and of trying to do something that is good for us – such as taking more exercise or going on a diet.

We start off full of enthusiasm and hope for change, but after a while our old ways creep back and it becomes harder and harder to stay on course.

We have seen that learning to develop a compassionate mind in order to work with stress involves changing habits on several different levels and there is no doubt that it requires effort, but it does not need to go the same way as our previous attempts to change. Once we begin applying compassion to our stress, we can see the benefits, and this will help us to continue to make changes step by step.

There is no need to set big targets or get ambitious about how you want to do this. Just start simply and build on what you can manage as you become more familiar with the material and more confident in using it. The key thing is to make working with compassion part of your life, rather than something extra, or something you feel you *have* to do. It also helps to be able to rejoice in your progress, however small the steps you take.

In this conclusion to the book we will look at some practical points to help you get started on working with what we have covered, and then we will look at a typical example of how all of this can be applied in everyday life.

## Some Practical Points

Remember, the formula of this book is:

- Define the problem – in our case, stress – and view it from all angles.
- Identify a helpful way of approaching it – applying compassion – and explore it fully.

- Realise that in order to apply compassion we will need to make some changes in our habits.
- Examine how our mind works in order to better understand our habits.
- Engage with mindfulness and meditation as a means to make a space for change and developing discernment, so we can identify which are our helpful habits and which are our unhelpful habits.
- Learn compassion techniques and how they can help us with our stress – thereby replacing unhelpful habits with helpful ones.
- Understand the importance of training our minds.

### *Working with all the exercises*

Chapter 5 offers practical advice on how to organise your circumstances so that you can do some meditation every day. Those points apply to all the exercises, so you might like to look over them again.

In addition, here are a few practical tips:

- Decide how much time you can spend each day sitting down to do these exercises.
- Spend at least half that time on meditation.
- Make yourself a schedule to help keep you on track.
- Apps such as Insight Timer can be helpful in supporting you.
- Choose another exercise to do in the remainder of your time – you may like to try one for a week, and then move on to another one and try that for a week until you have been through all the exercises.
- Once you are familiar with them all and you have decided which habits you want to focus on, you may decide to try a particular exercise for a longer period, such as a month or six weeks, until you feel some change happening.
- Choose a few of the exercises to try out at different times during the day. You could change these each week until you feel familiar with them all and can decide which ones help you most.
- Make yourself reminders for the habits you want to change and the exercises that you want to do – an alert on your phone, a screensaver on your laptop, a photo on your desk . . .

## Bringing it All Together

In order to bring all that we have learned together, let's take an imaginary scenario of moving house and see how we could put some of this into action. This could help us to see how to make all we have learned part of our everyday lives. Everybody moves house at some time or other and as it is considered to be on a par with divorce and bereavement in terms of stress, it gives us quite a bit of ground to cover.

> **TIP**
>
> As you read through this story, mark the places that resonate with your own experience.

### *Background*

In this scenario, we will be looking at moving house through the eyes of Kate, who is married to Keith and has two children aged nine and eleven. Kate runs her own website-design business from home. We could easily run into her at the supermarket we visited at the beginning of this book! This move is special in that the family is buying their first home and is moving from a rented flat into a house of their own. Let's say that she read this book about six months ago and has been using it to work with her stress levels.

Kate was drawn to the workbook because she was finding herself getting irritable easily and felt it was impacting on her family life. The information on the fight-or-flight response made sense to her and helped her to see that her stress response was indeed becoming overactivated and leading her to more easily become stressed. Using compassion as a way to address this seemed very attractive because it helps a person develop as a human being and, at the same time, it helps other people while helping you – this appealed to Kate.

When it came to the second part of the workbook and identifying habits, Kate realised that she is a bit of a perfectionist and that this can lead her to be quite judgemental of other people and even to treat them rather harshly. At the same time, she is also hard on herself – even though she is highly efficient and capable, she can drive herself too hard. This manifests in the making of endless lists and of her becoming quite hyper, which makes her tired and can leave her with a feeling that no one else – her husband and children included – are trying as hard as she is.

### Using the workbook to prepare for the move

Kate spent some time identifying her layers of stress so that she could be aware of them and therefore more likely to catch them before they became a problem. In terms of the stressful aspects of her world – the first layer – she felt there was plenty to work with: her children needing to change school, her husband needing to adjust to a different commute to work, keeping her business together as they packed up the house, and so on. She could see that all this was predictable, which helped, but that her habit would be to try and control everything to make it work. Pain settling in her neck helped Kate to notice that she was becoming stressed and she identified one of her stress alerts as being over-tired and feeling that things were getting on top of her. She decided to stop packing and preparing half an hour earlier than she'd been doing each day, in order not to let her tiredness build up and become a problem.

Over the six months since reading the workbook, Kate has been trying out techniques to be more present and mindful and now tries to use them as she is packing up the flat. She finds that if she can focus her attention on the acts of collecting and sorting items and packing them into boxes, her energy lasts much longer than if she worries about cooking dinner, how the new school will work for the children or how much the move is costing at the same time. She has also reflected a lot on how she is spending energy in hoping the new house will work well for them and fearing that something might go wrong. Applying what she has read in Chapter 3 about happiness and suffering, Kate tries to remember that, while the new house will be a big improvement, it cannot be the answer to all the family's needs, and that problems and difficulties will arise as a normal part of the life they will lead there. This helps her feel more settled and less anxious as she realises that levels of happiness are not just about how hard she works and how perfectly she arranges everything but simply the ups and downs of life. It is not all down to her! She is also aware that if she gets hyper and over-efficient she will affect the whole family and they will feel more anxious and stressed, whereas when she can manage to be patient and kind to herself everyone feels the benefit.

Since using this workbook, Kate has been trying to do some meditation for ten minutes every morning before the children wake up. It is still early days but already she is getting a sense of what it means to see her thoughts and emotions from the perspective of the space and calm that she sometimes feels in meditation, rather than from the perspective of the hustle and bustle of her daily life. She feels that she has been able to take a step back from her thoughts and emotions and can notice more how they affect her. She has chosen to work with her habit of being too perfectionist and its subsequent effect of making her judgemental of others and hard on herself. Kate has taken on board that there has been research into neuroplasticity, which confirms that she can indeed change these habits.

In the weeks immediately before the move, Kate has tried to add another five minutes to her morning meditation time. She feels that allowing this time for herself each morning is a way of showing kindness to herself, which eases her tendency to be self-critical. Along with sitting meditation she sometimes does the exercise on Working with Stress and Anxiety as she finds it helps her deal with her wish to get everything right. On some mornings she combines meditation with the Loving Kindness Meditation in which she includes all the other people involved in the move – the estate agent, the solicitors, the removal company, electricians, phone technicians and so on. She finds it helps her remember they are all human beings just trying their best and this reduces her irritation with them.

Her husband has a much more relaxed attitude to the move than she does, trusting everything will work out for the best. Sometimes Kate finds this very reassuring but when she is tired – a trigger of stress for her – it can really annoy her. She has been using the Don't Go There! exercise to help with this. Whenever she feels the possibility of getting irritated with her husband, she just says to herself, 'I am not going there!'

### *The day of the move*

When the day of the move comes, Kate has a sense that she has made some progress with her habits of irritation and control. Her family seem excited and relaxed and she herself feels that she has been less bossy with them and a bit kinder to herself. Of course, her habits have not just disappeared overnight – she still has lists for everything – but all the signs are that it is workable, and she is able to make real progress. Over breakfast she asks her husband and children to each name one thing about their present home that they have really appreciated, as a memory to take with them – this works really well and provides a pleasant way of saying goodbye to the flat.

When the removal men arrive, everything is ready. Kate finds one of the men a bit irritating. He is opinionated and loud and seems to have a comment to make about everything. Remembering her loving kindness meditation, Kate tries to repeat the phrases, 'May you be happy, may you be well' in her mind to help her transform her irritation.

While she is appreciating that this seems to be working, her husband's mobile rings. It's the carpet people who are laying carpet at the new house. They were supposed to have finished the evening before but fell behind schedule and still have one of the children's bedrooms to do. This is a potential disaster, as they will be in the way of the removal men when they arrive. For a moment Kate forgets all her good work and simply gives in to frustration and irritation.

Overhearing the conversation, the annoying removal man comes up with a great solution – they will pack the van with all the items for the bedroom that needs carpet at the front of the van. That way, these things will be unloaded last, by which time the carpet people have promised to be finished. This solution is accepted by everyone and gives Kate a chance to reflect on what has happened and her reaction. She tries to think of the carpet people as being just like her – people who are trying to do their best but sometimes cannot get things completely right. This helps the stress reaction from her earlier outburst subside a bit and helps her to feel more relaxed. She is also struck by how wrongly she had judged the removal man as being annoying, when in fact he just has lots of spare energy and more intelligence than the job demands of him, so his running commentary is a way of entertaining himself and not intended to harm anyone.

The next obstacle comes when the van is almost loaded but not completely finished. The people who are due to move into Kate's flat arrive early with all their furniture! For an instant, Kate feels that this is all her fault and that her organisation has somehow been incomplete, but she quickly catches herself and realises that the other family have simply decided to turn up early and nothing she could have done could have prevented it. She tries to catch her anxiety on her breath and to breathe it down into her belly so it can dissolve. This helps to calm her down and she simply puts on the kettle to make tea for everyone while the new family wait for their turn to unload.

She lets go of her wish to give the whole flat another clean – it's no longer possible. She realises that she wanted to clean for herself because the whole place would get disturbed by all the unpacking to come. As she hands out cups of tea she looks at the young couple and their baby who will live in her old home, and for a moment she is able to put herself in their shoes and see how excited they are to be moving in and how they simply forgot the time and got carried away. They had not intended to cause any trouble at all.

Eventually everything is ready. The removal van moves off and Kate's family follow in their car. On the short journey, Kate takes a moment to think about all the other people who might be moving house that day and sends them a silent good luck wish. She starts to play a game with her husband and children to make a list of all the people who have made it possible for them to live in their new house – the list gets very long and takes up the whole journey. Just as they arrive at their new home they say a big 'thank you' to all these people – most of whom they will never meet. For Kate it helps to connect with the bigger picture and takes some of the pressure off her own personal situation.

As they all get out of the car at the new house, Kate thinks ahead to all the work that needs to happen for everything to be in order but decides not to go there and instead tries to be mindful of one task at a time. She feels that so far the move has gone well, and she has managed to work with her triggers and reactions to stress quite well. This increases her confidence in the techniques she is working with and helps her to feel that change is happening. She feels less stressed than she expected to feel and does not feel overwhelmed about what is to come. She knows that it will take time for her new habits to feel like second nature but as she has been able to work with them during such a demanding time as the family has just gone through, she feels that the outlook is good.

### TIP

You could use sections of this story to write guidelines for yourself on how to use the exercises and practices. Play a bit and get creative. See what comes out of it.

# Useful Resources

If you are interested in finding out more about the work of ***Awareness in Action*** you could:

- Check out our website www.awarenessinaction.org
- Find us on Facebook www.facebook.com/awarenessinaction
- Or talk to us on Twitter @awareinaction or Instagram awarenessin

## Useful Books


*365 Thank Yous*, J. Kralik (Hyperion Books, 2010)

*Affluenza*, O. James (Vermilion, 2007)

*The Age of Absurdity*, M. Foley (Simon & Schuster, 2010)

*The Age of Empathy*, F. De Waal (Souvenir Press, 2011)

*Ancient Wisdom, Modern World*, HH the Dalai Lama (Little, Brown, 1999)

*Anger Kills*, R. Williams and V. Williams (Harper Perennial, 1993)

*The Art of Happiness at Work*, HH the Dalai Lama and H. Cutler (Hodder & Stoughton, 1998)

*The Art of Happiness*, HH the Dalai Lama and H. Cutler (Hodder & Stoughton, 1998)

*Authentic Happiness*, M. E. P. Seligman (Simon & Schuster, 2004)

*Awakening the Kind Heart*, K. McDonald (Wisdom Publications, 2010)

*Beyond Religion*, HH the Dalai Lama (Rider, 2012)

*Boeddhisme in een Notendop*, B. van Baar (Uitgeverij Bert Bakker, 2006)

*Born to be Good*, D. Keltner (W. W. Norton, 2009)

*Boundless Heart*, B. A. Wallace (Snow Lion Publications, 1999)

*The Brain that Changes Itself*, N. Doidge (Penguin, 2008)

*Buddha's Brain*, R. Hanson and R. Mendius (New Harbinger, 2009)

*Coming to Our Senses*, J. Kabat-Zinn (Piatkus, 2005)

*The Compassionate Brain*, G. Huther (Shambhala, 2006)

*The Compassionate Instinct*, D. Keltner, J. Marsh and J. A. Smith (eds) (W. W. Norton, 2010)

*The Compassionate Mind*, P. Gilbert (Robinson, 2009)

*The Compassionate Mind Approach to Managing Your Anger*, R. Kolts (Robinson, 2012)

*Dalai Lama, Wijze van Deze Tijd*, B. van Baar (Uitgeverij Bert Bakker, 2009)

*The Emotional Life of Your Brain*, R. Davidson and S. Begley (Hodder & Stoughton, 2012)

*Full Catastrophe Living*, J. Kabat-Zinn (Piatkus, 2001)

*The Geography of Bliss*, E. Weiner (Black Swan, 2008)

*The Happiness Advantage*, S. Achor (Virgin Books, 2010)

*Happiness*, M. Ricard (Atlantic Books, 2007)

*Happiness*, R. Layard (Allen Lane, 2005)

*The Happiness Project*, G. Rubin (Harper Paperbacks, 2011)

*The Healing Power of Doing Good*, A. Luks and P. Payne (iuniverse.com, 1991, 2001)

*The How of Happiness*, R. Lyubomirsky (Penguin Press, 2007)

*Hurry Up and Meditate*, D. Michie (Snow Lion Publications, 2008)

*I Shall Not Hate*, L. Abuelaish (Bloomsbury, 2011)

*The Joy of Living*, Yongey Mingyur Rinpoche (Bantam, 2009)

*Joyful Wisdom*, Yongey Mingyur Rinpoche (Harmony Books, 2009)

*The Mind's Own Physician*, J. Kabat-Zinn, R. Davidson and Z. Houshmand (New Harbinger, 2011)

*The Mindful Way through Depression*, M. Williams, J. Teasdale, Z. Segal and J. Kabat-Zinn (Guilford, 2007)

*The New Leaders*, D. Goleman, R. Boyatzis and A. McKee (Little, Brown, 2002)

*One City*, E. Nichtern (Wisdom Publications, 2007)

*The Paradox of Choice*, B. Schwartz (HarperCollins, 2005)

*The Path is the Goal*, Chogyam Trungpa (Shambhala, 1995)

*The Plastic Mind*, S. Begley (Robinson, 2009)

*The Pleasures and Sorrows of Work*, A. de Botton (Penguin, 2009)

*Real Happiness*, S. Salzberg (Hay House, 2011)

*Religion for Atheists*, A. de Botton (Hamish Hamilton, 2012)

*Search Inside Yourselfs*, D. Goleman, J. Kabat-Zinn and Chade-Meng Tan, (HarperCollins, 2012)

*Self-Compassion*, K. Neff (Hodder & Stoughton, 2011)

*Smile or Die*, B. Ehrenreich (Granta Books, 2010)

*Social Intelligence*, D. Goleman (Bantam, 2006)

*Stress*, F. Jones and J. Bright (Pearson Education, 2001)

*Stress and Emotion*, R. S. Lazarus (Springer, 1999)

*The Stress of Life*, H. Selye (McGraw Hill, 1978)

*Stumbling on Happiness*, D. Gilbert (Alfred A. Knopf, 2006)

*The Tibetan Book of Living and Dying*, Sogyal Rinpoche (Rider, rev. 2002)

*The Plastic Mind*, S. Begley (Robinson, 2009)

*The Truth About Stress*, A. Patmore (Atlantic Books, 2006)

*The Truth Of Suffering and the Path of Liberation*, Chogyam Trungpa (Shambhala, 2009)

*Twelve Steps to a Compassionate Life*, K. Armstrong (The Bodley Head, 2011)

*The Universe in a Single Atom*, HH the Dalai Lama (Abacus, 2005)

*Visions of Compassion* R. J. Davidson and A. Harrington (eds) (Oxford University Press, 2002)

*Why Kindness Is Good For You*, D. R. Hamilton (Hay House, 2010)

*Why Zebras Don't Get Ulcers*, R. M. Sapolsky (St Martin's Press, third edn. 2004)

## Organisations

### *UK/Europe*

#### Awareness in Action

Awareness in Action was founded by Maureen Cooper in 2004. We offer workshops and online courses on applying the approach and techniques shared in this book for yourself, in your relationships and in your work.

www.awarenessinaction.org

#### The Compassionate Mind Foundation

Set up in 2006, the Foundation aims to promote wellbeing through the scientific understanding and application of compassion.

PO Box 7505, Derby, DE1 0LT

www.compassionatemind.co.uk

#### Compassion in Politics

https://www.compassioninpolitics.com/about-us

#### Mind with Heart

Mind with Heart is a charity dedicated to equipping young people with the social and emotional skills necessary to their wellbeing and to building a more sustainable society.

4 Sanford Walk, London N16 7LB

www.mind-with-heart.blogspot.co.uk

### *USA*

#### The Center for Compassion and Altruism Research and Education

The Center for Compassion and Altruism Research and Education (CCARE) at Stanford

University School of Medicine was founded in 2008 with the explicit goal of promoting, supporting and conducting rigorous scientific studies of compassion and altruistic behaviour. Founded and directed by Dr James Doty, clinical professor of neurosurgery, CCARE is established within the Institute for Neuro-Innovation and Translational Neurosciences. Stanford University, 1070 Arastradero Road, 2nd Floor, Palo Alto, CA 94304 (650) 721-6142

www.stanford.edu/group/ccare/cgi-bin/wordpress/

## Center for Investigating Healthy Minds

The Center for Investigating Healthy Minds (CIHM) conducts rigorous interdisciplinary research on healthy qualities of mind such as kindness, compassion, forgiveness and mindfulness. Scientists at CIHM represent an integrated team with a broad array of research methodologies from behavioural to neuroscientific. The CIHM engages in translational research and outreach with the goal of cultivating healthy qualities of the mind at the individual, community and global levels.

Waisman Center, Suite S119, University of Wisconsin-Madison, 1500 Highland Avenue, Madison, WI 53705-2280

www.investigatinghealthyminds.org

## Charter for Compassion

The Charter for Compassion is a document that transcends religious, ideological and national differences. Supported by leading thinkers from many traditions, the Charter activates the Golden Rule around the world. The Charter for Compassion is a cooperative effort to restore not only compassionate thinking but, more importantly, compassionate action to the centre of religious, moral and political life. Compassion is the principled determination to put ourselves in the shoes of the other, and lies at the heart of all religious and ethical systems.

4669 Eastern Avenue N., Seattle, WA 98103

www.charterforcompassion.org

## The Greater Good

The Greater Good Science Center studies the psychology, sociology and neuroscience of wellbeing, and teaches skills that foster a thriving, resilient and compassionate society.

Greater Good Science Center, University of California, Berkeley, 2425 Atherton Street, #6070, Berkeley, CA 94720-6070

greatergood.berkeley.edu/

### Mind & Life Institute

The Mind & Life Institute is a non-profit organisation that seeks to understand the human mind and the benefits of contemplative practices through an integrated mode of knowing that combines first-person knowledge from the world's contemplative traditions with methods and findings from contemporary scientific enquiry. Ultimately, their goal is to relieve human suffering and advance wellbeing.

Mind & Life Institute, 4 Bay Road, Hadley, MA 01035 (413) 387-0710

www.mindandlife.org

# Endnotes

## Introduction

1 HH the Dalai Lama, *The Compassionate Life* (Wisdom Publications, 2001)

2 HH the Dalai Lama, *Ethics for the New Millennium* (Riverside Books, 2001)

3 HH the Dalai Lama, *Beyond Religion* (Rider, 2013)

4 In 2005 the Dalai Lama published his book entitled *The Universe in a Single Atom* (Broadway Books, 2005), which documents his lifelong interest in science and the beneficial role he believes a dialogue between science and spirituality has to play.

5 https://www.mindandlife.org

6 Davidson, R.J. with Begley, S., *The Emotional Life of Your Brain* (Hodder, 2013)

## Chapter 1

1. Sapolsky, R., *Why Zebras Don't Get Ulcers* (St Martin's Press, third edn, 2004)

2. Selye gained a medical degree and PhD from a German university in Prague and a D.Sc. from McGill university in Montreal. He is the author of 38 books and 1,600 technical articles.

3. https://www.mentalhealth.org.uk/statistics/mental-health-statistics-stress

4 https://www.hse.gov.uk/statistics/causdis/stress.pdf

5 Adrenaline and noradrenaline are the terms used in the UK. In the USA the terms used are epinephrine and norepinephrine.

6. Gilbert, P., *The Compassionate Mind* (Robinson, 2009)

7. An international team of researchers from Western Sydney University, Harvard University, Kings College, Oxford University and University of Manchester have found

the internet can produce both acute and sustained alterations in specific areas of cognition, which may reflect changes in the brain, affecting our attentional capacities, memory processes, and social interactions.

In a first-of-its-kind review, published in *World Psychiatry* – the world's leading psychiatric research journal – the researchers investigated leading hypotheses on how the Internet may alter cognitive processes, and further examined the extent to which these hypotheses were supported by recent findings from psychological, psychiatric and neuroimaging research.

8. Ronson, J., *So You've Been Publicly Shamed* (Riverhead Books, 2015)

9. A key factor was the work of Redford Williams of Duke University, North Caroline, who declared himself to be a Type A personality. Realising the destructive potential of Type A characteristics both from a social and health point of view, Williams set out to try and understand the pattern more deeply. He identified hostility as the key factor in the list of Type A symptoms. Williams wrote a book, *Anger Kills* (Harper Perennial, 1993), with his wife, who was an important influence in helping him overcome his own hostile behaviour as a way of safeguarding his marriage.

## Chapter 2

1. Davidson, R. J., and Harrington, A (eds), *Visions of Compassion* (Oxford University Press, 2002) 68
2. https://philosophyterms.com/golden-rule/
3. King James *Bible*, Matthew 7:12
4. https://en.wikisource.org/wiki/Universal_Declaration_of_Human_Responsibilities
5. This wish is what is known as *bodhicitta* in sanskrit – *bodhi* is enlightened essence; *citta* is heart, or mind. The Buddhist teachings on compassion are often referred to as bodhicitta teachings. There are two aspects to the practice of bodhicitta – absolute and relative. Absolute bodhicitta is the direct insight into the true nature of mind, and the realisation of our fundamental nature. For most of us, this is not something that can be easily accomplished and so there is the more gradual path of relative bodhicitta.
6. A., and Zajonc, A., *The Dalai Lama at MIT* (Harvard University Press, 2008)
7. HH the Dalai Lama, *Ancient Wisdom, Modern World* (Little, Brown, 1999) 72

8. Experiment carried out by Jack Nitschke at the University of Wisconsin
9 www.joshua-greene.net
10. https://webapps.pni.princeton.edu/ncc/JDC/Home_Page.htmlto
11. Carried out by James Rilling and Gregory Berns at Emory University, Atlanta
12. Keltner, D., Marsh J., and Smith, J. A. (eds), *The Compassionate Instinct* (W. W. Norton, 2010) 11. If you are interested in reading the details of Keltner's work, consult his book *Born to be Good* (W. W. Norton, 2009).

## Chapter 3

1. From a public talk given by the Dalai Lama to an audience in Arizona, USA in 1993. HH the Dalai Lama and Cutler, H., *The Art of Happiness* (Hodder & Stoughton, 1998)
2. Definition of flow: 'A sense that one's skills are adequate to cope with the challenges at hand in a goal directed, rule bound action system that provides clear clues as to how one is performing. Concentration is so intense that there is no attention left over to think about anything irrelevant or to worry about problems. Self-consciousness disappears, and the sense of time becomes distorted. An activity that produces such experiences is so gratifying that people are willing to do it for its own sake, with little concern for what they will get out of it, even when it is difficult or dangerous.' Csikszentmihalyi, M., *Flow* (Harper & Row, 1990).
3. M.E.P. Seligman, *Authentic Happiness* (Simon & Schuster, 2002) 46
4. Sonja Lyubomirsky in her book *The How of Happiness* (Penguin Press, 2007) uses the same format but calls it the Subjective Happiness Scale.
5. *The Happiness Formula:* news.bbc.co.uk/2/hi/programmes/happiness_formula/default.stm
6. Richard Easterlin's study of the hedonic treadmill, published in 'Does Economic Growth Improve the Human Lot?' in David, P. A., and Reder, M. W. (eds.), *Nations and Households in Economic Growth* (Academic Press, 1974).
7. Solnick, S. J., and Hemenway, D., 'Is more always better?', *Journal of Economic Behavior & Organization*, 37: 3 (1998), 373–83.

8. Medvec et al, 'When less is more: counterfactual thinking and satisfaction among Olympic athletes', *Journal of Personality and Social Psychology*, 69: 4 (October 1995), 603–10.

9. Layard, R., *Happiness*, op. cit., 49

10. Kahneman, Frederickson, Schreiber and Redelmeier, 1993

11. Harvard science section, *Harvard Gazette*, 15 February 2012 news.harvard.edu/gazette/story/2010/11/wandering-mind-not-a-happy-mind/

12. Schwartz, B., *The Paradox of Choice* (Ecco, 2003)

13. *Online NewsHour* with Paul Solman, 26 December 2003 www.pbs.org/newshour/bb/economy/july-dec03/paradox_12-26.html

14. Delingpole, J., 'The tyranny of choice', *Mail Online*, 5 July 2007

15. Gilbert, P., *The Compassionate Mind* (Robinson, 2009) 64

## Part 2

1. Chödrön, P., *The Places That Scare You*, (Harper Non-Fiction, 2004)

2. https://centerhealthyminds.org/join-the-movement/should-caring-be-a-new-currency

## Chapter 4

1. Milton, J., 'Paradise Lost' (1667)

2. This is based on research carried out by Daniel Kahneman, psychologist and economist

3. Frankl, V. E., *Man's Search for Meaning* (Rider, new edn 2004)

4. Germer, C. K., *The Mindful Path to Self-Compassion* (Guilford, 2009) 31

5. Goleman, D., with Boyatzis, R. and McKee, A., *The New Leaders* (Little, Brown, 2002) 202

6. Adapted from ibid., 201

## Chapter 5

1. Salzberg, S., *A Heart as Wide as the World* (Shambhala, 1999)

2. This exercise is a simplified version of: Williams, M., Teasdale, J., Segal, Z., and Kabat-Zinn, J., *The Mindful Way through Depression* (Guilford, 2007) 104–6
3. Michie, D., *Hurry Up and Meditate* (Snow Lion Publications, 2008) 8
4. Lutz, A., Ricard, M., and Davidson, R. J., 'Long-term meditators self-induce high-amplitude gamma synchrony during mental practice', *Proceedings of the National Academy of Sciences* 101: 46 (2004), and for a detailed account of this study see Kabat-Zinn, J., *Coming to Our Senses* (Hyperion, 2005) 368–74
5. Kaufman, M., 'Meditation Gives Brain a Charge, Study Finds' in the *Washington Post* (3 January 2005) A05

## Chapter 6

1. Hanh, T.N., *No Mud No Lotus* (Aleph Book Company, 2017)
2. Foley, M., *The Age of Absurdity* (Simon & Schuster, 2010) 36
3. James, O., *Affluenza* (Vermilion, 2007) vii
4. Sapolsky, R., *Why Zebras Don't Get Ulcers* (St Martin's Press, third edn, 2004) 260
5. HH the Dalai Lama, and Cutler, H., *The Art of Happiness* (Hodder & Stoughton, 1998)
6. https://ppc.sas.upenn.edu/sites/default/files/learnedhelplessness.pdf
7. The 'third sector' is the term used to describe the range of organisations that are neither public sector nor private sector. It includes voluntary and community organisations (both registered charities and other organisations such as associations, self-help groups and community groups, social enterprises, mutuals and cooperatives). Definition from the National Audit Office
8. Kabat-Zinn, J., *Coming to Our Senses* (Piatkus, 2005) 74
9. Hanson, R., with Mendius, R., *Buddha's Brain* (New Harbinger, 2009) 55

## Chapter 7

1. Trungpa, C., *Cutting Through Spiritual Materialism* (Shambhala, New edition 2002) p115
2. King, Jr., Dr. M. L., 'Christmas sermon on peace', CBC Massey Lectures (1967)

3. Rinpoche, Y. M., *Joyful Wisdom* (Harmony Books, 2009) 55
4. Cosley, B. J., Mccoy, S. K., Saslow, L. R., and Epel, E. S., 'Is Compassion for Others Stress Buffering? Consequences of Compassion and Social Support for Physiological Reactivity to Stress', *Journal of Experimental Social Psychology*, 46: 5 (September 2010), 816–23
5. Luks, A., and Payne, P., *The Healing Power of Doing Good* (iuniverse.com, 1991, 2001)
6. Sobel, D., and Ornstein, R., *Healthy Pleasures* (Addison-Wesley, 1989) 235, quoted in Luks and Payne, ibid., 115
7. Hanh, T.N., *Work* (Aleph Book Company, 2017)
8. Begley, S., *The Plastic Mind* (Robinson, 2009) 9
9. ibid., 24–5
10. Begley, S., 'How the Brain Rewires itself', *TIME* magazine (19 January 2007), article at http://content.time.com/time/magazine/article/0,9171,1580438,00.html
11. Quoted in Begley, S., *The Plastic Mind* (Robinson, 2009) 242

## Chapter 8

1. Chödrön, P., *When Things Fall Apart* (Element Books, 2007)
2. Germer, C. K., *The Mindful Path to Self-Compassion* (Guilford, 2009) 84
3. Neff, K., *Self-Compassion* (Hodder & Stoughton, 2011) 41 4 ibid., 47–8
4. Ibid., page 11
5. www.personalityresearch.org/papers/clark.html
6. https://www.nbcnews.com/better/health/good-company-why-we-need-other-people-be-happy-ncna836106
7. Sonja Lyubomirsky defines these three categories of social support in her book *The How of Happiness* (Penguin Press, 2007) 139
8. https://www.alustforlife.com/soul/you-are-alive/how-the-buddhist-metaphor-of-the-second-arrow-can-help-you-be-nicer-to-yourself
9. Kabat-Zinn, J., and Davidson, R., with Houshmand, Z. (ed), *The Mind's Own Physician* (New Harbinger, 2011) 50

10. https://www.njlifehacks.com/gratitude-benefits/

11. I recently talked to a man who had been a senior buyer for a large Irish retailer for almost thirty years. He was made redundant when the Irish economy crashed in 2008 and, at the time we met, was working as part of the airport assistance team in Dublin Airport. He could have felt bitter about his change in status but in the half hour we spent together all he talked about was his gratitude for having work in an economy in which so many people are unemployed, and his pleasure and satisfaction in having such a worthwhile and interesting job. He was a great example of someone who was capable of working through stressful situations by choosing to focus on the aspects of the situation that were beneficial for him, rather than the aspects that were disappointing and difficult.

## Chapter 9

1. Armstrong, K., quoted on *Bill Moyers Journal* PBS (13 March 2009), transcript at www.pbs.org/moyers/journal/03132009/transcript3.html
2. Kabat-Zinn, J., and Davidson, R., with Houshmand, Z. (ed), *The Mind's Own Physician* (New Harbinger, 2011) 50–1
3. Address at his enthronement as Anglican archbishop of Cape Town (7 September 1986). Fuente: https://citas.in/frases/1732418-desmond-tutu-a-person-is-a-person-because-he-recognizes-others/
4. Albert Schweitzer (1875–1965), philosopher, physician, Nobel Peace Prize winner
5. Scherwitz, L., Graham II, L. E., and Ornish, D., 'Self-involvement and the risk factors for coronary heart disease', *Advances*, 2: 2 (spring 1985), 6–18
6. https://www.theguardian.com/society/2012/jan/08/high-blood-pressure-mark-honigsbaum
7. Luks, A., and Payne, P., *The Healing Power of Doing Good* (iuniverse. com, 1991, 2001) 96
8. Goleman, D., *Social Intelligence* (Bantam Books, 2006) 308
9. Abuelaish, I., *I Shall Not Hate* (Bloomsbury, 2011)
10. Mandela, N., *Long Walk to Freedom* (Abacus, 1995)
11. Haidt, J., *The Happiness Hypothesis* (Arrow, 2007)

12. Albert Schweitzer, in *Kulturphilosophie* (1923), translated as *Philosophy of Civilisation* (1949).
13. Joseph Campbell (1904–87), American mythologist and author
14. *Prose Works of Henry Wadsworth Longfellow*, 1857, Volume 2, Section 'Table Talk'
15. Based on the work of Paul Ekman, psychologist. Explained by Daniel Goleman in Keltner, D., Marsh, J., and Smith, J. A. (eds), *The Compassionate Instinct* (W. W. Norton, 2010) 172–3
16. Roman Krznaric's book, *Empathy*, is very helpful on this.
17. cultureofempathy.com/Projects/Empathy-Tent/extras/Empathy-Circle-Training.htm
18. Quoted in 'Hope on the Battlefield' by Dave Grossman in Keltner, Marsh and Smith (eds), *The Compassionate Instinct* (W. W. Norton, 2010) 41

## Chapter 10

1. Rinpoche, S., *The Tibetan Book of Living and Dying* (Rider, rev. 2002) 367
2. *Tonglen* is a Tibetan Buddhist practice that can be practised in many ways and at many levels. If you would like to learn more about it you could look at *The Tibetan Book of Living and Dying*, op.cit., 206–11
3. de Botton, A., *The Pleasures and Sorrows of Work* (Penguin, 2009) 41&42

# Index

Note: page numbers in **bold** refer to diagrams.


7/11 breathing 243

Abuelaish, Izzeldin 264
acceptance, attitude of 73, **87**, 88, 155, 170, 178–9, 199, 231, 245, 251
accidents 91
action *see* compassionate action
adaptation 75
addiction, to stress 181–2
adrenal glands 18
adrenaline 18, 182
affection 49
Affluenza Virus 166
ageing 91
aggression 16, 59
alcohol consumption 41
altruism 38, 51–6, 110
amygdala 17, **17**, 31, 157, 182, 254, 272
ancestors, hunter-gatherer 14–15, 29, 30, 114, 182–3, 196–7, 230
anger
  antidote to 225, 264–6
  functions of 240
  as threat emotion 22
antibodies 158
antidotes 220–31, 264–6, 270, 278–9
  to anger 225, 264–6
  to attachment 270
  to craving 270
  to the 'freeze' response 219, 220
  to hatred 264–5
  to self-criticism 218, 220–4, 223–4
antisocial behaviour 166–7
anxiety 14, 306
  and the Affluenza Virus 166
  low-grade unspecified 183
  and physical exercise 235
  reduction 216–17, 235, 246
  and self-compassion 246
  and 'simmer' 182–3
  social anxiety 159–60
  and the stress response 16
  as threat emotion 22
  working with (exercise) 216–17
appearance, stress regarding 14
Apple 159
Armstrong, Karen 250
assumption-making 98
attachment, antidote to 270
attention
  bringing into the present moment 110, 132, 133–9, 141–2
  failing to pay 98–9, 176–7, 203, 204
  paying to our bodily sensations 135

paying to our breath 133–4
paying to the world 136
attitudes to life 5, **87**, 88
of acceptance 73, **87**, 88, 155, 170, 178–9, 199, 231, 245
choosing one's 119
gratitude 237, 272
limited/limiting 98
optimistic 246, 272
'them and us' 181
authority 278–9
automatic nervous system 18
automatic pilot mode 80, 130–2
Awareness in Action 5

balance 216
BBC *see* British Broadcasting Corporation
Begley, Sharon 206
'being in tune with life' 154
'big picture' 283–99, 307
biology
of compassion 56–60
of empathy 62
Blitz 170
blood pressure 18, 30, 64, 72, 173, 264
bodily sensations
awareness of 112–13, 135, 137
value labelling 136
body
changing nature of the 195
as stress barometer 31
body image 14
bosses 101–2, 254, 256–7, 285–6
boundaries, establishing 174
brain 16, **17**, 31, 60, 247
amygdala 17, **17**, 31, 157, 182, 254, 272
cerebellum 57
cerebral cortex 16, 58–9
cerebrum 58
changes in our 110, 124–6, 206
and compassion 62–3, 207
dopamine production 235–6
and emotion 71
and empathy 62
and evolutionary habits 182–3
and hanging onto old habits 196–7
hippocampus 17, **17**, 31, 182
how stress works in our 20–1
hypothalamus 17, **17**, 18, 58
limbic system 16–17
measuring the activity of 71
and meditation 156–9, 207
mood set point of 157
negative bias 230
neocortex 58, 247
'new' 58–9
'old' (Reptilian) 16–17, 57–9
pre-frontal cortex 71, 157, 158, 207, 255
rewiring our 124–6
and self-criticism 247
and self-kindness 247
and stress pollution 186
brain scans 156–7
brain stem 57
bravery 38, 42, 109, 169, 199, 251
breaks, learning to take 175
breast cancer 158
breastfeeding 247
breathing rate 18, 30
breathing techniques
7/11 breathing 243
diaphragmatic breathing 243
and meditation 145–6
and paying attention to our breath 133–4
and practising mindfulness 132–3

and Tonglen practice 290–1
for when our composure is disturbed 243
British Broadcasting Corporation (BBC) 71–2
Brown, Charlie (cartoon character) 169
Buddha 3–4, 227, 231–2
Buddhism 109, 206
approach to compassion 40, 56, 59, 258, 269
and meditation 151, 154, 156
and the mind 115
and suffering 43
Buddhist monks 156, 157
burnout 25, 235, 251

Campbell, Joseph 272
cancer 103–4, 158, 274
capitalism, selfish 166
cerebellum 57
cerebral cortex (grey matter) 16, 58–9
cerebrum 58
challenges 231–4
change 7, 96–8, 100
constant and relentless nature of 193–6
desiring/wanting **121**, 122, 155
formula for **121**, 155–6
identifying where to change 109–210
inspiration for **121**, 122
making it happen 8, 211–99
and routines 236
as threatening 97–8
*see also* impermanence
Cherokee folk tradition 118–19
Chödrön, Pema 213, 216
*The Places That Scare You* 109
choice, overwhelming 84
clinical psychology 110
cognitive empathy 277
Cohen, Jonathan 62
comfort-seeking behaviours 173
comparison-making *see* social comparison-making
compassion 1, 3, 6, 9, 26–9, 37–67, 108–14
and the big perspective 283–99, 307
biology of 56–60
and the brain 62–3, 207
and Buddhism 40, 59, 258, 269
and change 196
definition 3, 6, 39–43, 68, 213
developing habits based in 7
development 5, 40–1
and emotions 200, 201
and empathy 61–2, 277–80
extending our circle of 197–8
and the Four Immeasurables 258–63
and fundamental wholeness 43–56
Immeasurable Compassion 258, 259, 269–71
and interdependence 94, 192, 193
logic of 200–3, 201
and meditation 143–4, 155, 207, 270–1
natural capacity for 44, 49–51
for others 8, 191–2, 250–82
and putting other people's needs before our own 8
and relatability 190
as relationship of equality 109
research 62–4, 206–8
seeds of 198–200
and stress reduction 41, 51, 88, 111, 120–2, 124, 128, 200, 201, 207–8, 211, 246, 252–4, 303
and suffering 39–42, 53, 68
sustainable nature of 255
traditional teaching regarding 38
and wholeness 44, 49–51
*see also* self-compassion

compassion fatigue 251, 278
compassion meditation 270–1
compassion training 8, 51–6, 100–1, 109–10, 205, 207–8, 283–4
  and causing no harm 53, 252, 255–7
  five stages of 53
  and 'melting the ice in your heart' 53, 54, 252, 258–9
  and putting yourself in another person's shoes 53, 284–90
  and seeing other people as being like you 53, 55, 220, 252, 274–6
  and seeing others as more important than yourself 53, 56, 252, 283, 292
  and Tonglen practice 290–2
  and universal responsibility 292–7
compassionate action, taking 8, 88–9, 128–62, 211, 270
compassionate empathy 277
compassionate habits 7, 191–3, 203–5
Compassionate Mind Approach 22
compassionate reasoning 198–203
complexity 82–4
composure 241–3
conditioning 214
  desensitisation 279
confidence 155, 247
connection 218, 227–9, 237–8, 247
  exercise in 228–9
  *see also* friendships; interconnectedness; relationships
consciousness, delusion of 94
consumerism 25, 165–6
contempt, manufactured 280
contentment 88, 100, 155, 157, 296
  *see also* happiness; peace, inner
control, loss/lack of 119, 154, 170–1
coping mechanisms 90
  coping with other people's suffering 251
  coping with stress 7
  failure of 14
  unhelpful 175
corticosteroids 18
cortisol 72, 254–5
courage 38, 42, 109, 169, 199, 251
craving 270, 273
crystals 48
Csikszentmihalyi, Mihaly 70
culture, tone of our 165

Dalai Lama 1, 3, 4, 37, 47, 57, 59, 156, 206, 266
  *Beyond Religion* 4
Davidson, Richard 4, 62, 156, 157–9, 207
day-dreaming 129
death 91
debt, personal 166
defence mechanisms 251, 278–9, 280
dehumanisation 279
denial 278–9, 280
depression 14, 157, 227
  and the Affluenza Virus 166
  and drive emotions 25
  and self-compassion 246
  and 'simmer' 182
desensitisation conditioning 279
desire/longing
  for change **121**, 122, 155
  feelings of 240
diabetes, type 2 72
diaphragmatic breathing 243
Diener, Ed 70, 72
digestion 18, 30
discernment **87**, 89, 90, **121**
disgust 22

dissatisfaction 80–2, 90–1
distance 278–9
distraction 9, 98, 119, 173
divorce 265–6
dopamine 31, 85, 235–6, 239–40
dreams 168–9
drive 24–6, 235–7

East Germany 76
Eastern tradition 110
eating 9
egoism 110
Einstein, Albert 94
electricity 295
electroencephalogram (EEG) 157
'elevation' 268
emails 32
emotional empathy 277
emotional habits 179–80
emotional suppression 174
emotional systems 216
  incentive and resource-seeking system 22, 24–5, 26, **28**, 29
  soothing and contentment system 22, 25–6, **28**, 29
  and stress 21–31
  threat and self-protection system 16, 22–4, 26, **28**, 29, 31, 32, 114, 182–3
  Three Emotional Systems 21–31, 27, **28**
emotions 21, 100
  and brain activity 71
  and compassion 200, 201
  constructive 253, 254, 259
  destructive 240–4, 254, 255, 259, 260
  handling 240–4
  incentive/drive 24–6
  inner disarmament 254
  and meditation 147–50, 155–6, 159–60, 273
  metaphor for turbulent 179
  and 'putting things right' (exercise) 243–4
  and rumination 229–31
  and the 'sky and the clouds' metaphor 116–18, 147–8, 150
  as solid and real 114
  as transient 118, 147–8, 150, 179–80
  *see also specific emotions*
empathy 42, 61–3, 247, 277–80
  beginnings of 61–2
  biological roots of 62
  and the brain 62
  cognitive 277
  compassionate 277
  definition 61
  emotional 277
  obstacles to 277–80
empathy circles/cafés 278
endorphins 26
Engle, Adam 4
Equanimity, Immeasurable 258, 259, 260–3
ethics, secular 4
evaluation 115
evolution
  evolutionary habits 182–3, 196–7
  and pleasure 85
  and selflessness 202
exhaustion 25
  *see also* burnout
experience 43, 115, 136

Facebook 84
failure, learning from 225
fear
  and the stress response 16
  as threat emotion 22
  of what we don't want 178–9, 205
  *see also* suffering, fear of

Fear of Missing Out (FOMO) 238–40
fearlessness 247
  *see also* bravery
'fight or flight' response 18, 64, 182, 217, 220, 254, 303
  antidote to 218, 220
first impressions, misleading 262
flight 184
'flow' experience 70
flux, state of 196
fMRI *see* functional magnetic resonance imaging
Foley, Michael 165
FOMO *see* Fear of Missing Out
food production 294
forgiveness 200, 264–6
Four Immeasurables 54, 225, 258–63, 275, 291, 292
  Immeasurable Compassion 258, 259, 269–71
  Immeasurable Equanimity 258, 259, 260–3
  Immeasurable Joy 258, 259, 272–4
  Immeasurable Loving Kindness 258, 259, 263–9
Frankl, Viktor 119
freedom 119
'freeze' response 217
  antidote to 219, 220
Friedman, Meyer 33
friendships 228
  being a good friend to yourself 214, 216
  connecting with friends 237
  and Fear of Missing Out 238
  and stress reduction 268
functional magnetic resonance imaging (fMRI) 156, 157

gamma wave activity 157, 207
Gaza strip 264
General Happiness Scale 71
Germer, Christopher 120, 217, 220
Gilbert, Daniel 80–1
Gilbert, Paul 22, 90, 191, 215–16, 221, 223
Golden Rule 38–9, 180
Goleman, Daniel 124–5
'good life', the 74
Google 159
gratitude 237, 272
greed 38
Greene, Joshua 62
grudges, holding 264

habits
  addiction to stress as 181–2
  avoiding change regarding 98
  changing our 7, 52, 100, 102, 109–10, 117, 121–6, **121**, 301, 305
  compassionate 7, 191–3, 203–5
  emotional 179–80
  evolutionary 182–3
  examining our 7, 110, 111–27, 303–4
  the habit of hoping for what we want and fearing what we don't want 178–9, 205
  the habit of not paying attention in the present moment 176–7, 203, 204, 229
  helpful 7, 50, 123–4, 126, 156, 190–209, 210
  of our thoughts 114–15
  self-protective 99–100
  stress-increasing 176–83
  and suffering 98
  support for working with 124–6
  unhelpful 7, 89, 98–100, 102, 110, 121–2, **121**, 124–6, 156, 163–89, 196–7, 203–5, 210, 214
  when feeling discontent 85

Haidt, Jonathan 268
Hanson, Rick 182
happiness 304
  actions we take to find **87**
  and adaptation 75
  anticipating the causes of your 79–80
  and brain activity 157
  complicated nature of 85–7
  and consumerism 25
  expectations of 6
  exploring 69–70
  lasting 6, 87–90, **87**, 100, 155, 200, 231, 264, 275
  and longevity 71–3
  and loving kindness 263–4
  measurement 70–1
  and meditation 100, 231
  and money 74–6
  and pleasure 85–8
  pursuit of 49, 57, 68–90, 92, 104, 108, 178–9, 275, 276
  research 74–80
  and resilience 71–3
  and self-compassion 246
  short-term 86, 87–8, **87**
  and social support 228
  and stress 68–90
  and success 70
  *see also* contentment; unhappiness
*Happiness Formula, The* (TV show) 71–3
happiness set point 73, 88
harm
  causing harm to yourself 264–5
  trying not to cause 53, 252, 255–7
hatred 264–5, 273
having your own way, and happiness 77–8
health
  and meditation 158–9
  and stress 33–4, 264
  and volunteering 202
Health and Safety Executive 14
heart
  compassionate 100
  melting the ice in your 53, 54, 252, 258–9
heart disease 33–4, 264
heart rate 18, 30, 63, 64
heaven/hell 38
help, deflection 173–4, 174–5
'helper's high' 201
helping others
  as helping yourself 200–3
  *see also* volunteering
helplessness
  feelings of 119, 144
  learned 171–2
high blood pressure 72, 264
hippocampus 17, **17**, 31, 182
hope 178–9, 205
hormones
  oxytocin 26, 64, 247
  stress 72, 254–5, 264
hostility 33–4, 264
HPA *see* hypothalamic-pituitary-adrenal axis
human condition/nature 44, 57, 215
humanity, recognising common 53, 55, 220, 252, 274–6
hunter-gatherer ancestors 14–15, 29, 30, 114, 182–3, 196–7, 230
hypertension 72, 264
hypothalamic-pituitary-adrenal axis (HPA) 18, 19
hypothalamus 17, **17**, 18, 58

IBM 159
imagination 2, 20, 21, 42

immune system 30, 61, 158, 202
impermanence 96, **97**, 98, 193–6
improvement 82
incentive and resource-seeking system (emotional system) 22, 24–5, 26, **28**, 29
independence 93–4
individuality 93–4
inflammation 63
inner critic 215, 218, 220–5, 245–7
inner peace 88, 100, **121**, 122, 128–62
insecurity / inferiority 25, 91, 176
interconnectedness 44–7, 49, 96, **97**, 98, 109, 144, 192–3, 196, 204, 253, 297
interdependence 56, 93–5, 98, 186, 192–3, 196, 204
internet 9, 32–3, 238–40
introspection 252

James, Oliver 166
'jar of water' metaphor 43, 44
jealousy 272–4
Jesus 39
job interviews 219
Jordan, Bill 279–80
Joy, Immeasurable 258, 259, 272–4
'just being', state of 113, 122, 139

Kabat-Zinn, Jon 158, 176
Kagan, Jerome 56
Kahneman, Daniel 78
*karoshi* ('death from overwork') 186
Keltner, Dacher 64
killing, human resistance to 279–80
Killingsworth, Matthew 80–1
kindness 38
  loving kindness 28, 224–5, 258–9, 263–9, 305
  self-kindness 218, 220–31, 247, 252
King, Martin Luther 192
Korean War 280

'lake and storm' metaphor 179
Layard, Richard 74, 76
learned helplessness 171–2
left-brained people 71, 157, 158, 207
Lennon, John 227
letters, self-compassionate 234
life, 'being in tune with' 154
life challenges 231–4
life expectancy 29, 30
limbic system 16–17
limitations, self-imposed 99–100, 174
list-making 123, 303–4
live young 26, 58, 247
longevity 71–3
Longfellow, Henry Wadsworth 274, 276
lottery winners 2, 25, 74–5
love 59, 61, 146, 200, 266–8
  *see also* self-love
loving kindness
  and happiness 263–4
  Immeasurable Loving Kindness 258, 259, 263–9
  loving kindness meditation 224–5, 266–8, 305
  parental 28
low mood 85, 86
  *see also* sadness; unhappiness
Luks, Allan 201–2
Lutz, Antoine 156

Maier, Steven F. 171
*Mail Online* 84
mammals 58, 60, 63–4, 247
management styles, top-down 101–2
Mandela, Nelson 265

manufactured contempt 280
Marshall, Brigadier General S.L.A. 279
material possessions 74–5, 76, 296
MBSR *see* Mindfulness-Based Stress Reduction
meditation 5, 100–2, 128–62, 304–5
  and applying meditation practice 159–60
  and the benefits of a stable mind 154–6
  and the brain 156–9, 207
  and breathing techniques 145–6
  and Buddhism 151, 154, 156
  and compassion 143–4, 155, 207, 270–1
  compassion meditation 270–1
  and control issues 143–5
  duration 151
  and emotions 147–50, 155–6, 159–60, 273
  and happiness 100, 231
  and health 158–9
  on joy 273
  loving kindness meditations 224–5, 266–8, 305
  making time for 150–4, 175
  methods of 145–7
  and the mind 7, 81, 99–100, 128, 130–2, 137, 142–3, 147–51, 154–6
  and mindfulness 130–43, 158, 229–31
  props for 152
  research 156–9
  and self-awareness 98, 100, 122, 130, 141–3, 156
  and the soft spot 231
  and spaciousness 142–3
  and Stop Moments 153–4
  and stress reduction 100, 143, 147
  taking a break from 152
  and thought 147–50
  using a candle 147
  and wandering minds 7, 81, 100
  and wellbeing 158–9
  what it is not 128–9
  when to practice 151
  where to practice 152
'melting the ice in your heart' 53, 54, 252, 258–9
memory 17, 30, 31
mental health
  and meditation 158–9
  *see also* anxiety; depression
Mental Health Foundation 14
Milton, John 111, 112
mind 98–100, 109–18, 125
  benefits of a stable mind 154–6
  clarity of 43, **121**, 122, 130, 132, 142, 179
  and contentment 100
  emptying the 129
  evaluating (judging) aspect 115
  and experience 43, 115
  how our mind reacts 111–14
  and 'just being' 113, 122, 139
  'lake and the storm' metaphor of the 179
  and meditation 7, 81, 99–100, 128, 130–2, 137, 142–3, 147–51, 154–6
  peaceful 88, 100, **121**, 122, 128–62
  power of the 111
  quietening and calming the 7, 99–100
  reactions of the 7, 111
  'sky and the clouds' metaphor of the 116–18, 142, 147–9, 215
  spaciousness of the 117, **121**, 122, 142–3, 147
  and transforming suffering 98–9
  wandering/busy 80–2, 98, 100, 113–18, 130–2, 137, 147–51
  and the 'watching our mind' exercise 112–13
  *see also* self-awareness

Mind & Life Institute 4, 206
mind training 43, 51–6, 90, 101, 109–10, 114, 126, 128, 130, 159, 207–8, 283–4, 292
  and habit changing 206
  and meditation 128
  *see also* compassion training; meditation
mindfulness
  and 'a mindful cup of coffee' exercise 138
  and applying mindfulness practice 140–1
  and breathing techniques 132–3
  extending 134–6
  making time for 175
  and meditation 130–43, 158, 229–31
  research 156–9
  and self-compassion 220
  and wandering minds 81
  ways to practise 132–9
Mindfulness-Based Stress Reduction (MBSR) 158
mirror neurons 62–3, 186, 277
mishaps 91
modern life, complexity of 82–4
money 74–6
monkey studies 62–3
mood 112–13
mood set point 157
mother-infant relationship 26–8, 49, 59–60, 62
moving house 303–7
muscles 30

natural disasters 91
Neff, Kristin 220, 225–6
neocortex 58, 247
nerves, vagus 63–4
nervous system 18, 26
nervousness 19
neurons
  mirror 62–3, 186, 277
  new 236
neuroplasticity 100, 124–6, 156, 206, 305
neuroscience 62–4, 124, 156, 206, 236
news 199–200, 271
noise pollution 183–4
noradrenaline 18
'not good enough', feeling 159–60
nuns 72–3
nurturance 247

oestrogen 247
opportunities 197
optimism, as buffer against stress 246, 272
Ornstein, Robert 202
other people
  compassion for 8, 191–2, 250–82
  and coping with other people's suffering 251
  dehumanising 279
  helping 42–3, 191, 200–3, 201
  seeing as being like you 53, 55, 220, 252, 274–6
  seeing others as more important than yourself 53, 56, 252, 283, 292
  suffering of 39–42, 49, 53, 64, 68, 202, 250–1
  taking the perspective of 53, 55, 284–90, 296
  transmitting stress to 101
overdrive 235–7
overload 168–9
oversensitivity 187
overwhelm 1, 3, 14, 38, 41, 43, 123, 202
oxytocin 26, 64, 247

pain 90
  chronic 158

parasympathetic nervous system (PNS) 18, 26
parents 26, 58, 247
  and loving kindness 28
  working 140–1, 220–1
  *see also* mother-infant relationship
patience 200
Payne, Peggy 201
peace, inner 88, 100, **121**, 122, 128–62
perception
  of how things really are and how we actually see them 93–8
  of suffering 103–4
  threat 17, 19, 182–3, 213, 216, 254, 272
perfectionism 85, 225–7, 303–5
personal growth 225
personal strength 169
personality traits 7, 33–4
perspective-taking 53, 55, 110, 116–17, 122, 149, 156, 210, 284–90, 296
physical exercise 235–6
pituitary gland **17**, 18
planning 178–9
pleasure 85–8
PNS *see* parasympathetic nervous system
politics, short-termist 165
positive outlook 246, 272
positive psychology 70–1
post-traumatic stress disorder 280
pre-frontal cortex 157
  left 71, 157, 158, 207
  right 71, 157, 207
  ventromedial 255
predictability 170
prejudice 260, 262, 278–9
present moment
  bringing our attention into the 110, 132, 133–9, 141–2
  the habit of not paying attention in the present moment 176–7, 203, 204, 229
pride 240, 260
*Proceedings of the National Academy of Sciences* 156
prosocial behaviour, promotion 110
prostate cancer 158
psoriasis 158
psychological factors, affecting stress 170–2
psychology
  clinical 110
  positive 70–1
public shaming 33
pushing ourselves too hard 235–7
'putting things right' (exercise) 243–4

questionnaires 70–1
quick fixes 86, 87

radiotherapy 103
reactions to the world 99, 100, 109, 111–14, 145
  changing our 100, 104
  choosing our 118–23
  and coping with negative emotions 240–4
  and making things worse 183–5
  and our responses to the suffering of others 64
  and 'putting things right' (exercise) 243–4
reality, our limited view of 93–8
reasoning, compassionate 198–203
reciprocity 38–9
reflection 46
  on bodily changes 195
  on fundamental wholeness 50
  on interconnectedness 94
  on our reactions to stress 185

on perfectionism 226–7
on suffering 93
rejection, fear of 25
relationships 228
fluidity 261–2
mother-infant 26–8, 49, 59–60, 62
*see also* friendships; social contact; social networks; social support
reptiles 57–8
resilience 220
and happiness 71–3
and mindfulness meditation 230–1
and social support 200
and suffering 108
unknown levels of 169
ReSource Project, The 110
responsibility, universal 292–7
retail therapy 166
Ricard, Matthieu 156, 157
right-brained people 71, 157, 158, 207
Rinpoche, Sogyal 283
Rinpoche, Yongey Mingyur 194
Rizzolatti, Giacomo 62–3
Rosenman, Ray 33
routines, making changes in 236
rumination 15, 20–1, 23, 114–15, 229–31

sadness 71
*see also* low mood; unhappiness
Salzberg, Sharon 128
SAM *see* sympathetic adrenal medullary system
Sapolsky, Robert 11
Schulz, Charles M. 169
Schwartz, Barry 84
Schweitzer, Albert 263, 269
Second World War 170, 279
secular ethics 4
self
being a good friend to yourself 214, 216
changing nature 195
individual 20
and interconnectedness 96
unwanted parts of the 216
self-absorption 219, 229–31, 264
*see also* self-centredness
self-acceptance 245, 251
self-awareness 7, 81, 115–18
of flux 196
and happiness 86, 87, 88, 90, 92
of interconnectivity 97
and meditation 98, 100, 122, 130, 141–3, 156
and the 'sky and the clouds' metaphor 116–18
and stress-reduction 120, **121**, 122
and transforming suffering 98
and wholeness 44, 48
self-care 214, 252
self-centredness 270
*see also* self-absorption
self-compassion 8, 81, 213–49
and antidotes 220–31
and anxiety 246
benefits of 246–7
concerns regarding 245
core components 220
and crunch points 235–44
definition 214
and handling emotions 240–4
and happiness 88, 90, 246
and life's challenges 231–4
and meditation 100, 229–31
and mindfulness 220
and pushing ourselves too hard 235–7
and self-compassionate letters 234

and stress reduction 246
and the stress response 217–20
understanding the need for 215–17
view of 215
and wellbeing 246
withholding 214
self-correction, compassionate 223, 223–4
self-criticism 215, 220–5, 245–7
antidote to 218, 220–4
self-indulgence 245
self-interest 57, 59
*see also* selfishness
self-isolation 173, 218, 227–9
self-kindness 218, 220–31, 247, 252
self-love 227
self-pity 245, 272
self-protective mechanisms 251, 278–9, 280
self-reporting systems 70–1
selfish capitalism 166
selfishness 38, 202, 245
being wisely selfish 47, 255
cessation 53
*see also* self-interest
selflessness 202
Seligman, Martin 70–1, 171
Selye, Hans 13
senses, paying attention to your 136, 138
shame 215–16
shopping 9, 165
short-termism 165
'simmer' 182–3
Singer, Tania 110
'sky and the clouds' metaphor of the mind 116–18, 142, 147–9, 215
sleep 26
SNS *see* sympathetic nervous system
Sobel, David 202
sociability 49
social anxiety 159–60
social comparison-making 14, 75–6, 239
social contact, and helping others 202
social media 33, 238–40
social networks 61, 228, 268
social support 200, 228, 268
deflection 173–4, 174–5
society, conditions of our 165
soft spot 231
soldiers 279–80
soothing and contentment system (emotional system) 22, 25–6, **28**, 29
spaciousness 117, **121**, 122, 142–3, 147
Starbucks 159
status quo 52, 196–7
stereotyping 278
Stop Moments 153–4
Self-Compassion Stop Moment 232–3
stories, personal, and the stress response 183–5
strain 13
stress
addiction to 181–2
biology of 14–19
causes of 1–2, 15, 144–5
chronic 18
and control issues 170–1
definition 13
distracting ourselves from 9, 98, 119, 173
feelings about 11, 12
as habit 104, 181–2
habits which increase 163–89, 190
how stress works 6, 11–36
immediate 168–9
inevitable nature of 144, 154, 170, 221
and the internet 9, 32–3, 238–40
layers of 164–8, 304
and learned helplessness 171–2

'mechanical' approaches to 13
origins of the term 13–15
and our emotional systems 21–31
our experience of and how we react to it 109
and our fear of suffering 68–9, 90–104
and our longing for happiness 68–107
and predictability 170
prevalence 13
'psychological' approaches to 13
psychological factors affecting 170–2
and the pursuit of happiness 68–90
quick fixes 9
statistics 14
and suffering 68–9, 90–104, 104, 144
transmission to others 101
turning towards our/leaning into our 41, 119–20, **121**, 122, 125
understanding instead of avoiding 6, 9, 108
'wear and tear' 169
work-related 174–5
working with our perception of 171
*see also* coping mechanisms; reactions to the world
stress barometers, body as 31
stress disorders 158
stress hormones 72, 254–5, 264
stress pollution 186–7
stress reduction
and adopting beneficial habits 190–209
bringing it all together 303–7
and compassion 41, 51, 88, 111, 120–2, 124, 128, 200, 201, 207–8, 211, 246, 252–4, 303
exercise 216–17
incorporating into our lives 301–7
and meditation 100, 143–4, 147–50, 153–6, 158–9
and the mind 111
mindfulness based 158
and self-compassion 246
and social support 268
stress-combatting formula 5–6
survival mechanisms to deal with stress 173–6
and switching off automatic pilot 132
and universal responsibility 297
stress response 11, 13–15, 303, 306
chronic 15, 20, 29, 30–1, 182
cutting through the 90
downside of 29
evolutionary nature 14–15
experience of 15
and the internet 32–3
and oxytocin 64
paying attention to your 31
practical example of 16–19
purpose 14–15, 30
as response to threat 213
and self-compassion 217–20
short-term 15
and the stories we create 183–5
unhelpful nature in the modern world 173
stress thresholds 19
stress triggers 177, 184, 185
stress-related diseases 11
success 70
suffering
acceptance of 199
avoidance of 164, 276
causes of 90–1, 97, **97**, 163
closing down to 42
and compassion 39–42, 53, 68
fear of 6, 68–9, 90–104, 108, 163
feeling overwhelm in the face of 38

and habits 98
helping others with 42–3, 68, 191, 270–1
and how things are and we see them 93–8
inevitable nature of/leaning into 41–3, 69, 90–2, 104, 120, 144, 154, 163, 191, 199, 221
learning from 6, 90
of others 39–43, 49, 53, 64, 68, 191, 202, 250–1, 269–71
paying attention to 41–3, 49
perceived 103–4
reducing our 41
reflection on 93
and resilience 108
and stress 68–9, 90–104, 104, 144
transforming our 98–100
*see also* stress; unhappiness
supermarkets 1–2, 294
survival mechanisms 16, 29, 30, 57–8, 60
to deal with stress 173–6
sympathetic adrenal medullary system (SAM) 18
sympathetic nervous system (SNS) 18, 26

taking a step back **121**, 122, 156, 210
technological development 82–3
'tend and befriend' response 247
Teresa, Mother 266
terminology 2–3
'them and us' attitude 181
Thich Nhat Hanh 163, 203
thought loops 21, 23–4, 114–15, 216
thoughts
awareness of 112–13
blocking out 129
habits we have with our 114–15
and meditation 147–50, 155–6, 159–60
paying attention to our 135
and rumination 229–31
and the 'sky and the clouds' metaphor 116–18, 147–9
as transient 117–18, 147–9
treating as though they are solid and real 114
value labelling 136
threat perception 17, 19, 182–3, 213, 216, 254, 272
threat and self-protection system (emotional system) 16, 22–4, 26, **28**, 29, 31, 32, 114, 182–3
threats 217, 218
avoidance 197
and the 'tend and befriend' response 247
Tibetan Buddhism 3–4, 157
tolerance 200
Tonglen practice 290–2
trapped, feeling 236
tribalism 197
Trungpa, Chögyam 190
Tutu, Archbishop Desmond 3, 260
Type A personalities 33–4
Type B personalities 33–4

unhappiness
and our wandering mind 80–2
sources of 90–1
*see also* low mood; sadness
United Nations Universal Declaration of Human Rights 39
universal responsibility 292–7
universe, the 94

vagus nerve 63–4
values, of the Affluenza Virus 166
Varela, Francisco 4
Vietnam War 280

violence 38
volunteering 201–2, 256–7
vulnerability 226–7

Waisman Laboratory for Brain Imaging and Behaviour 4
*Wall Street Journal* 206
Walt Disney Company 159
wants
  the gap between what we want and how things are 229
  the habit of hoping for what we want and fearing what we don't want 178–9, 205
'we-centrism' 63
'wear and tear' 169
wellbeing
  and the chronic stress response 15
  and finding joy in the wellbeing of others 272–4
  and interconnectedness 297
  and meditation 158–9
  and self-compassion 246
  and taking responsibility for the wellbeing of others 292–7
wholeness 43–56, 231
  and awareness 44, 48
  and interconnectedness 44, 45–7
  and the natural capacity for compassion 44, 49–51
work absence 14
work-related stress 174–5
working parents 140–1, 220–1
world, experiencing the 136
worry 2, 20, 137